"Balance, balance, balance! In my opinion, Bill Hull's book *Straight Talk on Spiritual Power* is one of the most balanced books on the subject of spiritual power. He is honest and bold. For him spiritual power is not a matter of either/or, but of both/and. It is a part of becoming a disciple of Jesus. His argument, though simply written, is intently biblical in that it follows the scriptural path wherever it leads. I am convinced that this book will challenge and bless every reader not only in English-speaking countries, but also in other parts of the world, including here in Korea."

Dr. John Han Hum Oak,
Senior Pastor, SaRang Community Church, Seoul, Korea

"One of the most important topics facing the church today is that of authentic spiritual power. I believe that every reader will be both challenged and helped by Bill Hull's thoughtful 'straight talk' on this significant subject."

Dr. Paul Cedar, Chairman, Mission America Coalition

"Personal and deeply moving—honest, very helpful, and full of practical insight. I loved it."

Reverend Prebendary Sandy Millar, Holy Trinity Brompton

Straight Talk on
Spiritual Power

Other books by Bill Hull

Building High Commitment in a Low-Commitment World
The Disciple-Making Church
The Disciple-Making Pastor
Jesus Christ, Disciplemaker
New Century Disciplemaking
Revival That Reforms
Seven Steps to Transform Your Church
Right Thinking: Insights in Spiritual Growth
Anxious for Nothing

Straight Talk on Spiritual Power

Experiencing the Fullness of God in the Church

Bill Hull

Baker Books

A Division of Baker Book House Co
Grand Rapids, Michigan 49516

Published by Baker Books
a division of Baker Book House Company
P.O. Box 6287, Grand Rapids, MI 49516-6287

Printed in the United States of America

Library of Congress Cataloging-in-Publication Data

Hull, Bill, 1946–
    Straight talk on spiritual power : experiencing the fullness of God in the church / Bill Hull.
        p.   cm.
    Includes bibliographical references (p.   ).
    ISBN 0-8010-9136-5
    1. Church renewal. 2. Spiritual life—Christianity. 3. Jesus Christ—Spiritual life. 4. Holy Spirit. I. Title.
    BV600.3 .H85 2002
    262'.001'7—dc21   2002002256

For current information about all releases from Baker Book House, visit our web site:
                        http://www.bakerbooks.com

Contents

Introduction

My Journey

It was a warm spring night, the moon was full, and I was mad. I paced back and forth on the archery range. I yelled at God with all the frustration I could muster for the Deity. I wanted more of Jesus and every time I tried to get more, I came up empty. Getting more of Jesus at Oral Roberts University (ORU) in 1968 meant speaking in tongues. Whenever I tried—and believe me I turned my face toward heaven nightly asking God to loosen my tongue and saturate me with his power—I sputtered, spit, and then parrotted a phrase I had heard around the dorm "Shonadala. Sheroadahonda."

I had been a follower of Jesus for five months. My life had been transformed. I wanted what all the more seasoned people around me had, a touch of the supernatural, the "baptism of the Holy Spirit." A few minutes later I knocked on Roy Rogers's door. Roy was a singer but was no cowboy; he was someone who had befriended me. I knew Roy and his pal Eugene would be willing to help. They seemed overjoyed to see me in my time of desperation. Roy told me to sit in a chair. They laid hands on me and began to pray "in the Spirit," which means in their prayer language—in tongues. They told me to raise my hands and say, "Praise the Lord," over and over. I did it but evidently with too little emotion and at too slow a pace.

"Faster, Bill, faster," Eugene said.

"Praise the Lord. Praise the Lord. Praise the Lord." I was really moving out.

"Say, 'Praise the Lord; hallelujah; praise the Lord; hallelujah,' as fast as you can."

Before I knew it, my tongue seemed twisted and the sounds garbled.

"Praise God!" cried Roy. "He has received!"

I practiced my new gift every day. I got pretty good at it and even prayed "in the Spirit" out loud in small-group gatherings.

The next year was great. It was characterized by my fast-paced spiritual growth, giving my testimony at churches, preaching at jails and rescue missions, a trip to Africa, a 22.1-points-a-game average for the ORU basketball team, and I married the homecoming queen during spring break. Immediately following graduation, Jane, aka homecoming queen, and I went directly to Asbury Theological Seminary in Wilmore, Kentucky. Little did I know that in the next few weeks two events would dramatically change our lives.

The Asbury Reception

Asbury wouldn't let me in, even though we had moved to this tiny town in Kentucky by faith. Wilmore is located near many tobacco farms, and Kentucky is a strong tobacco-growing state. I knew Christians had a stronghold in this hamlet—there was only one cigarette machine in town. It was a very Christian place, even too Christian for many Christians. The seminary wouldn't let me in, not because they had no openings, but they had only a few openings for "charismatic students." Oral Roberts University had closed its seminary the previous spring, and Asbury was committed to seminarians from ORU who were already in the program. Since I was applying as a new student, I was placed on a waiting list. I was told unofficially, however, that they wanted to take only a limited number of charismatics. They might make chapel services too exciting.

This was a shock to me. It was the first I realized that there was a cleavage between evangelicals and charismatic Christians. I was determined to get in. Jane took a job as a secretary, and I became the best janitor Asbury College ever employed.

I preached weekends at Mount Pisgah United Methodist Church in Dry Ridge, Kentucky. You guessed it. It was a congregation of tobacco farmers and was like time travel backward. Many of the members didn't believe it when Neil Armstrong stepped onto the moon that July. But they believed in God and, because of a discovery I made, I thought they also believed in his healing power.

I had found a bottle of olive oil in the pulpit and was thrilled. *They have the oil right here for anointing the sick,* I said to myself. The next Sunday I preached on God's healing power and the altar was filled with needy people. I had never met a more physically needy group. They suffered from just about everything. I used the entire bottle. It was running down their faces, it got into their eyes, and it stained their clothes. I laid my hands on them, but nothing happened. I was destroyed.

I found out later the olive oil was for polishing the pulpit. I was learning that Christians disagreed about the ministry of the Holy Spirit, especially when it came to healing and speaking in tongues.

The Campus Crusade Ultimatum

Two days later I held a postcard in my hand. It was from my old buddy Bobby Hodge. He was playing basketball with a group called Athletes in Action. I had hung up my sneakers. I wanted to preach. Basketball was in my past. Yes, I was good at basketball; I held many of the scoring records at ORU. But after graduation, I was so overwhelmed with the desire to teach the Scriptures that I had put my love of basketball aside.

Two things about Bob's card grabbed my attention. The first was the phrase, "We could really use a shooter like you." The other was the statement at the bottom of the card, "Athletes in Action basketball teams travel the world telling others about the Good News of Jesus Christ."

Until I read that I didn't know this team was a Christian team. Then it dawned on me that I could both play basketball and preach. I made a couple of phone calls and discovered the team would take me on Bob's word alone. The only catch was that Jane and I would need to be in San Bernardino in one week for staff training. Oh, and, of course, every player had the privilege of raising his own financial support.

At dawn the next morning our '58 Buick station wagon was packed with all our possessions, and we were headed for California. Jane left a note on her employer's desk, and I had resigned both my jobs. We left Asbury behind agreeing that we could go back to seminary when my knees gave out.

The station wagon had two irritating characteristics. Every time we went over a large bump in the road, the hood would pop up and the rear doors would open. But what are ropes for? We made it to the Arrowhead Motel on Baseline Avenue in San Bernardino. The room came with a swamp cooler—a musty decor with the obligatory mildew. The restaurant was the burrito stand across the street. Being from Oklahoma we had no idea what a burrito was, but we found we liked them and ate them because they were cheap.

We discovered that we were not joining Athletes in Action. We were applying for employment with an organization called Campus Crusade for Christ. We had never heard of it. I remember how offended I was when we were told that you could be filled with the Holy Spirit by reading the blue booklet and saying a simple prayer. Jane and I were from a totally different branch of the church than most of the people we met who were part of Campus Crusade. During the training some students informed me that Campus Crusade did not allow people on their staff to speak in tongues. No one in authority spoke to us about it, however, and as the two weeks were coming to a close, I told Jane that maybe they were going to ignore it. Wrong. On the last day we were called in to discuss a few matters. We were informed of Campus Crusade's policy that they did not allow any staff to speak in tongues in public or private. I could understand the public part, but private—who cares about private? Yet they held fast.

"So the apostle Paul couldn't be on your staff?" I had to say it. I was ticked.

"That's right, but we don't expect him to apply." What an answer!

Still, the decision was ours. We retreated to our motel. We found it so sad that it had to be this way. What is wrong with people? The people at Asbury, now this group, don't they realize how wrong this is?

The church was divided, and we were stuck in the chasm. We determined that our calling to play basketball and tell others about Christ was stronger than the exercise of any particular spiritual gift. Therefore, we agreed to lay aside our prayer language for the greater calling, a decision to this day I believe was a good one.

The next spring Jane and I were attending a "senior panic" recruiting conference at the Adolphus Hotel in Dallas, Texas. At that meeting Bill Bright, the founder and president of Campus Crusade, made some comments about charismatics that I considered inappropriate. I asked for a meeting with Dr. Bright—a bit bold for a rookie staff member.

As I entered his room, Dr. Bright asked if he could brush his teeth while I told him what was on my mind. I stood at the door of the bathroom and I told him that I didn't know any charismatics who rolled on the floor and foamed at the mouth. I went on to say I thought he was wrong to have characterized charismatics in that way. I didn't know what to expect—a lecture, an assignment to open up the work at the University of Cuba. I just didn't know.

What happened next was a surprise. "You are right, Bill," Dr. Bright said. "Let's get down on our knees right now and ask God to forgive me." What an experience! What humility on his part! I learned that day why God has used Bill Bright in such a mighty way—his humility and his heart. He didn't have to see me. He certainly didn't need to agree with me. I knew that here was a man filled with the Holy Spirit. But the disdain that Campus

Crusade held for charismatics was still there and would remain there for years.

Being a Cessationist

My journey was just beginning. Two years later I became a cessationist. That is a person who believes that gifts, like tongues, healings, miracles, and prophecy are no longer operative in the church. And if they are, they are cheap imitations or counterfeited by the evil one. I had been influenced by several godly and good Bible teachers who believed this. This clearly illustrates the power of influence and of group culture. When a young person reads books, listens to tapes, and interacts with older, more learned teachers, he or she can be influenced. I found it more comfortable to be in step with those with whom I worked than to oppose them. I held my ground as a cessationist for several years until I entered seminary. I am a graduate of Talbot Theological Seminary and proud of it. I received an excellent education there that equipped me to study and teach the Scriptures. I found the faculty to be godly in character and good at their craft as theologians.

The teaching position of the faculty at that time was classic cessationist. We had several classes that in one way or another addressed the ministry of the Spirit and the role of spiritual gifts. It was while I was doing a class in Greek exegesis on 1 Corinthians 12–14 that I began to question what I had been taught. It is ironic that in the process of being indoctrinated in cessationist theology in the Greek New Testament, I concluded that not only was the argument on thin ice, but I had trouble finding the ice.

Thus began my "I believe that all the gifts are available to the church, but I don't want to open that can of worms" period. The beauty of this view is that you can be really nice to everyone; you can be comfortable in both worlds. But you still live in the cessationist world. And while your church may not speak out against the charismatic gifts, in practice you're still a cessationist.

It was during these years that I was pastoring and began to write. After eight published works I began my luminary phase—

teaching, traveling, and speaking around the world. For ten years I traveled the globe teaching about something I still believe and have not changed my mind about—making disciples.

The beauty of my subject was that it did not touch at all on the controversial aspects of the spiritual gifts. The happy result was that I was able to work with leaders across the entire spectrum of theological views. I learned from the Anglicans in Sydney, the Baptists in Bulgaria, the charismatic wing of the Church of England in London, and the Southern Baptists in the Carolinas. What I learned was that God was working in some significant ways, and much of it was because former cessationists were changing their minds because of the move of the Spirit. It also became clear that the chasm that had so impacted my life in the late sixties and early seventies was closing.

In the early 1990s I joined five hundred leaders in Orlando for two days of prayer and fasting. It seemed like the entire evangelical church was represented, from the Assemblies of God to the Episcopalians. Pat Robertson stood alongside many who at one time were his enemies. And who had called this meeting? Bill Bright. Campus Crusade had changed its policy, and, more important, God had changed the hearts of most of the evangelical world. We were coming together. The prayer of Jesus to his Father that his followers would be one just as he and the Father are one (John 17:21) was in the process of being answered.

The prayer movement, along with Promise Keepers, has broken down many barriers. Leaders have been reaching out to one another and the result has been fervent prayer for revival and an unleashing of power from a base of unity.

A Hunger for All of God

My interest in the full package of what God has provided was growing. My lifestyle, however, didn't provide much opportunity to do anything about it. At the time, I was leading a leadership training organization. The stated goal was: "Help return the church to its disciple-making roots." This required all my time and energy.

Primarily a reader, writer, and teacher—I actually experience physical pleasure when I read and write—I found my life was less what I love and more what was necessary to run an organization. Each day would bring a new fund-raising challenge or require a series of phone calls to sell our training to denominational executives. The times when I could concentrate on doing the things that created the need for the organization in the first place were fading away.

In an effort at international promotion of our training, in 1997 I spent two weeks on the Bristol Sea in the resort town of Minehead, England. I was there to teach daily seminars with the hope that the people of the UK would get to know me and my books. This afforded me some time to reflect on the changes going on inside me. It seemed like a force within was renewing my passion to experience God in a fresh and new way.

During three weeks each year, a total of seventy thousand people from the UK gather in two sites at an event known as Spring Harvest. There were seven thousand during the first week. I was assigned to teach a daily three-hour seminar based on my writing as well as a session on the Ten Commandments that I taught with two British pastors.

It was a strange approach in that each of us spent fifteen minutes on the same subject. There we were, a female captain in the Salvation Army from Yorkshire, an Anglican vicar from the largest congregation in the Church of England, and yours truly. The Anglican was Sandy Millar, well-known in England for the church he leads, Holy Trinity Brompton, near Harrods department store. His church is also the birthplace of the internationally known Alpha Course. Sandy was easy to like; his gracious manner and humility are powerfully used of God.

I was the only Yank among the seventy staff members, and frankly I had to initiate every conversation. When I went into the faculty lounge, I had to seek out someone to speak with. If I sat down, no one paid any attention to me. Most of them didn't know who I was or why I was there. I was not included in decision making. It was very lonely.

We were located at an amusement park with the Ferris wheels, roller coasters, and haunted house, right out of the 1960s. It reminded me of a dreary old black-and-white British horror film, in which a mummy or monster stalks innocent vacationers. The park was surrounded by cabins; it was a peasant's Disneyland.

I would take a daily walk into Minehead. Typically it was fifty degrees and the wind would be blowing forty miles per hour. One day was particularly brutal. I had on gloves, a stocking cap, and a winter coat as I leaned into the wind to make my way toward my cappuccino. The sand was peppering my face and I was miserable, but little English children were playing on the beach in swimsuits. No wonder Hitler couldn't defeat the British!

Sandy Millar was the first one to ask me to join him for lunch. Thus began a week of lunches and long discussions on the ministry of the Holy Spirit. In the evenings I would take in Sandy's ministry, and my heart was beginning to warm to what I heard. The first experience I had in ministry with Sandy was the second day of our teaching together. In his gracious way he asked, "Bill, would you mind if we did a little ministry at the close of our session?" Hey, I'm all for ministry. I had no idea what he meant. When we had finished that day's session, Sandy asked anyone who had needs to come up to the front and receive prayer. Many people came forward. I learned later that the seven people who came first were trained prayer counselors. They began to pray and then people began to fall, dropping all around our feet. We were in a large tent, the wind was whipping very powerfully, the Salvation Army captain and I kept backing up, backing up, stepping over fallen bodies, until our backs were against the tent wall.

At lunch I asked Sandy about the meaning and validity of "slaying in the Spirit." He didn't profess to understand it, but said only that it was the power of God coming on people and that in his experience many lives were changed after such a demonstration of power.

A few days later I was asked to pray with people at the end of the evening meetings. The venue was a circus tent called the Big Top. It held seven thousand for worship. The meeting began and it was a full charismatic service. The music started and the woman across from me began to shake and bob her upper torso up and down from the waist. Hands went immediately into the air. There was dancing, yelling, moaning, laughter, the full complement of human emotion on display. I am sure that much of this is learned behavior. Some groups learn to stand or sit stoically, calling it reverence. Others learn to jump up and down like kangaroos, calling it passion. To believe anything else is to stretch credulity. Think about it. God doesn't look down at the Big Top and say, "Oh, those are charismatics. I will instruct them by my Spirit to raise their hands, jump up and down, and at the end of the evening fall down."

Like anything else, some of what is experienced is genuine, some of it is people mimicking others, and some of it is foolishness. At the close, people came forward for prayer. I had prayed with a few people and then a young man began to tell me about his marriage problems. His wife was back in the hotel room because she was not open to God. I began to pray for him, my hands on his shoulders. Suddenly he was gone. I thought he had backed away. I thought my breath or my strong grip had caused him to put some separation between us. When I opened my eyes, I saw him on the floor, out cold. I had felt nothing myself and wanted to apologize, but there he lay, eyes closed; he seemed to be at peace. The next day our paths crossed. I asked him why he fell down and what difference it made. He claimed that he passed out. He said he hadn't done it on purpose. He and his wife were doing better, he said, and had started counseling that morning.

I still am unsure about slaying in the Spirit and its purpose, but the two weeks in England reawakened in me dormant feelings and thoughts that I had buried. I found myself reading books on the subject and restudying what the Bible really taught. I tried not to read my theological bias into the text, and I found that there was no theological reason to reject the full gifting of the Holy Spirit. But now I would need to seek God to see what he wanted me to do about it.

A hunger began to grow in me to experience all that God desired me to have. My hunger wasn't for any particular gift but for greater intimacy and greater power in ministry. I found myself being drawn to a search for God and desiring the dormant gifting in me to rise from its slumber. For this I realized I would need a different working environment. I would need to get out of traveling the world 60 percent of the time, raising money, and making deals. But I had founded the disciple-making organization. I had responsibilities to the staff and to our clients around the world. I would need to find a person to replace me and find a place to go that was right for my quest.

In 1998 the board of directors gave me time to determine what to do and where to do it. I began to explore returning to the pastoral life by preaching at a local church. At the same time I was talking with the cofounder of our organization to see if he would take over as president. Four months later he was president of the Training Network and I was pastor of Cypress Church. God had repositioned me for the next part of my journey.

The Pastoral Life

The pastorate provides an opportunity to hunker down and be contemplative. The daily pressure of making payroll is gone, the RPMs are slowed, the airline platinum card goes gold, then silver, and finally you're in row thirty-one in a middle seat. The peripatetic life militates against spending time with God, writing down your thoughts, and working in a community of fellow disciples. The pastoral life is filled with people problems and pettiness of every kind. And it is much more personal. Not only do people often disagree with you, but they get mad. It is a daunting challenge to maintain your focus when someone wants the pastoral head on a platter. But it provides the opportunity to seek God in the nitty-gritty of life, with friend and foe alike.

I had no grand strategy for my ministry apart from praying and feeling my way along. My church has a solid evangelical background and the preaching of the Word had always been central to worship. Like most churches of the ilk, we were not anticharismatic, just noncharismatic. The general attitude was, "We believe this stuff goes on somewhere; we are not against it; we just don't want any of it around here." The difficulty was and is that the Christian journey isn't about spiritual gifts per se; it is about knowing God and experiencing what he has planned for his church. But spiritual gifts are part of the story and somehow we must move into the realm of the fullness of God, but how?

The Separated Church

As I had observed in Florida the chasm between traditional evangelicals and evangelical charismatics is rapidly closing at the leadership level. But at the local church level, there is still cultural separation that is just as strong as any theological differences. I find there are more cessationists by custom than by study. Someone taught us that certain gifts and means of power are no longer active; therefore our church culture has been shaped around that teaching. The worship, the teaching, the praying, it all is slanted toward the cultural customs of the past. People's resistance is not theological. It is, however, a deeply inbred way of thinking. If the process of change affected only principles and logic, change would come a lot easier. Despite the baggage of our tradition, my desire for our church was to take them on a journey to experience all the fullness of God. But I knew that taking them on such a journey would require a great deal of prayer, team building, teaching, and patience.

The evangelical church is divided into two groups: those who are focused on the Scriptures and those who seek spiritual power.[1] The separation was never announced, just experienced. The Word-focused church gets periodic visitations of power, and the power church gets periodic visitations of the Word. For churches to continue like this is wrong. For me, the separation of my church from other bodies of believers became a matter of personal integrity.

I believed, along with the pastoral staff and elders, that all the gifts of the Spirit are active and available to the church. It became clear to me that our practice and our beliefs were not consistent. We had treated the gifts of 1 Cornithians 12 like the crazy uncle the men in white coats came and took away years ago. We all know he is alive but we don't talk about him. I began to see the duplicity in our practice. God convicted me.

God seemed to be saying, "If I have gifted my people for the common good, then why are you not teaching it? You are blocking the flow of my power. Why are you asking them to serve me without their tools and weapons?"

The congregations of many churches are not fully equipped for ministry. A good third of the Spirit's gifting lies dormant, because by custom or theology it is not available. How can the church serve God and fulfill the Great Commission with one arm tied behind its back? Since I believe that the full package of gifts was and is available to the church, my not teaching about them was wrong. I became convinced that I must move forward in a way that would be for the common good of the church. This would mean teaching on the subject; it would mean dealing with the unknown.

I have spent a good deal of my time teaching and advising leaders. When it comes to principles and programs that build Christians, I am comfortable and confident. I will never forget the first service when I felt out of control. I really hadn't planned it, but I asked people to come forward and pray. They came in good numbers; they were kneeling on the steps of our platform crying out to God. I thought, *I don't know what to do.* I felt helpless and scared. I drove away from church that day and I felt like a fifty-two-year old novice, completely out of my depth. Most of what I know two years later has been learned on the job. I am still frightened, I still don't know what is going to happen, but I've never been happier.

What follows is my journey. It includes my understanding of the issues and some advice on how to move ahead. But please be warned—I have no idea what I am doing.

Defining What Jesus Did

All Christian teachers tell us to follow Jesus, but most don't really mean it. What they really mean is follow the dispensational Jesus, the Wesleyan Jesus, the Baptist Jesus, or the Jesus in the white suit with the Rolex. It is so human to shape the person we are to follow into someone we are willing to follow. We want a Jesus we can live with, a Jesus who likes what we like, a Jesus who will take two days off a week, a Jesus who fits our customs and culture. We certainly don't want a leader who takes us over the hill into enemy territory. So do we really want to be like Jesus, to follow in his footsteps? (see 1 Peter 2:21).

What scares most of us is not *following* Jesus, it is *being like* Jesus. To follow him is to admire his courage and to glean lessons from his teachings. Jesus tells us that this is not enough, that simply to follow him and to honor him for the miracles is not the real call to discipleship. The real call is to be *like* Jesus; *it is to do what he did.*

"Do What I Am Doing"

I was frightened, a hundred thousand Africans were surging forward and only three strands of barbed wire separated us from them. Oral Roberts had just snatched the crutches from beneath a crippled woman, and she was walking down the ramp toward me. It was a hot July night in Nairobi, Kenya, and a collective cry of desperation rose from the needy mass. Many of the people in the front were in danger of being trampled; the barbs had already cut some of them. The crush of people demanded prayer. When the police allowed a few to come into the area immediately in front of the platform, we organized them into lines and we began to pray for them. I had been a Christian for six months, and now I am laying hands on Africans and asking God to heal them. "What a trip!" We said that a lot in 1968.

I was stationed at the end of the ramp where people would descend after receiving prayer. I remember laying hands on a deaf man. I prayed that he could hear, and then he could. I knew that God was present in a very strong way to heal. And even more remarkable was that he seemed to be present with *me* to heal (see Luke 5:17).

Over the din of music, prayer, and the exclamations of thousands, I heard someone yelling at me, "Bill, Bill Hull, come up here."

I knew that voice. It belonged to Oral Roberts. I ran up the ramp. "Yes, sir." We also said, "Yes, sir," a lot in 1968.

"You see what I've been doing?"

I looked him straight in the eye. "Yes, sir."

"Good. Do it. Do what I have been doing."

When I was a kid, I had seen Oral Roberts pray on television. And, frankly, he scared me. He would take that bulbous microphone and stick it in the face of a sick person. "What is your need?" he would ask. The person would state his or her condition. "Do you believe?" The person would nod yes, usually without speaking. Then O. R. would lay his huge hands on the person's head. "I pray in the name of Jesus of Nazareth that he heal you. From the crown of your head to the soles of your feet, be healed."

I had it memorized. "Go ahead." He had to coax me. I had never seen it done through an interpreter, but I started doing what he was doing.

That was a daunting experience, to be called on to do what Oral Roberts was doing in front of one hundred thousand people, television cameras, hot lights, and the expectations. But I must tell you that I was not afraid. Oral was trying to make a point. It's not the person who heals; it is God and God alone. Even a novice with faith is more powerful in prayer than the most learned person without faith. I was blessed with naïveté. I took what the Bible said at face value. I was not polluted with years of experience and too many alternative interpretations of what Jesus was really trying to say.

Now I must confess that I am afraid. The realities of life hammer one's faith. I have seen so many not healed; so many have suffered; so many have died too early. My prayer is that of the honest seeker: "Lord, I believe. Help me in my unbelief."

Doing What Jesus Did

It is one thing to have Oral Roberts say, "Do what I am doing." But what makes me tremble are the words of Jesus: "I tell you the truth, anyone who has faith in me will do what I have been doing. He will do even greater things than these, because I am going to the Father" (John 14:12).

Most Bible readers love this verse. The mind races with images of a string of miracles. I dream about praying for Pat, who has been bedridden for two months; for Sunny, who is suffering with bone cancer; Georgia, who is tormented by evil spirits. I just want to get into my car and drive to their homes and see them delivered. But these verses can't really mean what they say, can they?

Let me look up some of these key words in the Greek. The first key word is *anyone*. It says right here in my Greek New Testament that the literal rendering is "the one believing in me." I suppose that the English *anyone* means the same thing. Jesus could have said, "Okay, I am talking just to you, the eleven in this upper room." He could have qualified or modified the statement so we wouldn't have this special problem of taking him at face value.

The fact is that *anyone* who believes is qualified to do what Jesus did. He said *anyone* here for the same reason he said, "If *anyone* would come after me, he must deny himself and take up his cross daily and follow me" (Luke 9:23). "If *anyone* come to me and does not hate his father and mother, his wife and children, his brothers and sisters—yes, even his own life—he cannot be my disciple" (14:26).

When Jesus wants to specify his teaching to a limited application, he does so. He speaks to the fears of people listening to him and answers specific questions.[1] When Thomas asked how they could know where Jesus was going and if it was all true, Jesus answered, "I am the way and the truth and the life. No one comes to the Father except through me" (John 14:6).

For centuries this has been one of the clearest statements Jesus ever made about his being the only way to God. We have given it universal application. We have always taken Jesus' words "no one" to mean just that. There are no exceptions. The call to do what Jesus has been doing is just as universal in that he specifically says, "anyone."

This is not a promise or statement about apostles, pastors, and missionaries. It is an expectation for every believing disciple. This level of service to Christ is within our reach. And Jesus didn't stop with saying that we would do what he had been doing. What he says next challenges the best of us: "He will do even greater things than these, because I am going to the Father" (v. 12).

I don't know what we can do with this statement. I can track with and perhaps equal the works of Jesus—the healing, the casting out of demons, and the like. But how do we surpass raising the dead? I don't think anyone does exceed the works of Jesus in quality, but many have in quantity. There are thousands of disciples who have preached to more people than Jesus did. Certainly there are those who have seen more converts, more miracles, more wide-reaching revivals. Jesus never impacted first-century Hebraic culture like the First and Second Great Awakenings changed British and American life.

The key to understanding the meaning of Jesus' amazing prediction is the simple statement, "because I am going to the Father." Jesus promised that everything would be better because he was leaving and the Holy Spirit was coming. The disciples didn't believe that; they protested. If a vote had been taken, they would have stopped Jesus' plan. We don't believe it either. Who wouldn't rather have Jesus than the unknown Spirit? Yet Jesus was right—the Holy Spirit would come and be God present with us. Instead of God living in the temple in Jerusalem, he would now reside in each individual and in the collective people called the church.[2]

I have always loved following the idea of Jesus and the concepts of Jesus. The idea that I should do what Jesus did has laid siege to my mind. It has scaled the walls of my spirit and has penetrated my defenses. It is a struggle to think of oneself standing over a sick person and telling him or her to rise up in the name of Jesus. Even more frightening is hand-to-hand combat with demons. I don't do roller coasters, rock climbing, or water slides, and horror films curdle my blood. I can't even tolerate gremlins. I found the film *Exorcist* so scary, I left the theater before the exorcism. Dealing with demons is not something I want to do for excitement. I'd rather read about it and know it happened a very long time ago in a land far, far away. But now I am convinced that I have been wrong, that I have missed God's best for me and for those whom I lead because I have not been willing to do the works that Jesus did. I am his disciple; I am called to do what he did. Let us consider what that is.

Declaration of Intent

Jesus left the wilderness encounter with Satan and went directly to his hometown. It was an interesting choice. He was launching the rescue of the planet where he knew he wouldn't get a great reception, but he was doing it "in the power of the Spirit" (Luke 4:14).

Jesus had become a celebrity; news about his works had spread rapidly throughout the region. But even then the Palestinian cliché, "No prophet is accepted in his hometown" (v. 24), had been coined and would prove true in Jesus' case.

It was a custom to have a visiting teacher render a Scripture reading during Sabbath services, so Jesus stood to read. He didn't select the scroll of Isaiah; it was handed to him. He was supposed to give a nice reading and sit down. Jesus chose to read a messianic passage—the promised deliverance of Israel from the Romans and from all oppression. The passage also promised the beginning of the reign of the Messiah, when all the promises given to Abraham, Moses, and the prophets would be realized.

> The Spirit of the Lord is on me,
>   because he has anointed me
>   to preach good news to the poor.
> He has sent me to proclaim freedom for the prisoners
>   and recovery of sight for the blind,
>   to release the oppressed,
>   to proclaim the year of the Lord's favor.
>
>   Luke 4:18–19

At first they thought he was terrific, even when he said, "Today this scripture is fulfilled in your hearing" (v. 21). After his claim soaked in, the talk around town began to change. Around four hundred people lived in the village. Everyone remembered him, since he hadn't been gone more than a year. "Wasn't this Joseph's boy?" They began to question the stories of his miracles. "Why hasn't he done anything here but read the Scripture?" they asked. But Jesus knew what they were thinking. He wasn't one to let things go. He became a bit sarcastic and began to feed them their own thoughts: "Physician, heal yourself! Do here in your hometown what we have heard that you did in Capernaum" (v. 23).

Jesus believed that they wouldn't take him seriously. The parallel text makes it clear. He couldn't do many miracles there because of their unbelief (see Matt. 13:58). Using the ministries of Elijah and Elisha to show that God chose to bypass Israel and meet the needs of Gentiles, Jesus was teaching that Nazareth would be left out. They got the point and drove him from the city.

Jesus' intention was to launch his ministry in Nazareth, to proclaim himself Messiah. The nature of his ministry was to preach the good news, proclaim everyone free from the grip of Satan, heal the blind, and release the oppressed. It is a mistake to dissect each line of the Isaiah passage. The power is in the whole. Jesus came to bring spiritual and physical liberation. The priority is to give eternal life, the spiritual rescue of all humans, but it is also freedom for many from disease and spiritual oppression. Many of us have limited the application of this passage to the spiritual. After all, how many blind people get healed? So we conclude that it must refer to spiritual blindness.

Jesus had a holistic approach that met the multifaceted needs of society. To do what he did, we must have the same approach. When we operate only in the spiritual realm, we completely ignore God's willingness to intervene in the physical. We need the entire arsenal of God's power to reach those with physical needs, but our lack of faith keeps us from ministering to them.

Jesus' Bona Fides

When nations or companies want to demonstrate that they are acting in good faith, they provide bona fides. Normally these involve a negotiated concession between nations or a financial gesture between companies. It is the proof of their good intentions. When from prison John the Baptist sent a disciple to find out if Jesus was indeed Messiah, Jesus rendered his bona fides. One wonders what kind of negative propaganda John was fed by Herod.

"Go back and report to John what you hear and see: The blind receive sight, the lame walk, those who have leprosy are cured, the deaf hear, the dead are raised, and the good news is preached to the poor" (Matt. 11:4–5).

Jesus was saying to John, I am living out the messianic prophecy from Isaiah 61, which I announced when I launched my ministry in Nazareth. There can be no misunderstanding of the plain meaning of his words. He told John's disciple that his bona fides or proof could be seen in the physically blind, lame, and deaf who were healed and the physically dead who had been raised.

When God visits his people, there is great impact. Because we are spiritual and physical beings, our Creator ministers to us on both levels. The church's lack of impact can be partly explained by one simple fact—we have limited our impact to the spiritual alone. We have preached the gospel, usually not to the poor, and left it at that.

It was never God's intention to ask the church to reach the world on words alone. Christ modeled for us that it was both preaching and works of power that captured the world's attention. Paul said the same thing, "For we know, brothers loved by God, that he has chosen you, because our gospel came to you not simply with words, but also with power, with the Holy Spirit and with deep conviction" (1 Thess. 1:4–5).

Today church attendance has plateaued and even declined because of the lack of power in our meetings. Christ taught us that both the word and power are required to touch people.

A Powerful Combo

A most familiar story concerns the four imaginative friends of a paralytic who hoisted him onto the roof of a home. The house was crammed, Jesus was inside, and they were determined to get their friend into his presence. They proceeded to dig through the dirt roof, and then they lowered the pallet with the man on it to the feet of Jesus. "When Jesus saw their faith, he said to the paralytic, 'Son, your sins are forgiven'" (Mark 2:5).

The statement was inflammatory. Immediately the teaching scholars challenged Jesus. It seems obvious they weren't there to be ministered to but to scrutinize. It is not unusual for people to challenge teaching, but to call it blasphemy, that is unusual. Jesus knew their objections were about theological training, about the huge threat he was to the religious establishment's way of life.

They questioned Jesus' authority to forgive sins. By doing so he was playing the role of God. They could have argued for hours, days, months, years, and as it has turned out, centuries. But most of the people jammed into the house were hungry for God, and Jesus determined to end the debate.

> "Which is easier: to say to the paralytic, 'Your sins are forgiven,'
> or to say, 'Get up, take your mat and walk'? But that you may
> know that the Son of Man has authority on earth to forgive
> sins. . . ." He said to the paralytic, "I tell you, get up, take your
> mat and go home.". . . This amazed everyone and they praised
> God saying, "We have never seen anything like this!"
>
> Mark 2:9–12

There will always be some who don't get it. The teaching
scholars' accusations remind me of those so committed to their
teaching position they cannot afford to change. I have great
respect for many who disagree with me, but I can't allow their
disagreement to paralyze me. There are people who need Christ;
they aren't interested in our intramural games.

When the man took up his bed and walked, the argument
ended. Jesus' authority to forgive sins was unquestioned by the
openhearted. The people were amazed and they praised God. If
Jesus had argued for another hour, people would have wandered
away because of boredom. "Just as I thought," they would have
sighed. "These holy men are all the same." But Jesus *did* something, and they were convinced.

Doing what Jesus did means working with the Word *and*
power. It begins with a careful examination of what we believe.
Unless I can find solid and clear teaching that convinces me not
to follow and be like Jesus, then regardless of how foreign it
feels, I must do it.

Whatever Happened to Awe?

The very first church in Jerusalem has been trumpeted as the
crème de la crème. Dr. Luke summarized the strong points as
the early Christians lived in the afterglow of Pentecost. One way
to understand their strength is through their five commitments
found in Acts 2:42–47:

1. A commitment to the apostles' teaching
2. A commitment to fellowship
3. A commitment to prayer

4. A commitment to worship
5. A commitment to outreach

I doubt if there is an evangelical church in America that would not sign off on the above priorities. These five transformational activities are the gold standard for right practices. The search for a pastor or church that would claim not to practice the above principles would be long and arduous. Yet there is one dimension of the Jerusalem church that is missing in nearly all the churches that claim to honor and practice the five transformational activities. There is little sense of awe. "Everyone was filled with awe, and many wonders and miraculous signs were done by the apostles" (v. 43).

When you witness the birth of a child, there is a sense of awe. If you are standing near Niagara Falls or on the floor of Yosemite National Park, the beauty and power amaze. I can't forget the experience I had with Oral Roberts in East Africa. It was awe inspiring.

The first night of the crusade was a disappointment, though. There were more than one hundred thousand people in attendance. The Word was preached, and many committed their lives to Christ. That would be considered a success by most, but not by Oral. There were no visible miracles the first evening. The Muslim-controlled press blasted Roberts for his lack of physical healings. William Holden, the American actor, had a real interest in Africa and preserving its wildlife. The newspaper asked, "Who will save Kenya, Oral Roberts or William Holden?" The paper endorsed Holden.

At the staff prayer meeting the next morning, Oral was burdened with the way God wasn't being glorified. He prayed that God would strongly reveal himself during the rest of the crusade. That evening, after the worship and preaching were complete, Oral instructed those wanting salvation to walk across the field and go to a tent where they could get help. Then the healing time began. The first person up the ramp was a woman crippled from birth. She walked with crutches. Oral prayed for her. The cameras were rolling when he snatched the crutches from her and commanded her to walk in the name of Jesus. She began to walk normally. There was an audible gasp from the throng, and they surged forward. There was a sense of awe.

So many of us have strived for years to practice these commitments or principles, and yet we can honestly report that we have very little awe. The reason is there are very few signs and wonders or works of power that amaze. I have been to enough good church meetings to last a lifetime. I am tired of having a good praise time, a good sermon, and a good chat with friends, then returning home to consider how everyone performed. I long for an encounter with God, so powerful an encounter that he reveals himself in our worship. I desire to see wonders and miracles as a normal part of our ministry. This is our Achilles' heel—the reason we have little impact in our society. It is the missing encounter with the revealed presence of God. In some church services, it is beginning to happen, and once you taste it, you can never get enough. My goal for each church gathering is to experience God. I want always to be prepared to open the door and let him in.

Peter the Apostle

The first story recorded on the heels of Pentecost was Peter and John's encounter with the crippled beggar in Acts 3:1–10. Crippled from birth would mean no history of muscle use. Peter looked the man in the eye and commanded him to walk in the name of Jesus. Then he reached out to help the man up. That is faith. His reaching out his hand was supernatural. The man went running and jumping, which is what any totally transformed person would do. People jump up and down on game shows when they win the camper trailer. One can only imagine this man's joy. The power of God ends the debate; it melts the cynicism; it brings joy and amazement to everyone near. The people were filled with wonder and amazement.

Philip the Deacon

Philip wasn't an apostle. He had been chosen as one of the first deacons. When the church was scattered by persecution, he went into Samaria to preach. "When the crowds heard Philip and saw the miraculous signs he did, they all paid close attention to what he said. With shrieks, evil spirits came out of many, and many paralytics and cripples were healed. So there was great joy in that city" (Acts 8:6–8).

The ministry of Philip, like that of Jesus and of Peter, included miracles. After people saw the miraculous, they paid attention to his teaching. You get the strong impression that without the works of power, Philip would have been just another street preacher.

In all three ministries, the miracles had dramatic impact, and many believed. Works of power have been and always should be integral to evangelism. Too many of us can't remember the last time we witnessed God's miraculous power that brought people to Christ. Yes, I know that the greatest miracle is salvation, that a changed life is the most powerful witness possible. I also know that observers interpret changed lives subjectively. In a relativistic culture, the changed life gets lost in all the other truths. "I'm happy that it works for you" is the condescending mantra. I must say, however, when a person is freed from an evil spirit or the lame walk or the blind see, it makes a broader and deeper impact. It suspends the normal truth debate, because a deeper, more powerful truth has washed away the resistance.

I have also noticed how in the face of need, unstudied theology changes fast. You may doubt the existence of the gift of healing. But when your child becomes gravely ill and you hear of God working through someone to heal, you rush to that person, though you don't believe in his or her gift of healing. My purpose is not to ridicule; it is to demonstrate that if our need is great enough, we become more open to God.

Paul and Barnabas the Church Planters

Iconium was the first stop on Paul and Barnabas's first missionary trip. Through their ministry many believed in Jesus, Jews and Gentiles alike. These two missionaries also stirred up some significant opposition, which caused them to stay longer. They spoke "boldly for the Lord, who confirmed the message of his grace by enabling them to do miraculous signs and wonders" (Acts 14:3).

God uses miracles to amaze people, to give joy, and to confirm the authority of the message. What amazes me is how long many faithful servants have persistently preached the Word without the confirming power of signs and wonders. It is remarkable how many have been reached, but it's sad to contemplate what might have been.

Churches are growing. The number of megachurches is multiplying in the United States and around the world, but this fact is deceptive. Only 5 percent of all U.S. churches have one thousand or more members, and the actual number of people going to church has declined. People are coming to Christ in our country, but only enough to replace those promoted to heaven.

The not so well kept secret is that many smaller churches are in decline and closing. Part of the reason the smaller church—with an average Sunday morning attendance of two hundred or less—is struggling is cultural. We live in a celebrity-driven culture. The bigger the church, the better the show. People love to go where the action is, to the grandest mall, the most important sporting events, the biggest singing Christmas tree. You get the idea.

When a church really starts growing, the flaky and frustrated Christians flock to it. Growth takes on a life of its own, and the big get bigger. This also taps into the temptation to get lost in the crowd and escape accountability. More Christians going to fewer but larger churches is bad. But considering the anemia in the majority of smaller churches, it is the lesser of two evils. Regardless, at least in theory, attending a large church transforms accountable servants into freelancing consumers. I say in theory, because the assumption is that a church of three hundred is optimum for loving relationships, accountability, and the best use of personnel.[3]

The second reason for the "what might have been" in our churches is that they are weak and boring. The services are boring and the outreach is nearly nonexistent. This is easily documented, and I would recommend your doing some research.[4] This explains why so many bored, ineffective disciples go to the megachurches; at least they're interesting. Many smaller churches are so bad at worship, mission, and accountability that even the watered-down forms in many larger churches are better.

The most common missing element in solid evangelical churches is the miraculous. The "what might have been" disappointment comes from a lack of impact. If we would commit ourselves to doing what Jesus did, our impact would be dramatically better.

The Transition Argument

Some would say that what we read in the Gospels and Acts is not transferable to contemporary experience, that the experience of the church in the first few years was a transition. I would agree it was a transition from an Old Covenant relationship to God to a New Covenant relationship. I would agree that it was a transition from Jesus' earthly ministry and the apostles to the Holy Spirit's ministry and the church. I don't agree, however, that it was a transition from works of power to fewer works of power. What kind of a transition is that? We have gone from "the Lord added to their number daily those who were being saved" (Acts 2:47) to 1.7 converts a year per 100 in attendance; from a sense of awe to "this is boring"; from the people were amazed to "who cares?" Can this be the "transition" God desired?

The end game in the transition argument is the existence of the written record we call the Bible. The idea is that once we have a sufficient accounting of what we need to know, the power, which is the confirmation of the message, is no longer an integral part of our toolbox. My first objection is theological, a subject I will take up later. But my other objection is practical; the idea that the Bible replaces works of power is false. Are we really any less in need now of works of power to confirm the message than people were in the early days of the church?

Modernity has had a devastating effect on absolute truth. Modernity is commonly held to be the latent effect of the Enlightenment that sought to replace revelation with reason. Then, once revelation is replaced, reason becomes a traitor. You can't depend on it because you find yourself lost in a sea of relativism, and absolute truth is gone. This is where we find ourselves in the twenty-first century. Many nonbelievers are unwilling to accept our assertion that the Bible is truth. They say it may be truth for us but not for them. That's why works of power that will confirm the truth are so essential.

In 1972 I spent a lot of time on the college campus talking with students about the claims of Christ. I was armed with many good, objective reasons why one should believe in Christ. We used to say that Christianity was rooted in the truth of history. We would discuss the proofs for the Scriptures, the proofs for the deity of Christ, the proofs for the resurrection. The proof approach doesn't work anymore. Even twenty years ago Professor Allan Bloom at the University of Chicago said, "The only absolute truth about incoming freshmen is that they believe there is no absolute truth."[5]

Our church has been engaged in a wonderful outreach program called the Alpha Course. People come for dinner and then discussions ensue concerning the crucial elements of who Christ is and what is required for one to become a Christian. One of the first lessons considers the "radical claims of Jesus."

When I told college students, "Jesus said, 'I am the way, the truth and the life. No one comes to the Father but through me,'" a heated argument would be expected, because they thought: *The nerve of a prophet to make such an outrageous claim!* Today, however, our Alpha students say, "What's so radical about that? What do you expect him to say? That was his worldview. God expresses himself differently through his prophets. That doesn't make Jesus any truer than Buddha."

Rules of logic are not relevant for many in the metaphysical or spiritual realm. Do you think God saw this coming? He not only saw it coming, he planned to address it with more works of power, not fewer. As truth becomes more subjective and logic itself also becomes subjective, God will pour out his power. He will melt away defenses and crush resistance.

When Peter stood to explain the Pentecostal phenomenon of tongues, he placed it in cultural and theological context by citing the prophet Joel:

> This is what was spoken by the prophet Joel:
>   "In the last days, God says,
>   I will pour out my Spirit on all people.
>   Your sons and daughters will prophesy,
>   your young men will see visions,
>   your old men will dream dreams.
>   Even on my servants, both men and women,

I will pour out my Spirit in those days,
and they will prophesy."

Acts 2:16–18

The passage fundamentally speaks to the fulfillment of the inauguration of the New Covenant as concerns the coming of the Holy Spirit to the church. It's immediate application was the gospel being preached in languages never learned. The passage then jumps forward to the climax of the redemptive drama and the second coming of Christ.

The message of Christ needs affirmation and confirmation now more than ever. I believe that as the second coming of Christ nears, there will be an increase in the outpouring of his Spirit. Such demonstrative works of power are found slipped into Scripture as an assumed need. Paul referred his readers to the miracles to authenticate his work: "I will not venture to speak of anything except what Christ has accomplished through me in leading the Gentiles to obey God by what I have said and done—by the power of signs and miracles, through the power of the Spirit" (Rom. 15:18–19).

We need to accept what Paul and others readily believed—that works of power are central to the church. They are as natural to the Christian walk as prayer or Bible reading. To live robust lives in Christ, we need them and we should expect them as the norm. "This salvation, which was first announced by the Lord, was confirmed to us by those who heard him. God also testified to it by signs, wonders and various miracles, and gifts of the Holy Spirit distributed according to his will" (Heb. 2:3–4).

Confirmation for God's People

God testified and confirmed the Good News to his own people through works of power. That is because God's people are renewed and encouraged when they witness God at work. One of the reasons charismatic churches worldwide are growing fast is that people's hearts are touched at a deep level by the evidences of God's power. Yes, there are churches that are growing fast that don't experience demonstrative works of power.

Those churches are always pastored by a highly gifted communicator, assisted by a great music program. The problem with that as a model is that it represents less than 1 percent of the church. It leaves the other 99 percent out in the cold.

Two years ago I had a conversation with a young man who attends our church. He was losing interest in the church because he didn't see God working in our services. I immediately challenged his premise based on what I still believe to be solid theological truths. "You may not see anything visible going on, but there is plenty happening in the invisible realm." I went on to explain that God's Word never returns void and that I had received notes and had numerous conversations that testified to the changing of lives. I warned him of being too emotional and too dependent on signs.

While I made some good points, my friend was right when he claimed, "People have a need to see God at work when they are gathered." I admitted that I wanted to see God work as well, but I wanted it to be authentic. I didn't want to orchestrate what wasn't there or create an exotic playground for the emotionally needy.

The normal pressure on a pastor in the noncharismatic, evangelical church is to give invitations and get people to come down front. My genre of the church has avoided this in reaction to churches that abuse it. I have seen churches where the sermon's value was measured by the number who responded to the invitation at the end of the service. I believe that is a trap that creates a devastating success-failure environment.

I have reached the conclusion that the people's need for confirmation is greater than the dangers of abuse. It's like driving a car. The benefits outweigh the dangers. I started to ask people to come to the altar for prayer, and the most interesting thing happened—they came.

All the church-guru literature warns us against doing anything that would make the seekers uncomfortable. You know what? I think that is bunk. Seekers are looking for authentic faith. If they see it, they will be drawn to it (see 1 Cor. 14:24–25). My advice is, Don't allow a few seekers to keep you from doing what the church needs. Based on my experience, there are very few seekers coming to most churches. If works of power were central to our gatherings, there would be many more seekers.

And I believe that they would like what they would see. Demonstrations of God's power would draw them to Christ more than any other single factor.

We started praying for people at the end of the services. We had people come forward and say things like, "Last night I held a gun to my head. I was going to end it all, but a voice told me no, go to church. And here I am. Can you help me?" We prayed for Lisa who had a growth in her brain. We anointed her with oil. The church prayed for several days; the tumor went away and has stayed away. We had Lisa share with the church and then we asked all who needed healing to come and have Lisa pray for them. They came in great numbers. I haven't had to talk people into coming for prayer. They are naturally drawn to it, despite the fact that this is a church that rarely did such things.

I began to notice the look on people's faces. There were tears and many smiles. People were being edified and encouraged. They were moved at a very deep level. God's people need to see their God at work among them in a visible way.

I had to change my mind and then change my behavior before God's power was seen at our church. God appointed me the gatekeeper. I have the awesome responsibility of opening the door or keeping it closed. God forgive me for the years that I kept the door closed.

Authentication for Unbelievers

Christians are encouraged by works of power, but so are unbelievers. I have already given several examples of how Jesus and others drew the attention of people outside the church. Multitudes followed Jesus because of the combination of teaching with authority and the demonstration of power. Three thousand gathered at Pentecost because of the tongues of fire. People listened to Philip, Barnabas, and Paul because of the authentication of the miracles.

Paul puts it so well to the Corinthian church:

> But if an unbeliever or someone who does not understand comes in while everybody is prophesying, he will be convinced by all that he is a sinner and will be judged by all, and the secrets of his

heart will be laid bare. So he will fall down and worship God, exclaiming, "God is really among you!"

1 Corinthians 14:24–25

Isn't this what we all want—that our gathering environment would be so powerful and captivating that people would experience the presence of God and that they could not resist the message because it is authenticated with the powerful display of gifts? The immediate context is the advantage of prophecy over tongues as a ministry to believers and unbelievers alike. The broader principle is in play as well, that the supernatural combined with the teaching of God's Word authenticates the message. People will draw the conclusion—God is among you.

I propose that, rather than create seeker services that cater to a small percentage of people who may actually show up, we should develop services that demonstrate authentic power and the operation of the gifts of the Spirit. Scripture gives us more hope that the latter will bring people to Christ. A fascinating quandary faces any church that wants to take reaching out seriously. If you design your services to be sensitive to unbelievers, the traditionalists attack you. If you design your services to allow time for God and works of power, the traditionalists attack you. It seems any attempt on the part of brave leaders to break out of the evangelical box of customs and traditions is met with opposition. It still must be done, but you can expect some problems. There are many good books on change. Prime yourself by reading a couple and talk with others who have gone before you.[6]

I believe there is a consensus among church members and leaders alike that there is far too much talking about and not enough demonstration of power. As our worship has become more passionate and the demonstration of God's power more visible, the hunger has only increased. People know God's presence when they experience it. Once they taste it, they want more. There are a few nervous people; I would count myself as one of them—nervous that this might spin out of control. But the taste is in our mouths; we want that sweet savor to rest within us every day for the rest of our lives.

But can we experience God without self-destructing? Can we navigate through the dangerous waters of ambition and the pressing need for the new? There will always be disagreement and criticism that will emerge from fear and miscommunication. But how can we do anything less than try if we want to keep our integrity? Jesus did only what he saw the Father doing. Now we are to do what we see Jesus doing (John 5:19–20), what we see the early church doing, and what those brave souls before us have been doing. They have had the proper combination of naïveté and faith to actually believe that they can do what Jesus did.

Where do we go from here? I like what Charles Kraft writes:

> In order to understand and appropriate New Testament power, though, we have had to fight a rather formidable enemy. The cultural conditioning passed on to us through family, school, and church has not been conducive to understanding and following our Master and his early followers in the area of spiritual power.[7]

In 1984 my first book, *Jesus Christ, Disciplemaker*, was published. The new edition is called *New Century Disciplemaking*. That work and the remainder of the corpus on disciple making were rooted in a basic premise—that disciple making is the heart of the church's mission. It is doing what Jesus did in developing his followers and preparing them for the mission. I mused as to why something so obvious had been marginalized in church life. Now I wonder the same thing about the miraculous. Why is doing what Jesus did so off the charts and out of reach? I think I know why—the enemy doesn't want the church making disciples, because that is what Jesus did and told us to do. Neither does he want us to do what Jesus did in power, because that would revolutionize our lives and we would be everything God intended. Too many would fall at the feet of Jesus and say, "I am sinful. I need help. God is among you. I want Christ now!"

Knowing How Jesus Did It

How did Jesus do what he did? Where do we draw the line between the way Jesus did things and how we do things? Are they exactly the same, largely the same with a few exceptions, or totally different? When we consider Jesus' prediction, that we can equal and exceed his works (John 14:12–13), we must ask, How is that accomplished?

We are to follow Jesus in suffering (1 Peter 2:21), leadership technique (Matt. 28:20), and in works of power (John 14:12–13). Some would limit following Jesus to following his lessons and principles. The appeal of such a premise is that it can be done, based entirely on technique, innovation, communication gifts, and intellect. The frightening thing about including works of power in what we do is you can't fake it. Okay, there are some people who have faked it, but most of them have been caught.[1]

Two Tragedies

Trying to do what Jesus did is not optional. Jesus promised it and expects us to follow through. But there are risks to both our faith and the nature of the mission. There are two separate but equal tragedies that can result. *The first is for us to try to do what Jesus did and then conclude that it can't be done,* that he didn't really mean it the way it reads in Scripture. He could have been speaking in general terms not specifically talking about healing, for example. While this is a remote possibility, a more present danger is for us to try to do the works of Jesus exactly the way Jesus did them. There seem to be those occasions when Jesus healed everyone. He simply called on demons to leave people and they did (Mark 1:29–34).

The mistake is for us to go around ordering things to happen, decreeing people to get out of their wheelchairs or pop right out of their beds. When people don't start running and jumping and praising God, we begin to doubt, we feel like failures, and we back off. The tragedy is that we come up with a mistaken analysis of what went wrong. We conclude either that God didn't really mean that we would do the works of Jesus or that we just don't have what it takes to do them. The real problem is that we have tried to do what Jesus did the way Jesus did it without factoring in his divinity. Since we don't possess any divinity at all, it can appear that we have failed. The truth is that Jesus will equip us to do the same works, but we will accomplish the same things differently.

The second tragedy is not trying at all to do what Jesus did, believing it cannot be done. This is the person who spends life with his or her nose pressed against the window of the miraculous. This person claims that we are reading someone else's mail. Jesus never meant for us to do works of power and that is why we are disappointed. Not only that, we are leading many naive people astray.

These are twin tragedies because they end up in the same place—the church not doing what Jesus did, not experiencing an important dimension of God's desire to help his creation. One group is misguided by the idea that there is no difference between Jesus and us. The second group, equally misguided, never tries to do what Jesus did. We can avoid such tragedies by committing ourselves to learning how to do what Jesus said we would do.

How Did Jesus Do It?

R. A. Torrey, who wrote from a noncharismatic perspective, put it this way: "Jesus Christ obtained power for His divine works not by His inherent divinity, but by His anointing through the Holy Spirit. He was subject to the same conditions of power as other men."[2]

Torrey based his argument on Peter's words at the house of Cornelius. "How God anointed Jesus of Nazareth with the Holy Spirit and power, and how he went around doing good and healing all who were under the power of the devil, because God was with him" (Acts 10:38).

This position plainly stated is that Jesus had no more resources for working miracles than we do. Jesus could not heal at will. He had to pray and ask in faith like we do. Just think, the only thing standing between me and a raft of miracles is my faith. It may appeal to those with the gift of faith, but it breaks down horribly in practice.

I was fresh out of university and had assumed the pastoral position at the Mount Pisgah United Methodist Church in Dry Ridge, Kentucky. I was paid twenty-five dollars a week, and my job description included cleaning the church on Saturday. Every Saturday morning Jane and I would drive the seventy miles to this country church nestled in the tobacco fields of northeastern Kentucky. We would clean the church and then make a few visits. One of our regular stops was at a skilled-nursing facility. In 1969 they were called rest homes and were filled mostly with the elderly. We were shocked, you could say horrified, as we walked the hallways. The place was a trash bin for the unwanted of society. The rooms were filled with young and old alike. Witnessing the last days of life for those damaged by stroke, Alzheimer's disease, and general dementia is heart wrenching. A great sadness comes over you and begs the question, "God, why do so many need to suffer so much?" But that was not what shocked us the most.

We entered a room filled with cages, each cage had a mattress on the floor and on each mattress was a child. Most of these poor children were from two to sixteen years old and suffered from birth defects. We would walk up to a cage and put our hands through the bars, and the child would grab hold. None of them could talk, and they loved a human touch.

I am sure it was not easy for the parents of these kids, but putting them in that pit was a wretched act. We weren't parents then, but now after experiencing parenthood, I understand how painful and horrific it all is. But that wasn't the cruelest thing we saw. That prize goes to Kenny.

Kenny was seventeen; he was a totally normal teenager except that he couldn't walk. I was puzzled as to why he was in such a place. I was only twenty-three myself, and we enjoyed the same kind of music. He had a new, bright-red electric guitar that he was learning to play. I couldn't understand why his parents would place Kenny in such a horrid place when he would have been able to live at home. Instead of helping him get an education and become a productive member of society, they had hidden him away in this facility.

Week after week I visited Kenny. We finally got to his pain of being placed in the facility. We talked about God and what he thought about a God who would allow this to happen to him, not the accident that caused his disability but the way his parents were treating him. That is when I started talking to Kenny about God healing him. I read some verses and told him that I would pray all week and the next Saturday I would pray for his healing. I spent the week in prayer, reviewing the cases where Jesus and his followers healed the paralytics.

The next Saturday my step was quickened as I entered Kenny's room. After a few moments of pleasantries, I told Kenny it was time. I unbuckled his seat belt so when he was healed he could get out of his wheelchair. I laid my hands on him; I prayed with all my faith; I released my faith to God. Then I told Kenny to stand, but he couldn't. I cried out, "In the name of Jesus of Nazareth, I command you to stand up and walk." He couldn't move. I extended my hand. "Kenny, take hold of my hand." Kenny did, and I pulled hard. His body flopped up and then back down into the chair. I grabbed him under the arms and tried to lift him. He was dead weight.

Tears filled both our eyes. Kenny diverted his eyes from mine. I was devastated. I don't have words to describe what Kenny must have been feeling. Was I foolish? Did I make matters worse? What kind of damage had I done to Kenny?

I know this—I hadn't matched the works of Jesus, exceeding them wasn't even in play. The only real damage I had done to Kenny was to leave him with the impression that my faith didn't meet the standard, that if my prayer could have been more pristine, he would be walking. I am happy to say that I told him my faith was too weak, that it wasn't his fault. That was a wrong conclusion on my part, but at least I didn't leave the responsibility on his shoulders.

What would I do differently now? I would tell Kenny that God might heal him. I would also tell him that God would make the final call, that our responsibility would be to pray in faith, that God's responsibility would be to decide. I still believe it is the task of the person who prays to believe, and if we at least try, it is possible that God will heal. It is vital that we avoid the naive position that God will do anything we can believe him for. Equally dangerous is the belief that because of my experience with Kenny and others like it, I should just back off and not hurt people. So let's try to find out how Jesus really did the works he did and how we are to do them.

Option One: Jesus Operated by Faith Alone

There is a body of Scripture that seems to indicate that what Torrey wrote and I quoted above is absolutely true. I have a couple of questions concerning this body of teaching. Those questions will emerge as we interact with the key evidence.

When Jesus was challenged by religious leaders because he was healing on the Sabbath, he replied, "My Father is always at his work to this very day, and I, too, am working" (John 5:17). This of course created serious consternation among his enemies. The text serves as its own commentary—Jesus was making himself equal to God. When it comes to how Jesus accomplished his works, again he tells us: "I tell you the truth, the Son can do nothing by himself; he can do only what he sees his Father doing, because whatever the Father does the Son also does. For the Father loves the Son and shows him all he does" (vv. 19–20).

These words are plainly spoken. Jesus is subservient to the Father. It could even be interpreted to say that Jesus was not a part of the decision-making process when it came to ministry and mission. Jesus could not heal at will, because he was completely obedient to the sovereign will of his Father. Jesus could not heal on his own, because he was committed not to do anything independent of his Father's will.

Jesus is more emphatic later: "By myself I can do nothing; I judge only as I hear, and my judgment is just, for I seek not to please myself but him who sent me" (v. 30). "My teaching is not my own. It comes from him who sent me" (7:16).

Question One

My first question is how could Jesus, being God, not know what the Father wanted ahead of time? It seems impossible that Jesus could have been totally in the dark about the Father's will. How can you exist in eternity past with the Father, be equal with the Father, have perfect intimacy, then throw a switch and start over on earth as a finite being? One possible explanation is that the Godhead made a choice to cause Jesus to behave as a human and to model faith for his followers. It seems as though Jesus had a pristine connection to his Father, neither polluted by a fallen nature nor hampered by the limitations of a finite mind. This creates even more questions about the validity of Jesus' modeling the life of faith. If you know with absolute certainty that God exists, then how can that qualify as faith?

Question Two

Did Jesus really need to be taught, sent, and commanded?

So Jesus said, "When you have lifted up the Son of Man, then you will know that I am the one I claim to be and that I do nothing on my own but speak just what the Father has taught me (John 8:28).

For I did not speak of my own accord, but the Father who sent me commanded me what to say and how to say it. I know that his command leads to eternal life. So whatever I say is just what the Father has told me to say (12:49–50).

Don't you believe that I am in the Father and that the Father is in me? The words I say to you are not just my own. Rather, it is the Father, living in me, who is doing his work (14:10).

But the world must learn that I love the Father and that I do exactly what my Father has commanded me (v. 31).

It appears that Jesus didn't know what to say, that the Father had to give him the words. It also seems evident that Jesus didn't have a mission in mind, but the Father had to send him. Jesus didn't know what to do. He had to listen to the voice of the Father before acting. Jesus was sent on a mission and he chose to limit the exercise of his deity for a period of time. Is this how we should interpret these Scriptures or was Jesus making a case for his special connection and dependence on the Father in order to evangelize the Jewish leaders? Did Jesus just move from one mode to the other? Or was all that is in the above verses merely to serve as a model for us?

Not All the Truth

The axiom goes, either you were a Baptist, you are a Baptist, or you will be a Baptist. I was a Baptist and I married a Baptist and I played basketball on the Baptist church team. I found church league basketball much more dangerous than the games I played in Division One NCAA.

I am six feet, six inches tall. The senior pastor in our Baptist church was five feet, six inches tall. We played our games on Saturdays and he would always comment on the game during his Sunday sermon. One Sunday was particularly funny when he proudly proclaimed that he and I combined for a total of forty points the day before. He scored two points and I filled in the other thirty-eight. Everyone had a good laugh. It was true that we combined for forty points, but it wasn't all the truth that was needed to understand what had happened.

Everything Jesus said in the above body of teaching is true, but the questions left in its wake are significant. They have a major impact on what it means to do what Jesus did. We are still in search of how he did his works and then how we can comply with his promise and command to do the same. There are too many unanswered questions to believe that Jesus operated *exactly* as we do.

Option Two: Jesus Used His Divine Qualities

The rest of the truth is found in several texts that reveal that Jesus did use his divinity. His omnipotence (his power) and his omniscience (his knowledge) were resident within him, though not fully activated.

His Power

Jesus was asleep in the boat when the storm placed his and the disciples' lives in peril. When, in a panic, they woke him,

> He replied, "You of little faith, why are you so afraid?" Then he got up and rebuked the winds and the waves, and it was completely calm. The men were amazed and asked, "What kind of man is this? Even the winds and the waves obey him!"
>
> Matthew 8:26–27

Jesus rebuked the winds. At his command, they died down. The operative word is *command*. We pray, we seek, we beg, but God alone commands. The only exception I can think of is when we can command evil spirits to come out of a demonized person (see Luke 10:17). Commanding nature to behave and it does is godlike. The disciples had seen plenty of healings, but this was different in kind. That's why they were so astonished. Two other parallel acts were the changing of water into wine (John 2:1–11) and the multiplying of the loaves and fishes (6:1–15).

Wayne Grudem writes, "The contextual explanations do not point to the Holy Spirit, but to Jesus Himself."[3] For instance, concerning his turning water into wine, the commentary in 2:11 says "This, the first of his miraculous signs, Jesus performed at Cana in Galilee. He thus revealed his glory, and his disciples put their faith in him." These actions were not about how the Holy Spirit worked through Jesus; they were about his glory and power. His disciples believed in him because they believed it was he who was doing the miracles. They believed he was God, and they were ready to worship him. John, the author of the Gospel, was there. He could be accused of reading deity back into the text, but I see that as a plus. When you are on the good side of the resurrection, many things become clearer. John's comments reflect the godlike character of Jesus.

His Claims

If it had not been for his godlike actions, some of the things Jesus claimed would have been ridiculous. He claimed to be the only way to God (John 14:6), "I am the resurrection and the life" (11:25), "I am the light of the world" (8:12), "I am the good shepherd" (10:11). But his most outrageous statement was his claim to be eternal (8:58).

The conversation with the Jewish leaders began because they claimed Jesus was possessed by a demon. They challenged his claim to being greater than Abraham. Jesus' response was to invoke the name of God, "Before Abraham was born, I am!"[4] Jesus was claiming to have existed in eternity past, before Abraham. Jesus even said that he and Abraham knew each other (v. 56). By using "I am," the idiom the Jewish leaders understood to mean the God of Israel, Jesus had, according to them, both claimed deity and committed blasphemy.

I don't see how we can extract ourselves from these statements and claim that Jesus was operating on the same level as you and I. This, of course, has serious ramifications on our doing what Jesus did. There is more going on here than Jesus' living entirely by faith, doing all his works in the power of the Holy Spirit.

His Knowledge

Jesus seemed to have an uncommon inside track as to what people were thinking. There are people who exercise the gift of discerning of spirits or the word of knowledge and wisdom, but they cannot exercise these gifts at will. The difference between deity and the flow of the Spirit through a gifted follower is access. It would be similar to the difference between a standard phone line and a dedicated service line (DSL). One you access periodically while the latter is always open.

I sometimes have people approach me with a prophecy or word for me or the church. I always take them seriously. I pray about their message and then determine what I should do. I consider each case with optimism but also place it under the scrutiny of Scripture and the witness of the Spirit, realizing that we can have a bad connection on the phone line between us and God; there can be a lot of static on the line.

Contrast that with Jesus who never seemed to misunderstand what his Father was revealing. After forgiving the sins of the lame man in that crowded home near Capernaum, Jesus immediately knew what his enemies were thinking (Mark 2:8). When Jesus first met Nathanael, Jesus told him he had seen him under the fig tree before Philip called him (John 1:43–51). Nathanael's response was "Rabbi, you are the Son of God; you are the King of Israel" (v. 49). Jesus went on to promise that Nathanael would see heaven open and the angels of God moving in and out. Jesus' knowledge demanded belief in his deity, and Jesus promised what only God can.

Jesus entrusted himself to no person because he knew what was in the heart of man (2:25). He knew who would believe in him and who wouldn't. He knew about Judas; he knew what was in the heart of the young ruler. His disciples made note of his special knowledge in the upper room. "Then Jesus' disciples said, 'Now you are speaking clearly and without figures of speech. Now we can see that you know all things and that you do not even need to have anyone ask you questions. This makes us believe that you came from God'" (16:29–30).

It was clear to those closest to Jesus that he knew everything. They saw also that he didn't need to ask questions to find out what people were thinking; he knew already. I find this convincing proof that Jesus exercised his deity. How he was actually God and man remains a mystery. I won't be resolving that mystery, but I will discuss the practical application of the God-Man—how it all works out in practice—based on the conclusion that orthodox Christians have reached. There cannot be any doubt, however, about the fact that Jesus chose at times to display his divine attributes.

His Sovereignty

There are three instances that reveal Jesus behaving in a way that only God could. The first is the healing of the paralytic in that crowded home in Capernaum (Mark 2:1–12). The first thing Jesus did was not to heal the man, it was to forgive his sins. The healing was only to demonstrate his authority to cleanse the man. It was recognized by theologians then and now that God alone has the power to forgive sins. Doing what Jesus did does not give us the right to forgive other people's sins. I don't ask my good Christian friends to forgive my sins. I do ask them to forgive me for hurting them.

Another interesting divine act was Jesus' promise to be present with his followers when two or three would get together (Matt. 18:20). The promise of his presence is remarkable because it requires omnipresence and immortality. Whether it is two saints in Singapore in 1972 or thousands in Seoul, Korea, in 2005, he promised to be there. He promised to be many places simultaneously, and the promise applies to the undetermined future. That means Jesus was teaching that he was sovereign, all knowing, and present everywhere.

The third way Jesus exercised his sovereignty is when he appeared to his disciples to issue the Great Commission (28:16–20). It is telling that Jesus accepted the worship of his disciples.

What a mystery this all is! Based on just the points I have made, he has my worship. I embrace the mystery and I embrace him.

The Power of Life and Death

Jesus frustrated the Jewish leaders and baffled his disciples. A case in point is his cryptic answer as to why he had reacted so violently to the selling of sacrificial animals in the temple: "Destroy this temple, and I will raise it again in three days" (John 2:19). Later the disciples understood this was in reference to his own death and resurrection. The operative words are *I will raise*, meaning, I have the power to do so. Jesus claimed this power in another famous passage. One of Jesus' most memorable sermons included the assertion that he is the good shepherd. Four times he speaks of laying his life down for the sheep (10:11, 15, 17, 18).

The nexus of his claim is this:

> The reason my Father loves me is that I lay down my life—only to take it up again. No one takes it from me, but I lay it down of my own accord. I have authority to lay it down and authority to take it up again. This command I received from my Father.
>
> John 10:17–18

Much of Jesus' teaching had to be contextualized for Israel's consumption. He taught that he is God, having existed from eternity past, not having been created by the Father but equal to the Father. With this understanding, we know that God the Father has always loved God the Son. Jesus teaches this way to relate the intimate connection between Israel's God and himself.

Jesus said that he received a *command* from the Father, but he uses the word *command* as an accommodation to the listeners. In actual fact God the Father and God the Son agreed on the redemptive plan. Jesus' language seeks to communicate truth in a way his listeners will understand. The language honors the place of the Father in the Jewish mind. At the same time the language portrays an intimate relationship. That makes it impossible for the Jewish leaders or his disciples to ignore what he says. The establishment's response is that Jesus is demon possessed. But others conclude that you can't heal the blind and at the same time be possessed. The bottom line is that Jesus already possessed the power of life and death. He teaches it as a delegated authority, but in fact, by divine nature, he already had the authority.

It is fair to conclude that Jesus at times behaved as deity and even allowed others to treat him as such. It is also true that he operated by faith as a model for all who would believe in him. Those of us separated from Jesus by two thousand years of human interpretation are still called to do what Jesus did. We are not alone in our confusion. Our spiritual forefathers also struggled to find the right chord to strike. The two options we have considered—that Jesus operated by faith or that he used his divine qualities—are suspended in theological tension. Both seem to be true, so we must go where others have gone before and discuss the nature of the God-Man.

The God-Man's Nature

The God-Man's nature and practice while on earth is described in Paul's letter to the Philippian church.

> Your attitude should be the same as that of Christ Jesus:
> Who, being in very nature God,
>   did not consider equality with God something to be grasped,
> *but made himself nothing,*
>   taking the very nature of a servant,
>   being made in human likeness.
> And being found in appearance as a man,
>   he humbled himself
>   and became obedient to death—even death on a cross!
>
> Philippians 2:5–8

The italicized words above come from the Greek verb *keno,* meaning "to empty." This is commonly referred to as the kenosis passage. The classic understanding has been that Jesus voluntarily laid aside his right to be recognized as God while on earth. He also humbled himself to take a subservient role to the Father. This was an act of love that went as far as giving up his life on the cross.

The controversy concerns what he emptied himself of. Was it the actual departure of his divinity or the regular exercise of his powers? The passage never really says he emptied himself of divinity.

The kenosis theory was championed by theologians in both England and Germany, from about 1860 to 1880 in Germany and from 1890 to 1910 in England.[5] The theory teaches that "to empty" means that Jesus laid aside some of his divine attributes while on earth, that they actually left him and he lived totally by faith in the power of the Father and/or the Holy Spirit. This was a strategy that the Father and Son agreed on and was a voluntary act on the part of Jesus.

Wayne Grudem gives three reasons that the kenosis theory is wrong.

1. No recognized teacher in the first eighteen hundred years of church history, including those who were native speakers of Greek, thought that "emptied himself" meant that the Son of God gave up some of his divine attributes.
2. The text does not say that Christ emptied himself of any powers.
3. The text does describe what Jesus did in "emptying." He did not do it by giving up any of his attributes but rather by taking the form of a servant. The context itself interprets this "emptying" as equivalent to "humbling himself" and taking on a lowly status.[6]

Jesus gave up status and privilege. He didn't grasp for the accolades, for the advantage. The main thrust of the passage is for all followers of Jesus to look out for others, to consider other people's needs more important than their own. Jesus is our model of such humility and service. If Jesus intended to shelve his deity, such a momentous event would be expressed more clearly than one word with a questionable interpretation in the New Testament.

Controversy as to who the God-Man really was challenged the early church. It wasn't until the Chalcedonian definition of A.D. 451 that a clear conclusion was reached. In the city of Chalcedon, near modern Istanbul, a large group of leaders met for three weeks. There had been three theories concerning the God-Man that had gained some momentum. Apollinarianism taught that Jesus had a human body but not a human mind. Nestorianism said that Jesus was two separate persons, one human, the other divine. This violated the scriptural position that Jesus was

one person. Eutychianism believed that Jesus had only one nature. The human nature was absorbed in the divine nature.
The council arrived at four conclusions:

1. "The human and the divine natures were not confused or changed when Christ became a man, but the human nature remained a truly human nature, and the divine nature remained a truly divine nature."
2. "It [the council] taught that Christ definitely had two natures, a human nature and a divine nature. It taught that his divine nature is exactly the same as that of the Father. And it maintained that the human nature is exactly like our human nature, yet without sin."
3. "It affirmed that in the person of Christ the human nature retains its distinctive characteristics, and the divine nature retains its distinctive characteristics."
4. "It is affirmed that, whether we can understand it or not, these two natures are united together in the one person of Christ."[7]

The summary statement I learned in seminary is "Jesus is fully God and fully man, united in one person forever."

God-Man Anomalies

At the same time, Jesus was in the manger and was holding the universe together. The mystery of the God-Man is also the God-Baby who created all things but became an infant and while in the crib was holding the universe together by his power:

> For by him all things were created: things in heaven and on earth.
> . . . all things were created by him and for him. . . . He is before all things and in him all things hold together . . . for God was pleased to have all his fullness dwell in him.

Tired yet Omnipotent

Jesus was weary from a day's work and fell asleep in the boat. He was awakened and then calmed the storm. How could Jesus be omnipotent and yet weak? How could he leave the world and yet be present everywhere? How could he learn things and be omniscient?

Subject to Death yet Eternal

Jesus died on the cross, but God cannot die. When we say that Jesus died for our sins, we must ask, what part of Jesus died? We are forced to reason within the limits of our language and intellect. We would say something like Jesus' perfect humanity died. For the purposes of discussion we would need to split the God-Man, yet we believe that both are there and fully integrated in a way we cannot comprehend. Once again we must embrace that Jesus is one person, not two. We are forced to admit that the nature of the God-Man is outside of our intellectual purview.

Tempted yet Unable to Sin

Jesus was tempted at every point as we are, but God cannot be tempted and he himself tempts no one (see James 1:13). Here is another anomaly. Jesus' temptation plays a major role in both his victory over evil and his being a role model for us.[8]

Since Jesus possessed no sin nature in his perfect humanity, he could not sin. And since God cannot be tempted, what significance could Jesus' temptation have? My answer has always been that while most of us give in to temptation before it reaches its full intensity, Jesus took the full hit every time. Since Jesus stood at the center of the redemptive drama, his temptations were directly from Satan, thus more difficult. Jesus can sympathize with our temptations, but not with our sins.

The Answer to the Anomalies

About the God-Man, Grudem writes, "Anything either nature does, the person of Christ does."[9] Anything that is true of the human Jesus is true of the divine Jesus. If I said I took a test, my mind and hands were central to the task. But the rest of me was present also, so the whole of me took the test. Jesus will-

ingly laid aside the free exercise of his divinity while on earth.
He did not, however, cease to be fully God and fully man. He
was the same person we believe him to be, but he made choices
to activate his deity on special occasions. When it gets down to
it, we can't really understand him. The mystery of the Godhead,
the intimacy, the strategy, the inner workings of Jesus are above
and beyond us. Yet we are called to be like him and to do the
works he did. He modeled some things for us and we are to follow. I have concluded there are three levels of living. Jesus alone
operates on the first two; we are limited to the third.

Deity in Action

When Jesus turned water into wine, fed the five thousand,
calmed the storm, and raised Lazarus from the dead, he was
operating on a level that is above and beyond even the greatest
human faith. When Jesus knew exactly what people were thinking and even more dramatically what was in their hearts, he was
exercising deity, for God alone knows the heart of man (see Jer.
17:9–10). Not only did he know a specific person's heart about
a certain subject, he knew the overall condition of a person's
heart continually. As I have studied these acts of Jesus, and more,
I have become convinced that some of the things Jesus did and
said are his alone. We will never do them, nor should we try.

Pristine Faith in Perfect Humanity

It is clear that Jesus operated by faith. He was "the author
and perfecter of our faith" (Heb. 12:2). Faith is defined as "being
sure of what we hope for and certain of what we do not see"
(11:1). Jesus was sure and certain because he had been there—
done that! What role does faith play when you have existed since
eternity past? Jesus played a part in the creation of the world
and had absolute certitude concerning the eternal state and the
existence of God. I don't think his faith was the faith that humans
normally experience. It could be faith in that in his humanity
Jesus was tempted to doubt and to be swayed by the environs
of earth. His spirit was troubled over the resistance of Jerusa-

lem, the battle with Satan in the wilderness, and the thought in Gethsemane of physical death.

All the faith challenges Jesus experienced in his humanity were legitimate tests. Jesus could have called angels to help him. He could have opted out of the long and agonizing procedure to save the world. The greatest temptations that prisoners of war faced during Vietnam were the offers of early release, but honor and duty encouraged most of the men to resist the temptation. Jesus had the option through the exercise of his divinity to blast Satan and emerge victorious. He chose the more honorable way that would also rescue humankind. But please remember, Jesus' faith was a pristine faith, unhindered by the pollutants of a sin nature.

I don't think Jesus lay awake at night like me, wondering if the human experience is a water bubble on the thumb of a superior creature in a larger world. I struggle with my faith when I think of the great suffering of humanity. I sometimes question the strangeness of the gospel story and wonder why it is superior to other religious stories. Why would God allow people to spend eternity in hell when they messed up only seventy years on earth? Isn't that overkill? These journeys of doubt don't last long, but they are real.

In my quest to equal and exceed the works of Jesus, there will be interruptions of the power flow. My doubts and sins will cause my faith to be weak and sometimes missing in action. Whatever I experience in doing the works of Jesus will be somewhat inferior because my humanity is fallen and my faith polluted. That leaves me with the third level of living in which I can endeavor to do the works that Jesus did.

Fallen but Regenerated Faith

Doing what Jesus did in a limited way, that is our reality. Yes, it is true that as we walk by faith, it is the Holy Spirit who works through us. So we are not doing our works in our own power. But we are not as pure an instrument as Jesus; therein lies the difference. We can do the works of Jesus—we can even exceed the works of Jesus in quantity—but it would be wrong for us to start acting as though we have the authority to command anything to happen like Jesus did. On the other hand it is crucial for us to believe that many more people will be helped in a supernatural way if we believe that God will do Jesus' works through us.

I can't know the heart of every person continually, but periodically I can discern spirits or receive prophecy in which God gives me specific information about an individual to help him or her in time of need. Perhaps only 40 percent of the people I pray for will be healed, but that is 40 percent more than if I hadn't prayed for healing. Our level of operation in doing the works of Jesus is imperfect and a faith challenge, but we must go forward anyway.

Properly Relating
to the Written Record

Rudolf Bultmann was a bad guy because he wanted to take the miracles out of the New Testament. That is what I was told in my contemporary theology class at Oral Roberts University. It seemed like the German brigade of Barth, Brunner, Bonhoeffer, and Bultmann were dedicated to removing the miraculous from God's Word.[1] Actually Bultmann was a devout Lutheran, modest in demeanor and careful in his study. He was passionate about his spiritual life and well intentioned in trying to help others find Christ. He is best-known for his essay to pastors, delivered in lecture form in Frankfurt in 1941. Spending his life teaching theology at several German universities, Bultmann retired to writing and speaking in 1951.

Bultmann's goal was to make the Christian faith more relevant in modern society. To this end he introduced a new method of biblical interpretation to the theological world that would demythologize the New Testament, divesting it of its primitive worldview.[2] Bultmann's passion was to encourage the proclamation of the gospel in terms that modern society could accept.

Bultmann proposed a system of interpretation that would change the meaning of the miracles of Christ. He did not propose removing the stories but rather finding the meaning behind them. To Bultmann, myths were ways that man expressed his own understanding of his existence. It was man's way of talking about the mysteries of God in human terms.

Bultmann's rather elaborate system of interpretation, however well intentioned, yielded devastating results. It led to many not believing in the works of Jesus. His feeding the five thousand, changing water into wine, walking on water, or raising Lazarus were just stories, not real events. Bultmann's well-intentioned attempts to make Christ more relevant ended up making Christ less than he is.

Bultmann's mistake was to begin with a false assumption and then apply a false method that led to a false conclusion. He wrongly assumed that the average person could not relate to the myths or miracles. Actually it was the average German professor with the predisposition to doubt that had the problem. He therefore used a scientific hermeneutic with the predisposition to eliminate any metaphysical phenomena. This led to false interpretations, such as his conclusion that Jesus' resurrection is a lesson on improvement, rather than the means by which Jesus can come to live in us.

Making Jesus less is not the exclusive assignment of the liberal or neoorthodox theologian. Some evangelicals have made the same mistake as Bultmann. Bultmann thought the miracles never happened; many evangelicals say they happened, but they don't happen anymore. In our own way we have removed God's power from our lives. For Bultmann the power was never there. Some evangelicals say the power was there but is now gone. Either way you get the same results—diminished power.

The cessationists[3] of today are trying to make the Bible more palatable to their experience. Bultmann reached his conclusions based on his view of Scripture and his predisposition to doubt miracles. Evangelicals who doubt the continuation of certain gifts also have approached Scripture with a predisposition not to believe it as it is plainly written.

Theological Bias

Reading the Bible is a challenging quest. It is difficult to grasp its meaning without an understanding of history, culture, and language. But the more we study history, culture, and language, the more we are influenced by our teachers who have a theological bias. We then become products of interpretive subgroups, with the natural tendency to read our theology into the Scriptures. There are study Bibles that explain the meaning of passages to us so that we don't need to do any independent thinking. The old axiom when reading a study Bible goes, "Start reading at the top of the page." In other words, read the Scripture and attempt to understand it before reading the commentary on it. We are products of our theological systems, and they generally govern our understanding. If the subject is the security of the believer, there are two schools of thought and the student is told how to handle the difficult passages. They are difficult because they are the proof texts for the other view. The same is true of the charismatic and cessationist viewpoints regarding the gifts of the Spirit. Each view has its proof texts and its interpretations of those that are used to support the opposing view.

As previously mentioned I was for years a convinced and articulate cessationist. There were several events that worked together to cause me to reconsider my position. I then engaged in a serious study of the relevant passages that exposed my bias. I simply asked the question, Does the Bible really teach this? When I studied the Scripture without a certain predisposition, the evidence for the cessationist position evaporated.

I didn't have a name for what I was until I read Jack Deere's article, "Confessions of a Biblical Deist."[4] Many of the framers of the U.S. Constitution were Deist in theological persuasion. They believed in the religion of morality based on natural reason. They rejected divine revelation and taught that God created the universe, wound it up like a clock, then stepped back to let it run down.

The biblical Deist has a lot in common with the natural Deist. They both worship the wrong thing. The Deist of the eighteenth century worshiped human reason. The biblical Deist worships the Bible. This is not a conscious or intended belief, but, for the biblical Deist, Christ and the Bible have merged into one. Since I was of this mind for a very long time, I can vouch for the subtle nature of this malady. Usually one does not set out to be a biblical Deist. It is certainly not a matter of confession. It is a subtle belief, and it is significant. The biblical Deist has lost the distinction between knowing God and knowing the Scriptures, between worshiping the Bible and worshiping God. Therefore, the language and focus of this genre of the faith is "being biblical," and the key to spiritual growth is to know more about the Bible. This person thinks of obedience to the Bible, rather than following Jesus. The practice seems impersonal and sometimes it is. I want to make it clear that I had a strong relationship with Christ during my years of being a biblical Deist. It naturally follows that I believe many in the biblical Deist camp also have a warm and strong relationship with Jesus. But I found myself relating to the written record more than to Jesus. The reason for this is the biblical Deist's inherent belief that God has finished talking to us.

Knowing Jesus Is a Bible Study

There was a time when I didn't care what music the choir sang or whether we used hymnals, sang from song sheets, or played CDs. I just wanted to get the preliminaries over so I could learn. Like many well-intentioned believers, I shut out all other stimuli. I just wanted the Word. We desperately need to study the Scriptures; in fact we can't grow without them.[5] But the danger in making the study of the Word the main or only thing is that we can't hear God's voice when he decides to comment on his Word. I never expected God to impress anything on me through other people or events. I was to follow biblical principles. As you can see, this entire discussion is rather tricky. It is not a matter of either/or, but of both/and. God can and does communicate to us in other ways besides his Word.

I have started taking time to listen to the voice of God. This is an uncut trail for me and for most of the people in my ministry. I am also taking more time with others to listen. This means five minutes of quiet reflection after praying specifically that God would speak to us. It can seem like five hours. The longer the silence, the thicker the tension. This is because we are so success-failure trained that if God doesn't say something, we think we have failed. The only way that God comments on his Word is if we give him the time and opportunity. Normally it is through an impression or a Scripture that is laser sharp in its application. Try it in a small gathering first. Take five minutes and wait. If nothing happens, so be it, but continue it week after week, and the listening ability will improve. Its value is the personalized touch of God in application and the development of an ear for God.

The biblical Deist's position is that Christ cannot or has chosen not to speak apart from the Bible.[6] He used to speak in an audible voice. He would appear in dreams and visions. He did miracles through his followers. The irony is that a good share of Christians believe that the only one who does these things now is Satan. Satan does what Jesus used to do—he appears to people; he speaks in an audible voice; he gives people dreams and visions. I have at least twenty volumes in my library that deal with the activity of Satan. There seems to be no end to the ways he communicates. Christians believe Satan is a chatterbox. When someone feels guilty about a forgiven sin, with great confidence we say, "That is the voice of Satan." It is that still small voice that makes us feel smaller still. We believe that Satan manifests himself through the voice box of persons he inhabits. We believe that he manifests himself in a séance. Some even believe that he manifests himself in flying objects, UFOs that are meant to confuse people about ultimate meaning.

I will need to say this several times. I believe that the Scriptures are the authoritative communication of God to his church. I even believe they are without error in the original autographs.

But there must be a discussion about the difference between the Bible and God himself.

The Bible is a tool that God has provided for us so we can have a basis on which to relate to him. It is the story about God and man and how our relationship was broken and how God did what was needed to repair it. God wants a relationship with us. Where there is a relationship, there must be fresh communication to keep it alive.

Let's say that on my wedding day I presented my bride with a thick book of all my opinions, beliefs, wishes, and wise sayings. "My darling, I want you to have this book. Whenever you think of something you want to know about me, please look it up. You can talk to me, but the only answer I will give you is already in the book. I know that sometimes the book is not specifically suited to answer your questions, but you can figure it out if you are patient." I'm sure she would protest, "Hey, wait a minute. This is a marriage, a relationship. We need to communicate."

I believe that all impressions, visions, dreams, prophecies, and other messages must be tested by the authority of Scripture. But I believe that God desires that we continue to have a vital and live communication with him. God speaks primarily through his written Word, but not exclusively. We can have it both ways. We can have an authoritative written record in the Scriptures. We can also have affirming signs from God that encourage our hearts and strengthen our faith. We can have our cake and eat it too.

How do we properly relate to the Word of God? There are three questions to ask and answer. What is the Word of God? How do I know if I am limiting the Word of God? And how do I connect with God on a deeper level through his Word?

What Is the Word of God?

May I be the master of the obvious? It is the Word *of God*. The word *of* denotes possession. The origin of any communication is God. The Word *of* God preceded any written documents, the Word *of* God is whatever God says. God created language. Words are symbols that when heard or seen represent images that have meaning to us. Since the Word of God is whatever God says, his communication cannot be limited to the Bible. He has spoken many more words than are found in the written record. That doesn't make it any less God's Word because it is not in the Bible. God said more to Adam than is recorded. Whatever God told Adam was just as much God's Word as what is recorded.

God communicated to many of his followers, and we have no record of what was said. Job is a prime example. How did he know the only true God? How did Job come to understand the nature and plan of God? There is no answer except that God must have communicated with Job. He told Job enough to cause him to trust God through one of the most horrific episodes of suffering in history.

The apostle John tells us that Jesus did and taught so much that all the books in the world, or the world itself could not contain them (John 21:25). There were not many books in the first century, and the world was considered flat and small. Even so, John was engaging in some hyperbole. His point, however, supplements the truth that Jesus said many things that were not recorded in the written record. There were many words that Jesus spoke that were not teaching. If he told Peter to get some firewood or pass the bread, that would not be included in the written record unless it happened to be integral to the story. In the case of feeding the five thousand, Jesus gave some pedestrian instructions that were important to the story. But when we are speaking of the Word of God, it would be safe to restrict the term to mean Jesus' teachings.

The accumulated words of Jesus, then, are no less the Word of God than our Bibles. If Jesus said them, they originated in God. The Word of God is all the words that God has spoken or intended for man to hear. The words of man, however, even if they are impressions given by the Spirit of God, are not equal to Scripture. The Bible is unique in its claim to inspiration and in its acceptance by the church. The Bible is the written record that God has seen fit to leave with us for our instruction. The Word of God, then, has three primary vehicles: the living word, the spoken word, and the written word.

THE LIVING WORD

Jesus was called the Word in the first few lines of John's Gospel: "In the beginning was the Word, and the Word was with God, and the Word was God" (1:1). John describes two personages, the same in essence, nature, and deity. In eternity past they coexisted. They were different but also the same. This reminds us of the axiom, "Deny the Trinity and lose your soul. Try to explain it and you will lose your mind."

Later the text identifies the Word as Jesus: "The Word became flesh and made his dwelling among us. We have seen his glory, the glory of the One and Only, who came from the Father, full of grace and truth" (v. 14).

The Greek *logos* in English is *word*. Jesus is communication. He is the Word of God because Jesus is God speaking to the world. The Father says, "If you want to know what God is like, look at Jesus." I am reminded of E. Stanley Jones's statement, "If God isn't like Jesus, he ought to be." Jesus is the compelling and life-changing communication from God to humankind. Through both actions and teachings, Jesus is the explainer of God.

Immediately we can see that the Word of God is broader than the written record. This in no way diminishes the Bible. It does, however, put the Scriptures into a larger context. God has created multifaceted ways to speak to his creation.

THE SPOKEN WORD

It is a challenge for Christians living at the turn of the twenty-first century to fully grasp the fluidity of the Word of God in the first century. We have always used the term, "Word of God" to mean the Bible. The early Christians had the "Word of God" converging on them from four directions. They studied and heard sermons on the Old Testament. There were also the oral teachings of the apostles, their circulating letters, as well as the oral traditions of Christ's teaching. Additionally, there had to be overlap among the latter three sources. By the third century it had all been sorted out and canonized into what we know as the Bible.[7] The verbal teachings of Christ were not recorded the moment he said them. There was no court stenographer, but they were nonetheless the Word of God. "I tell you the truth, whoever hears my word and believes him who sent me has eternal life and will not be condemned; he has crossed over from death to life" (John 5:24).

It is obvious but important to know that words from God not found in our Bibles were as divinely powerful to change a person's life as the Scripture. These were spoken words, not canonized words. The words spoken to the five thousand recently fed listeners or the many conversations with the disciples, all carried the impact of the Word of God because their source *was* God. The spoken words that come from God are living and active as self-described in Hebrews 4:12.

I am not making a case for present-day communication through prophecies and such as equal to the written record. I am saying that the Word of God is divine because it comes from God. Words spoken by a Christian employing the gift of prophecy are polluted words of God, polluted by the ravages of the fallen nature; whereas words spoken by God himself are no less the Word of God than what we have in our Bibles. God spoke volumes more than are recorded in the Bible. He simply selected a limited edition of all his thoughts and teachings that would be included in Scripture.

THE WRITTEN WORD

Paul was advising Timothy and in the process gave us our most definitive declaration concerning the written record.

> But as for you, continue in what you have learned and have become convinced of, because you know those from whom you learned it, and how from infancy you have known the holy Scriptures, which are able to make you wise for salvation through faith in Christ Jesus. All Scripture is God-breathed and is useful for teaching, rebuking, correcting and training in righteousness, so that the man of God may be thoroughly equipped for every good work.
>
> 2 Timothy 3:14–17

It doesn't naturally occur to contemporary Christians that Paul is speaking here of the Old Testament. It is obvious that in Timothy's youth there was no New Testament. In fact there was no New Testament at the time Paul is writing to Timothy. Of course, it was in the process of being written and it very well could have been 50 percent completed. There was no debate between Jesus and Jewish scholars as to the canon of the Old Testament. It is also significant that by A.D. 397 there was agreement among church leaders as to the canon of the New Testament.[8] The reason that the Old Testament could make Timothy wise to salvation was the fulfillment of prophecy and the christological passages now interpreted in the light of completed events.

Now, while Paul's reference is primarily to the Old Testament, anything that was later accepted as Scripture also qualified as God-breathed and authoritative. Our Bibles are the written record, inspired by God, and without error in the original writings. The Bible serves as our standard against all other thoughts and ideologies. If someone came to me and claimed to have a word from God, it would have to be tested against the standard of Scripture. Whatever communication comes to the church via the supernatural manifestations, the gifts of the Spirit, this communication would always play a supporting role to Scripture.

A MEANS TO AN END

When it is said that the Word of God will endure forever, it doesn't mean the fifty-plus English translations of the Bible. We won't all be issued King James Bibles in our heavenly starter kits. There will be no need for Bible study in heaven. We will be in God's presence and we will know the truth fully as we have been fully known. Then, the word of God will expand beyond even the pre-fall relationship with Adam. He will speak to us for eternity. Then it will be literally true that all the books in the world cannot contain what he will tell us. The end is to know God, to experience him fully, to worship him, to be with him. *This is why, in the end, we will not be worshiping the Bible.*

The creation was rocked by the fall, and the point of the entire redemptive drama is getting us back to perfect communion with God. The Bible is a primary tool God has chosen to get us into his unadulterated presence. That is why we worship God, not his Word.

Learn the Beauty of *And*

The canon is closed. We have an authoritative Scripture that is sufficient for living (see 2 Peter 1:3–4). *And* God is still talking to us. I think of God as the author who wants to comment on his work.

My first book was published in 1984. I have spent a great deal of time since then commenting on my writing. Each time I publish a work, there is an effort launched by the publisher to promote it. There are many authors who employ agents to get them interviews, book reviews, and appearances on the *Larry King Show*. Writers want to explain and comment on their work. They also want to affirm their points of view and persuade readers to subscribe to those ideas. The writer's motivation usually is self-serving. After all, there is money and fame involved.

Unlike the contemporary author, God's motivation is unquestioned. God desires to give a loving personal touch to his children, so he comments on his written Word primarily through spiritual gifts.

Recently I was discouraged. I sat in my office wondering if God was ever going to give us *the breakthrough*. I have been praying for not just any breakthrough, but *the* breakthrough. For me that means God pouring out his Spirit on our church as he predicted in Acts 2:6–18:

> No, this is what was spoken by the prophet Joel:
>   "In the last days, God says,
>   I will pour out my Spirit on all people.
>   Your sons and daughters will prophesy,
>   your young men will see visions,
>   your old men will dream dreams.
>   Even on my servants, both men and women,
>   I will pour out my Spirit in those days,
>   and they will prophesy."
>
>   Acts 2:16–18

People demanded an explanation for a group of people running into the streets preaching the gospel in various languages. The observers decided they were drunk. Peter says, no, this is not a group of drunks. This isn't Belfast on St. Paddy's Day. This is the promised outpouring of God's Spirit on all people, Jews and Gentiles. I believe this fulfillment of prophecy on the day of Pentecost was a foretaste of what God has planned for us. As time moves toward history's climax, the frequency and intensity of such phenomena will increase. I know God has already filled his church with the Spirit. But God's presence is thin and we are only ankle deep in the waters of renewal. I thirst for more and expect more as we seek God with all our hearts. It is in this context that God hears our prayers and begins to comment on his writing. He affirms and speaks personally to us.

It was a typical Sunday morning, but I had gone into the service that day a depressed spirit. My only hope was what I prayed before I left my office. "O, God, encourage me; give me something; speak to me in a way that I can grab hold."

At the end of the service people were coming to the front for prayer. A member sat down next to me and said, "God has given me a word for you. While you were preaching, I saw you making bread. You were stirring the dough. Then you placed the dough in the oven. I saw you continually going to the oven and looking through the little window to see if the dough would rise." I immediately understood. The dough was the church. I was working, stirring, doing everything I knew how to get it to grow or rise.

She went on. "You need to know that God says the dough will rise. You have nothing to worry about." Wow! That was it. God gave me what I needed through one of his daughters. She had been obedient and, through her gift, God gave me exactly what I needed. We learn from the Scriptures that people can communicate what God has revealed to them. Through that gift God confirmed my efforts and my direction. We can have both—the written record and fresh, personal words from God. We do have both. But do you have both?

Have you, like Thomas Jefferson, removed the miracles from the Bible?[9] Or, like Bultmann, have you left them there but redefined their meaning? My guess is that many have created a hybrid Bible, leaving the miracles in, but saying they no longer happen. Have you considered the net effect of this approach? If you are a leader, your decision could hamstring your ministry by eliminating some of the gifts the church desperately needs. So I ask you to consider with me some of the dangers of taking that position.

How Do I Know If I Am Limiting the Word of God?

Jesus battled with the theologically biased. No group enjoyed hours of in-depth Bible study more than Jesus' opponents. John's Gospel referred to Jesus' nemeses as simply the Jews. They were more than mere Jews. They were Pharisees, Sadducees, and scribes. The Pharisees were conservative and political, the Sadducees were theologically liberal, and the scribes were scholars. These men studied the Scriptures carefully and reverently. They were sincere, and their primary interest was to protect the Scriptures from subjectivism.

They also had preconceived notions of what the Messiah would be like, and Jesus wasn't it. There were numerous holy men wandering first-century Israel claiming to be some type of messiah. The Jewish leaders' skepticism was grounded in good motives. They were zealots for the faith and would go to almost any length to protect it. Jesus' confrontation with the leaders reveals their bias and how it affected their interpretation of the Scripture.

The Jews were not great fans of the Baptist, but at least he didn't claim to be God. Jesus compared himself to John: "I have testimony weightier than that of John. For the very work that the Father has given me to finish, and which I am doing, testifies that the Father has sent me" (John 5:36). Then Jesus goes on to make an accusation. "And the Father who sent me has himself testified concerning me. You have never heard his voice nor seen his form, nor does his word dwell in you, for you do not believe the one he sent" (vv. 37–38).

The nature of conversion was a bit fuzzy during this period, but the core of it was a heart belief in Jesus as Messiah. The well-intentioned men standing before him didn't have the capacity to understand. The Word had not taken root.

LISTENING WITHOUT HEARING

"You diligently study the Scriptures because you think that by them you possess eternal life. These are the Scriptures that testify about me, yet you refuse to come to me to have life" (vv. 39–40).

Have you ever had the experience of carefully explaining a technique or procedure to someone and they can't seem to get it? You could teach me for hours how to assemble an easy-to-assemble appliance, and I would not get it. I have mechanical dyslexia. I am not equipped to get it.

These scholars were carefully studying the Scriptures but were coming up empty when it came to Jesus. Why hadn't the Word found good soil in the souls of these very religious men? The reason was they had already decided that Jesus couldn't be the Messiah. Whenever you make up your mind what you believe before you read the Scriptures, then your interpretation is predetermined. The Jews were reading Scripture, but it was having no effect. There are many who Sunday after Sunday listen to the Word preached, but they don't change. Compiling more and more information, their minds implode under the weight of the unused knowledge. These are spiritual schizophrenics, experts on what they are not experiencing. I am not equating believing evangelicals to unbelieving Jewish scholars, but a believing Christian can predetermine what he or she will believe before an honest study of the text. There are well-studied cessationists, but there are far more by custom than by study.

Searching without Finding

It is startling what Jesus says to people who knew their Bibles better than most of us. He said they thought eternal life comes from more knowledge and a better grasp of the documents. They considered themselves the supersleuths of scholarship, but they had missed the point. He said that the Scriptures were about him, but they wouldn't open their hearts to him. Because of political reasons, theological bias, or cultural history, the established Jewish leaders couldn't see Jesus as the main character in their redemptive story. Their primary relationship was to the written record. Their interpretation was geared to their comfort zone. They wanted to study the Scriptures, cultivate the intellect, and feel in control. Jesus challenged not only their interpretation but their way of life. There is a fallacy that teaches the more you know about the Bible, the closer you are to God. These leaders prove that philosophy wrong. They knew more, but they understood less. Knowledge is power says the contemporary culture. But the story of Scripture reveals knowing God is power.

The Jewish scholars believed in the truth of Scripture. They believed the stories of Abraham leaving Ur and risking all to obey God. They believed the stories about Sodom and Gomorrah and the rescue of Lot, Moses and the burning bush, the ten plagues, and the Passover. These were all dearly held traditions. We could go on, David and Goliath, Samson and Delilah, Elijah on Mount Carmel; they didn't doubt any of them. They just never expected anything as significant to happen to them. The Scriptures were a book of inspirational memories, more of a scrapbook than a living document. It would have been great to have been there, to know the heroes, but they believed their place was to remember—not to expect to duplicate the experiences. Their pride and theological bias didn't allow them to experience God's mercy and power.

Making the Same Mistake

Liberals deny that miracles ever happened. The Jesus Seminar[10] is proof enough that a predisposition to doubt is followed by an interpretation that discounts the miraculous. I remember a professor teaching that the Israelites crossed, not the Red Sea but the Reed Sea. This was in a different location and it was only knee deep. One wonders how the Egyptian army drowned in two feet of water.

You have to have a deep moral or cultural reason to spend your life explaining away the Bible as it was written and normally interpreted. After the liberals are finished with the Bible, there is precious little to believe in. What you have left is the instruction to be nice to each other, form a circle, join hands, sway back and forth—it's a Pepsi commercial!

But are Bible-believing evangelicals any better? Sadly not much, because many of us are filled with the same unbelief. We worship the biblical characters and the miraculous stories of the early church, but functionally we end up in the same place as the other skeptics. The stories, starting with Jesus' changing water into wine, thrill the soul, but we don't expect any of that stuff to happen to us. If California Christians could change water into Merlot, they could put Robert Mondavi and the Napa Valley out of business.

I confess that unskilled winemaking is frivolous, but experiencing the relevant power of God is not. On the whole, miracles might as well be religious fairy tales, because we don't believe they are to be part of our experience. The Bible then becomes a book of abstract truth about God. It is a guide to a moral life, and if we mix the holy tips with a little discipline, we can live better lives. For too many, that is where it all ends. The Scriptures do give guidelines on raising children, but it also teaches that through prayer God will heal a rebellious teen. How about overcoming drug addiction or restoring trust to a broken marriage?

In the spring of 1987, while working on a sermon, I took a call from my oldest son's high school. I was told he had violated school rules by smoking marijuana. I will never forget walking into the principal's office and seeing my son's glazed eyes, filled with shame and anger. This heartbreaking episode began a four-year trip into hell for our family. This included Bob's placement in two treatment programs, the first for three months, the second for two and a half years. The latter was a fine school that really turned it around for him and us.[11] Today he is happily married, a college graduate and a graphic designer living in Southern California. But for a number of years we thought we might lose him. God provided some wonderful people who have dedicated their lives to help the hard-to-parent child. But at its root, what saved our son's life was God's mercy and our commitment as parents to what the Scriptures teach about rebellion.

We got a lot of advice, and almost everyone thought we should identify what mistakes we had made. No doubt we had made mistakes and we have faced those over the years. But I knew in my heart that we had neither abused nor neglected our son. We had not even forced on him a certain script that we had written for him. We did, however, understand that he had a strong spirit of rebellion. The key to success is often just knowing the right question. The right question was, What breaks the back of rebellion?

Jane and I began to pray and fast. One day Jane went away to be alone with God. She returned with what I consider to be a prophetic word. She found it in Psalm 107. The psalm is long and it details the nature of rebellion and what it takes to break rebellion's back. It shows levels of rebellion and explains how some people's rebellion requires more discipline from God to break. The bottom line is that it takes pain and desperation for many to call out to God for help.

The prophetic word was that God would break the chains that held our son; he would be rescued from darkness and gloom, and there would be songs of rejoicing. One day we would sing for joy. The vital importance to all this is that we believed in the miraculous work and promises of God. We had many choices and approaches that were offered to us by others. Many of these ideas were well intended, but they did not really deal with the rebellious spirit. We placed our son's life in the hands of God based on his Word, and we did so by sending him to a Christian treatment program.

It is a terrible thing to have to admit to yourself that you can no longer parent your child. Little did we know how our prophetic message would be challenged. The first program just didn't fit our son. He tried to make it work, but his personality didn't respond. He fought with the counselors—some of these were knock-down-drag-out physical battles with several teachers trying to control him. In the end he ran away and spent several days living at a truck stop in Colorado. We brought him home with an agreement, which he immediately refused to follow.

We placed him in a special local school. He only got worse because of his drug use. I finally had to ask him to leave home. I gave him the money he had saved and drove him to his desired location. I told him that I loved him, but he could not come home until he would agree to go to a new treatment program. The next thirty-one days were the worst. He lived on the streets, and we prayed. He asked to come home. He had counselors call us, trying to make deals. This is where we really had to stand strong against the temptation to give in, letting our parental feelings betray us.

One night Bob asked if he could come home and get some clothes. He wanted to know when I would be gone so he wouldn't have to see me. I happened to be there when he arrived. He gave me a hate-filled look as he walked past me to his room. His mother asked if he was hungry; he agreed to have a hamburger. When he was ready to leave, I asked him if he wanted a ride. He said yes.

We rode along in silence. I wasn't sure what to say. I didn't want to make it worse. I have always possessed a very large vocabulary, but I get tongue-tied at moments like this. I would often ask Jane to explain what I meant to the boys. She just had a way of saying it that made it clear and understandable.

I broke the silence with a plea from deep within me. "Bob, what has happened to us? You're living on the street; you are miserable; your mother and I are miserable. What happened to my little boy, the one I used rock to sleep at night, who would run into my arms when I got home from work? I love you. I just want you to turn this around before your life is destroyed. There is a place where you can go and work on your life."

He seemed to soften. "Okay, I'll think about it."

I dropped him off and went home.

At 1:00 A.M. he called. "I'm ready to go. Come get me."

I was there in record time. The next two and a half years were a gift from God. Bob changed; much of the poisoning of culture was drained from him. He did a great job, worked hard, and overcame many obstacles. His mother and I are very proud of his accomplishments.

I was privileged to speak at my son's high school commencement. We rejoiced at his graduation from university. Today we have a very good relationship, one that is open and loving. God gave us a promise through his Word, and we acted on it. God promised us that we would get our boy back, and he delivered. The Scriptures are a powerful tool God uses. But before we can take advantage of their teaching, we must believe it and then act on it by faith. That is the deeper dimension that so many of us have removed from our lives. We need to get it back. That is what I want to talk about now.

How Do I Connect with God on a Deeper Level through His Word?

I thank God for my formal education. I learned much from godly, scholarly professors. My gift is teaching and I love to study, read, write, and interact with words. My idea of a good time is spending several hours in front of a crackling fire reading or writing. It is even better if someone else is stoking the fire for me. I am fond of a California fire—a fake log and a gas jet. You never need to tend it, so it goes on and on and on. I love those hours that I can get lost in the world of words and ideas. Some might even call me a bookworm. I love ideas and the cultivation of the mind, but I must admit that the key to understanding the Bible and knowing God is not primarily intellectual.

Study Is Not Enough

"My message and my preaching were not with wise and persuasive words, but with a demonstration of the Spirit's power, so that your faith might not rest on men's wisdom, but on God's power" (1 Cor. 2:4–5). Paul's first issue here is that we should not depend on human talent. Some seem to think that Paul dumbed down his message so the common person could understand. It really doesn't matter if he did or if the language he used was his own. Regardless, the rhetoric was plain because it had to be affirmed by God's power. Paul's reasoning is that we should be smart enough to be impressed by the right thing. The right thing is to witness the demonstration of God's power as a result of the proclamation of the Scriptures. But it must be more than the proclamation. It must be the belief in and application of the Scriptures. Paul reaffirms the earlier point that it must be the Word plus power, not the words alone.[12] Really grasping the meaning of Scripture goes beyond the mere intellectual understanding of words and concepts. It means experiencing the changes of attitude, the healing of memories, and the intervention of God in transforming culture. It is the difference between an interesting idea and a changed life.

Beyond the Human Mind

We do, however, speak a message of wisdom among the mature, but not the wisdom of this age or of the rulers of this age, who are coming to nothing. No, we speak of God's secret wisdom, a wisdom that has been hidden and that God destined for our glory before time began. None of the rulers of this age understood it. . . .

> "No eye has seen,
>   no ear has heard,
> no mind has conceived
>   what God has prepared for those who love him"—
> but God has revealed it to us by his Spirit.

1 Corinthians 2:6–10

God's Word is a mystery. We can't figure it out on our own. Not only are God's thoughts mysterious, but they are unlike anything even the most fertile imagination could create. So how do we get God's thoughts into our thoughts? This is supernatural activity, and only God can provide the help necessary. A common mistake we make in trying to have God's Word really come to life in us is to depend on our intellect and training. We defer far too much to our professor of choice. I love and respect those who have taught me. They are bright and good teachers. The problem arises when we defer to them before we even try to understand God's message on our own. I think we should consult the learned, but they should not always make the call.

It is common for people to wonder what the Bible is saying in a particularly difficult or cryptic passage. We have been trained then to ask, What does it say in Greek or Hebrew? But the real secrets to the kingdom cannot be found in the biblical languages. As one who has studied the original languages of Scripture, I can assure you the keys to the kingdom are not to be found on the pages of the Greek or Hebrew text.

Paul's point is that the great minds and great leaders of his day were never wise or smart enough to understand the Bible's message. We can study and memorize the Scripture and never really understand it. We can teach the Scriptures without the wisdom of the Holy Spirit. How can we connect to this mysterious document so that our hearts will burn for God?

Know the Author

Study isn't the key, neither is intellect or wisdom. Paul introduces the secret to rightly relating to the Scriptures:

> But God has revealed it to us by his Spirit.
> The Spirit searches all things, even the deep things of God. For who among men knows the thoughts of a man except the man's spirit within him? In the same way no one knows the thoughts of God except the Spirit of God. . . . The man without the Spirit does not accept the things that come from the Spirit of God, for they are foolishness to him, and he cannot understand them, because they are spiritually discerned. The spiritual man makes judgments about all things.
>
> 1 Corinthians 2:10–11, 14–15

The phrase "revealed it to us by his Spirit" is the key. If one is going to understand God's mind, he must be connected to God's Spirit. The most crucial step to getting the thoughts of Scripture into our thoughts is to know the author. This is more important than biblical knowledge, theological systems, or educational background. Being filled with the Holy Spirit is the core factor in understanding and knowing God and his Word. And beyond that, the determinative factor in understanding God is the condition of my heart when I read the Bible. An omniscient being isn't impressed with my intellect, but he is a pushover for a broken and contrite heart.

INSIGHT AND INTERPRETATION

Good insight is based on good interpretation. If you have a wrong interpretation, you may get a wrong insight. Therefore a baseline understanding of Scripture is crucial. That is why God created the church, so believers could gather and try to understand the Bible together. For example, if the Bible were interpreted to say that a Christian is not called on to forgive until someone asks for it, then there would be a lot less forgiveness. There would be more broken relationships, and families would be filled with much more bitterness. The Bible actually teaches that we are to forgive even if a person does not ask. It is about more than the person being forgiven; it is also about our freedom from bitterness.

The Spirit of God helps his children understand the meaning of Scripture far beyond their own education or intelligence. Am I saying that God will give better insights to the uneducated than the highly trained theologian? Yes, very often the best and brightest who don't meditate on the Word, who don't really seek God, will come up empty. At the same time the ten-year-old with simple faith and an open heart will receive much more from God. The child may see much more in the Word than the more mature and learned. The best of both worlds would be the highly trained with a heart that seeks God. But the percentage of Christians who have studied theology and are professional scholars and who are committed to the truthfulness of Scripture has to be less than 1 percent of the Christian population. Therefore, God's normative pattern for teaching his children his great truths cannot be primarily intellectual. It is primarily a spiritual exercise. Yes, there must be simple rules of how to interpret the Bible, but insight on how to apply what we learn is a different matter.

Transformation begins with interpretation and insight, but it cannot remain in the mind, or it isn't true transformation.[13] Paul taught that transformation begins in the mind as a necessity but is proven only in behavior. Jesus taught the same thing when he promised ongoing knowledge of God as a result of good behavior: "Whoever has my commands and obeys them, he is the one who loves me. He who loves me will be loved by my Father, and I too will love him and show myself to him" (John 14:21).

Knowing God is walking down the path of obedience. God tells us in his Word what to do. The Holy Spirit gives us insight into how to apply it to our life. Then our part is to step out in obedience and do it. As I walk down the path of obedience, God shows me his love by teaching me more and more what he is like. It is partly an intellectual exercise, but also it is an ongoing exercise in obedience. A Christian can learn enough to live for God in a very short time frame. The rest of the challenge is doing it and staying with it for a lifetime. God will continue to teach those who are following.

The Bible is like a map. When I want to travel into unknown territory, I look at a map. There are far too many who become experts on what the map says but do very little traveling. When you actually go on a trip, you learn far more than you would by just studying the map. You discover the beauty of the land and you experience the physical and mental challenges of travel. You find beautiful spots, eat at interesting restaurants, and meet fascinating people.

Christians who travel down the road of obedience learn a great deal more about God and are closer to God than those who refuse to set out on the journey. During these faith journeys, God speaks to us and affirms his love for us in ways that we could have never known otherwise. I am advocating adventure, allowing God to use all his gifts and tools to teach us. The person who knows the author of the map and is filled with the Holy Spirit is going to live in a multidimensional world, this world where God is affirming, speaking, and showing his power regularly.

A Learning Posture

God could have limited Paul's teaching to the reading of the Old Testament. Instead, he struck him down on the Damascus road and took him up to the abode of God. Paul had visions and dreams. God chose to affirm his Word through signs and wonders, because Paul needed them, the church needed them, and the watching world needed them.

This chapter has been about editing the power from our Bibles. Liberals do it by predetermining that the miracles never happened. Moderate theologians like Bultmann do it by redefining the meaning of miracles. Evangelicals do it by studying the miracles, believing the miracles, and then placing them in a theological lockbox, so they can't get out. We must unlock the box and throw away the key. We must read the Bible and believe it as it is plainly written.

Seminary taught us the wrong question. We were taught to ask, "How am I doing as a teacher?" This is not a bad question. It needs to be asked, but it isn't the primary question. The first question for a teacher is, "Are people learning?"

At our church we asked this question, and the answer made us take a big step. We determined that we needed to change the way we were teaching the Bible. One change is that we have added personal testimonies to many of the sermons. This helps people grasp what biblical application really means. In the Bible teaching genre of evangelicalism, too many think application means writing down something in the fill-in-the-blanks part of the sermon notes. But actually hearing someone talk about how he applied the concept of accountability to overcoming outbursts of anger is an eye-opener.

Another big change is a greatly reduced lecture time in our adult Bible study classes. In many churches the adult Sunday school has been in an attendance free fall for twenty years. The reason is that it provided an inferior worship service. Say hello, grab a pastry, sing a song or two, and sit and listen to a lecture. The law of competition tells us that people will not attend more than one meeting a week that meets the same need. The worship service is generally better in its quality than a class; therefore, the worship service usually wins.

At our church we are now using a guided discussion format that focuses on application and interaction between members. The objective is to help people learn in a practical way and express their needs. It also encourages them to ask deeper and more relevant questions. Freud accused the church of asking only the questions for which they already had the answers. We are attempting to build a caring community that asks the hard questions.

The Word of God is alive and active. We need to create forums for it to be activated in our lives, allowing God to keep it fresh and relevant through the exercise of the gifts of the Holy Spirit.

Properly relating to the written record means adopting a learning posture. It is believing the Bible as plainly written and attempting by faith to live it. For some of us it calls on us to launch out into the deep of spiritual power. I for one have spent too many years playing it safe. I'm ready for God to melt me down and reshape me. I want to jump into the pages of the Bible and live it.

4

Experiencing God
Present with Us

Jesus left us with a commandment and a commission—to love him with everything we've got and to obey him with everything we've got.[1] A more specific challenge is to do what he did.[2] "Anyone who has faith" qualifies as a candidate to equal and exceed the works of Jesus. We have learned, however, that there is a huge difference between the way Jesus did what he did and how we are to do it. As I like to say, being God is an advantage. He left us with a written record and a promise. We must understand and obey his written Word and receive the promise that God will be present with us in the person of the Holy Spirit.

Presence is a delicious word—nothing can take the place of presence, not gifts, not telephone calls, pictures, mementos, or videos, nothing. When you talk to a person who has just lost her life's partner and ask what she misses the most, almost always the answer is *presence*. The person left behind misses the joy of being in the same room with her loved one—or at least in the same house together watching separate televisions. It is the assurance of not being alone in this world, of having someone to share your life with.

When we are ill, we don't long so much for flowers and cards; we desire to have our loved ones present, at least the ones we are getting along with! What make board games pleasurable or a concert memorable are the people with you. Why do family reunions exist? In our dot-com world we can e-mail pictures, mail cards, and send flowers. But still people get on airplanes and travel. My wife and I traveled recently from Los Angeles to Morgantown, West Virginia, for my niece's wedding. We could have sent an expensive present and asked for a video, but we knew it would be much more meaningful if we were present. So we were present and still got the expensive gift. It was one of those special events when presence is delicious. And of course who would have cleaned up the fireman's hall if the family hadn't been there? It's all about presence.[3]

The Restoration of His Presence

One of the many tragedies of the fall is that humankind lost God's pure presence. We have been living east of Eden ever since. The entire redemptive drama is about God's restoring his presence to the creation. God has been inching us back toward a stronger and clearer presence. Of course God has always been omnipresent and present in the world, generally to restrain evil (see 2 Thess. 2:7), but God's goal is to have all his people experience his pristine presence (see Rev. 21:1–5). There is an interesting progression in how God has gradually restored people to his presence.

Moses and Company

God was present among his people in the wilderness. His dwelling place was the tent of meeting, a precursor to the tabernacle and temple. Whenever Moses inquired of the Lord, he would go into the tent, and a pillar of cloud would sit at the entrance. The people both feared and sought the presence of God. They would stand a safe distance from the presence and worship while Moses spoke with God. And what a conversation they had!

After the tumultuous ups and downs of the idolatrous debacle surrounding the golden calf, God was more angry than Moses. Moses smashed the tablets; God wanted to smash the people. God told Moses he wouldn't go with them to the Promised Land because he might destroy everyone.[4] One thing led to another and the people repented.

The Comfort and Power of God's Presence

Moses' number one issue was his need for God's presence. Moses asked God to reconsider going with his people. In fact Moses said he couldn't go without God's visible presence. He begged God not to send them if he would not go before them to prepare the way. Moses makes a point for all of us for all time: "If your Presence does not go with us, do not send us up from here. How will anyone know that you are pleased with me and with your people unless you go with us? What else will distinguish me and your people from all the other people on the face of the earth?" (Exod. 33:15–16).

Moses needed something tangible to demonstrate to the people that God supported his ongoing leadership. The nature of people is to very quickly forget salient facts, like who is in charge. When Moses was on the mountain for forty days, the people were referring to him as "that guy, whatever his name is or was." Spiritual leaders live in a "what have you done for me lately?" world. Revolt was a bump in the road away.

Moses needed that cloud by day and pillar of fire by night— God's presence with them. The fearful, the proud, the rebellious, the weak could all see the cloud as they traveled. It gave them rest from fear and a willingness to follow Moses. It meant God's hand of blessing was on him.

I call out to God daily to reveal his presence. I don't mean his omnipresence. We are all aware that he is everywhere. I ask him to manifest himself more specifically—in our ministry. I ask him to enter our worship and challenge and change people. I ask him to speak to us through the gifts of the Spirit, to deliver the unbelievers from the grip of sin, to heal some instantly, to heal memories and deliver people from demonic oppression. I ask him to do it in front of everyone, so that the weak, the rebellious, the proud, and the fearful will all bow to his power and authority. I want this to happen because it is proof that God's hand is on our church. But as Moses said, it will also distinguish us from all the other people on the earth. Like Moses, I ask God to show us his glory and blow the roof off our building, our lives, our community. God's presence is life changing; it is what makes the church different.

I used to think of a worship service as primarily a cognitive experience. I still think the teaching of Scriptures is the foundational core when the church gathers. But sermons and songs are not going to change people and communities like God's manifest presence can. When God is present in a way that is noticed, sermons and songs fade to black.

In the recent past my focus has been praying for and expecting God to show us his glory in church. And he has. One week it is a testimony of a family who lost a child and how God met them in their sorrow. Then others with similar needs pour forward for prayer and counseling. The next week it is working with a member who is demonically oppressed. Those struggling with pornography, drugs, and various maladies come for prayer and deliverance. The difference between now and the past is emphasis. We used to rely on a good sermon with the results of: "that was good teaching." Now people are saying, "We met God today." God does work through sermons and songs, but they are only vehicles for the encounter with him. Everything else is cannon fodder.

Learning from the Pilgrims

There is much to learn from the pilgrims—not the Plymouth Rock Pilgrims, but those who made long, arduous journeys to Jerusalem. The people of Israel longed for Jerusalem, because that was where God lived. He resided there when he desired to manifest himself in the Holy of Holies in the temple that was built to his specifications. Three times a year the people would gather in Jerusalem for rituals of remembrance. That is why today thousands stand at the Western Wall and pray for their needs. That remnant of a wall is all that is left of God's house, where God lived, where God's presence was revealed. We can learn from the pilgrims' inner longings for God's presence, their willingness to make the trip, to stand and wait long hours in line to make a sacrifice, to meet and be forgiven by their God.

God with Us

God sent Jesus to confirm that the story of history really is about God's presence. He is Immanuel or "God with us." Because of him we know what God is like. The disciples who lived and worked with Jesus loved being with him. They were so enamored with him that they protested his leaving. Jesus promised not to leave the disciples as orphans. He would send the comforter, the helper, the teacher, the Holy Spirit. Now the apostles themselves would become the temples of God. God would dwell in them.

As the apostles stood around the upper room, they were skeptical. They were not so sure who the Holy Spirit is or how he could help them. They periodically glanced down at their chests and contemplated how God was going to get in there. They had forgotten their theological training from childhood, the Weeping Prophet's promise that God would indwell his people.[5] This was to be the first installment on the fulfillment of the restoration of God's presence in the hearts of his people. *The Holy Spirit, then, is the renewed presence of God in us and in his church*. Jesus taught that the Holy Spirit was God present with us.

When God Moves In

Jane and I found Francis and Edith Schaeffer inspirational. They lived and ministered in Switzerland, taking people into their alpine community, aptly named L'Abri, meaning "shelter." Young people would come for study and reflection in their quest to find God. The Schaeffers lived in a Swiss chalet surrounded by the magnificence of the Alps.

When we were a young family, we lived in a three-bedroom condo directly under the flight path to El Toro Marine Base. We told our two toddler sons that we were going to take in a young lady with a big belly who needed some help. So Joan moved in and the adventure began. She had her own private room and the run of the house. She was young, naive, and six-months pregnant. She drank the kids' milk and used all the hot water and three towels every time she showered. She changed our home. Jane did more laundry. I ran to the store for milk twice as many times as usual. The boys complained about having to share a room and their missing candy.

Joan claimed that taking care of a newborn would be no big deal. She didn't know why people wouldn't baby-sit infants for free—all they do is sleep. A week after she brought her baby home she wanted to send him back. She was crying, "This baby never sleeps! He's always crying. I never have any time for myself." Joan was beginning to discover what every seasoned parent knows—kids don't start life caring about their parents' needs. In fact the caring doesn't start until they turn thirty. Jane was a gracious teacher who didn't laugh in Joan's face. She saved that for behind closed doors.

Was it worth the trouble to help Joan? A few weeks after she moved in, she committed her life to Christ. Joan then wanted the father of her baby back in her life. Enter Jerry, a long-haired hippie who moved in too. Jerry came to know Christ. Joan's parents accepted the baby, Jerry, and Jesus. Jerry and Joan were my first wedding. It was held, of course, at Laguna Beach. What a wonderful experience, except for that dog pile that Joan's mother tripped and fell into on the beach. No one had invited the dog.

Jerry and Joan now have five kids; they go to church; they do right; it was our privilege. If someone comes to live in your home, it will make a difference. When Jesus moves in, the changes are dramatic.

God does more than move into our house, he inhabits our bodies. The film industry has done its best to depict the human being inhabited by an alien force. The classic is *Invasion of the Body Snatchers* where aliens crawl out of pods and replace the earthlings. If you like comedy, there is Dennis Quaid traveling through Martin Short's body in *Inner Space.* Short contorts his body and portrays what it would be like to have an alien force controlling one's thoughts and actions. My personal favorite is *All of Me* in which Steve Martin plays a very confused man whose second brain belongs to Lily Tomlin. Just remembering the scenes makes me laugh out loud. These portrayals attempt to show what would happen when a strange force lives inside a human being. It is interesting that with the vast creative imagination resident in the entertainment community, when it comes to alien inhabitation, they have limited themselves to horror or comedy. Both are exaggerated and not to be taken seriously.

But God does inhabit millions of earthlings around the planet. They live among us and most look normal. God inside you is the normal paranormal. It is paranormal because it is outside the norm. It is normal, however, because we were created for it; thus God fits in our soul very nicely, thank-you. Those in whom God lives don't seem as out of control as Short or as confused as Martin. They aren't as scary as the alien itself that Sigourney Weaver fought off in *Alien I, II, III,* and *IV.* Let's end it all—*Alien V* meets *Rocky V* in the final conflict!

God in Each Disciple

God living in us means radical change. Paul makes this point to the Corinthians who lived in a moral morass. The first century was much like the twenty-first in that people practiced a "cut-and-paste" spirituality. The primal temptation for the Corinthians was to combine their newfound Christian faith and temple worship. The temple worship included two activities prohibited by Christian teaching. The first was the use of alcohol as a spiritual aphrodisiac. Once you were high on the spirits, you entered into an altered state that enabled you to worship without inhibitions. The derivation of the word *spirits* for liquor can be traced to the supposed enhancement of worship via alcohol.

The second temptation was to indulge oneself through the use of a temple prostitute. Paul's use of the contemporary philosophy "Let us eat and drink for tomorrow we die" was a product of such "spirituality." Paul's appeal was simple and direct, "Do you not know that your bodies are members of Christ himself? Shall I then take the members of Christ and unite them with a prostitute? Never!" (1 Cor. 6:15). His logical conclusion was "Flee from sexual immorality. All other sins a man commits are outside his body, but he who sins sexually sins against his own body. Do you not know that your body is a temple of the Holy Spirit, who is in you, whom you have received from God?" (vv. 18–19).

Christ gave his life for us. He now resides in us so we can honor him by our lives. If God living in us does not change our behavior and attitude, then we must wonder if God does indeed live in us. The Christian popular culture treasures and celebrates God living in each believer, but it must be said, without evidence of the fruit of the Spirit, there is nothing to celebrate. God living in us should make some difference. *God in us, present in us, is the power we need to equal and exceed the works of Jesus.*

God Living in His Church

It is so common for Christians to talk about the Christ within that the wonder of it is diminished. But at least it is taught and understood as central to God's restoring relationship to his people. What is underreported and not believed is that Christ indwells his church corporately. When the body gathers, God is present in a special way that can be experienced in no other place. God promised through Ezekiel that he would one day again be among his people. And Paul uses Ezekiel's words to make the point: "I will live with them and walk among them, and I will be their God, and they will be my people" (2 Cor. 6:16).

There is a special presence of God when the church gathers that is not there in just one person. This idea smacks of institutionalism to many, like the "man" is trying to power grab. People like to think spirituality is disconnected from established structure, even enhanced when organization is absent. God thinks of us not only as individuals but as a community of people.

> Consequently, you are no longer foreigners and aliens, but fellow citizens with God's people and members of God's household, built on the foundation of the apostles and prophets, with Christ Jesus himself as the chief cornerstone. In him the whole building is joined together and rises to become a holy temple in the Lord. And in him you too are being built together to become a dwelling in which God lives by his Spirit.
>
> Ephesians 2:19–22

God inhabits us collectively as surely as he does individually. There is a power of God's presence in the gathered church. When disciples stay away from church, they have less power. They then have limited access to all that God has provided. Just as God was present more powerfully to heal in some cases—see Luke 5:17—he is present to minister in the church gathered in a way that he may not be with an individual who is alone on a prayer walk through the woods. There really is something to the idea that where two or three are gathered together in Christ's name, he is there in their midst.

One can argue about what constitutes a church, but it must be admitted that we enter into a special and exclusive presence when we gather in the name of Christ to worship him. I like what Gordon Fee says, "God is not just saving individuals and preparing them for heaven; rather, he is creating a people among whom he can live and who in their life together will reproduce God's life and character."[6] Paul keeps calling the church a body, a temple, a people, a household—all meant to bring out the communal part of faith.

When we gather to worship, we enter into his already established presence. Just as God chose to manifest himself to Israel in a variety of tangible ways, he does so now through spiritual gifts. When we stay away from church and the rich dynamic that is there, we are missing most of the edifying work that God has planned for our lives.

A fifty-year psychological siege has captured major sections of our culture. It has brought with it a new lexicon of self-hyphenated words. There is an insane preoccupation with self and getting our own needs met. Self-help is an oxymoron because no one really means to say it can be done alone. The very existence of books, tapes, seminars, and elongated counseling regimes is indication enough that we can't do it alone. The growth of clinics designed to provide structure, peer accountability, and professional counseling again belies the naive notion of self-help.

Whether it's solving our psychological problems or practicing our religion, we do want to do it our way. The assimilation of Eastern mysticism into popular thinking has contributed to a designer god mentality. So often we hear, "I'm not into organized religion, but I am very spiritual." In other words, I went to the Shirley MacLaine school of theology, where you make up whatever beliefs suit you and call them right. The psychological river has converged with the Eastern mysticism river to form a very strong current of selfish individualism that now harms Christians.

The Christian is swimming upstream when he or she commits to a "common good" ethos, because so many disciples' commitment to the community of faith is challenged by the above forces plus those of technology. With access to the best of everything through one hundred-plus television channels and the Internet, we feel little need for the company of other people. In fact people outside the immediate family become expendable. So talking about responsibility to be at church because it's the right thing to do falls flat with most people.

Called into His Promised Presence

Once you have tasted the revealed presence of God, you never want to go back. The best church growth method I know is experiencing the manifest presence of God. That is what God wants for us and that is why he sent the Holy Spirit to reveal himself to us when we are gathered. When he is present, the dynamic is definitely different. I think God is pleased when we invite him to manifest himself among the gathered congregation.

You might be protesting, "This presence thing is too amorphous. I can't get my hands or mind around it. Could you give me something concrete?" My first response is, I know what you mean. I have struggled with that as well. How often we have seen the televangelist strutting around the stage telling people that he feels the presence of God. Then he claims because he feels it that God's anointing is on him. The organ music follows and increases his emotional level as the people are swept into the evening's froth. I would argue that there is a difference between the talented speaker whipping up an emotionally charged environment and the presence of God. I think the manifest presence of God comes with a sense of awe. It is what the early church felt when they committed themselves to the five transformational activities.[7] And when they combined these five experiences, God manifested himself in signs and wonders that created a sense of awe. When this happens, the people are struck with God, not his spokesperson, not the talent, not anyone's brilliance.

It is difficult for us to extract from our thinking the authority of celebrity. The popular culture listens to the successful, regardless of whether they are qualified to speak. Every day the airwaves are filled with the words of actors, athletes, and captains of Wall Street. We listen to them because they are famous, because they have money, because they are on TV.

A church can draw a much bigger crowd with a cultural celebrity than with an articulate spokesperson for the faith. The runaway success of the television series *Survivor* gives us our example. In the first series of shows one of the cast members who was voted off the island is a professing Christian. He has been touring the country and for a handsome fee is speaking in churches. The only thing that qualifies the young man to speak in place of the pastor is that he has been on TV. And many people show up to hear him, a less qualified person than a pastor, give an inferior presentation.

What this means is that we are much more susceptible to the creation of a phony God presence than we would like to admit. The show business aspect of church can produce a very strong emotional force that may or may not be God. There are no cut-and-dried answers except that whatever happens must be squared with God's Word and the witness of our spirits that it is the Spirit of God.

There is a real danger in seeking experience as the primary guide to life. And our experiencing God's presence is subjective. Some people will say it was felt; others will say, "Nope, didn't feel it." God is present when we gather in his name for his purposes (see Heb. 10:24–25). I also believe that we can invite him to manifest his presence among us.

Revealed through the Gifts

I often ask God to be present with us and to minister to us. I'll pray, "Come, Holy Spirit. Move among us; have your way; reveal yourself."

A man approached me and asked, "If God is already here per 'where two or three are gathered in my name, I am in the midst of them,' do we need to ask him to be among us?"

I asked him if before teaching a class, he ever prays for God to be with him? I went on to ask him why we ask God for anything if he knows everything we need before we ask? We ask God to be with us and enter into our experience for two reasons. The first is for our own encouragement; the second is that God will reveal himself in a special way because we have asked him. Conversely, without our request, he will remain unrevealed. It is the difference between positional truth and experienced truth, between the cognitive realm and the application realm. We know that God is always with us, takes care of us, and so on, but there is another realm of relating to God that is intimate. As I called it earlier, it is the normal paranormal experience of God. It is God speaking to us and relating to us with a personal touch. It is the supernatural, mixed intricately with the natural. Dallas Willard puts it this way, "God comes to us precisely in and through our thoughts, perceptions, and experiences and can approach our conscious life only through them, for they are the substance of our lives."[8] And God has chosen to use the entire body and the tools he has provided so that we experience his personalized presence.

The Holy Spirit is God's presence personalized through the gifts of the Spirit. Rather than an ever-present cloud or pillar of fire or extremely loud organ music, God has chosen to be present among us through spiritual gifts. That way his presence doesn't rely on the culture of celebrity or the worship leader's ability to raise the people's spiritual temperature. What it does rely on are the many members of the body of Christ knowing how to minister to each other. Remember, the setting for God's being present among us is the church gathered.[9] And that is the exact context for Paul's teaching on gifts to the Corinthian church.

The listing of nine gifts of the Spirit in Paul's first letter to the Corinthians is connected to worship. There has been a trend to lift the gifts from their context and treat all gifts the same. Gordon Fee puts his concern this way:

> My problems with this fad are several: taking the texts out of context, rearranging the gifts under our own convenient groupings thus leveling the various passages in Paul to a card-catalogue form and focusing on discovering what the Corinthians would have known by experience. But the greatest problem for me is the nearly universal tendency to divorce the list of "Spirit manifestations" in 1 Corinthians 12:8–10 from its clear setting of Christian worship.[10]

It is hard to fathom why it took me so long to understand the power of God's presence. I always said the right things like, "If Jesus were to enter this room right now, we would all fall on our faces in worship." And I meant it. It is easy to see how important God's presence was and is when you reflect on the stories of the ark of the covenant, the tabernacle, and temple. It is clear that a glorified Christ would change any room he chose to enter. But for us, it goes back to the same problem the scholars had with Jesus. They believed in all those miracles; they just never thought any of them would happen to them. Christians believe in the power of God's presence, but we just never think he would present himself to us now in a dramatic way. God desires to manifest himself through us and be powerful among us. The primary way he has chosen seems to be through the personalized touch of the gifts of the Holy Spirit when we are gathered.

This realization changed what I pray for and what I value when we gather. I now pray for God to manifest himself when we worship, knowing that my role is to facilitate the move of his Spirit. For that is what really counts, directing people to the

throne of his grace. It is only there they can be changed. My sermons are only a tool to help people connect with God. It is about
him and them. It's not about me and my sermon. What I value
is a focus on him through praise, prayers, teaching, and asking
the people to respond. What I am praying for when I use the
word *manifest* is found in Paul's response to the Corinthians:
"Now to each one the manifestation of the Spirit is given for the
common good" (1 Cor. 12:7).

Satan's strategy has always been to divide and destroy. God's
has always been to unite and build. The gifts of the Spirit are
for the common good of the church, to unite it and build it.
Often, however, it has been said that the gifts are divisive, and
it is fair to say that the gifts have proven to be the center of much
controversy. But God is not going to divide his church with the
very tools he intended for building it. It has been the carnal
response of one group of Christians to another that has caused
the division. I am not going to enter that debate, but I do believe
that those who consider these gifts illegitimate for our time are
a shrinking minority.

Satan fights against our experiencing God's manifest presence, for once we taste it, we won't ever go back. By going back
I mean being satisfied with the pedantic and often boring church
experience that addresses the intellect alone, or the uncritical,
unthinking, lathered-up emotionalism that is the other extreme.

Manifest *Means to Reveal*

The nature of the nine gifts mentioned in the 1 Corinthians
12 passage are that they manifest God's presence. Through their
use, God will reveal himself to his people. The nine gifts are message of wisdom, message of knowledge, faith, gift of healing,
miraculous powers, prophecy, distinguishing between spirits,
speaking in tongues, and interpretation of tongues. The context
is worship and their use is focused on the gathering (see 14:26).
Later in the book I will address the miraculous in worship. For
now my focus remains a more general point. When we gather,
each gifted disciple, when exercising a gift, becomes God present with us.

There are many people who need prayer yet lack the faith to believe God. I often ask our prayer team members to pray for those weak in faith. We know who seems to have great capacity to believe and we have them pray for the weaker ones. If that isn't God's personalized touch, I don't know what is. Many come asking for prayer to battle overwhelming problems. What is going on in my head when I lay hands on a brother suffering from cocaine addiction? Do I really believe God will deliver him? We have everything from child abuse to smoking, and we call on members to pray who have some idea of what the person is experiencing. That may require the discernment of spirits, the gift of healing, or someone to prophesy over a needy soul.

During one of my messages, something exciting happened. I was speaking on restoring broken relationships and how we throw away relationships over petty differences. This is particularly true of adult children and their aged parents. I was lamenting the pain and loss of unfinished business that hits us hard when the parent dies. At this point a woman in the second row burst into tears and ran out of the sanctuary. A woman who didn't know her followed and they began to pray and talk in the hallway. The first woman was in anguish over the unfinished business with her mother who was dying of cancer. As the other woman ministered to her, she found herself coming under conviction about her own mother. Then the tables turned and the other woman ministered to her. Both of them exercised their gifts with each other, and God became powerful and personal in the moment.

We have many who come for prayer during the ministry time as we close the service. But even more come after the close of the service and that is when a deeper kind of work can take place. On one occasion our team told me that a woman was having problems with demonic oppression. It was the Halloween season and at that time her battles are always more intense. A few of us went into a private area and began to minister. It was a wonderful thing to see gifts being exercised that helped this woman in a significant way. People took turns, some talked to the woman, others to the spirit within. God gave relief and helped her with the ongoing battle.

On another occasion a woman walked into the service and leaned against the wall. She then moved incrementally around the room, stopping at points to lean against the wall. She had her head down, chin tucked tightly to her chest. After the service a woman with a discerning gift went to her and asked what was wrong. She was considering suicide and walked into our church looking for help. We ministered to her for a few minutes, the prayer team member followed up, and the woman passed safely through the troubled time.

A dimension that is missing in too many churches is a personal touch, a comforting sense that God is with me, he loves me, he knows my name, and he understands my pain. It is one thing to learn from the Bible that God knows you; it is quite another when you sense his personal presence.

Early in my ministry life I was questioning if I had the gift of teaching. I loved to study and present the findings of my labor. But at twenty-five years of age, I lacked confidence. I asked God to encourage me, to somehow confirm that I was headed in the right direction. A couple of nights later I gave a message to a student gathering. Afterward a parent approached me. "Bill, I really thought you did a good job tonight. I think you have the gift of teaching, I want to encourage you to keep pursuing your teaching gift." That was it, exactly what I asked God for, and he gave it to me from one of his own with the gift of encouragement. If we are open and alert to God's speaking to us through others, our level of ministry will increase in multiples.

The Church without the Gifts

The church without the manifestational gifts given in 1 Corinthians 12 means there will be little revealing of God's power and presence. It is simply wrong for us to live without them. We Christians are paying a high price for our lack of experience in this realm of the Spirit. There are sick people who are unhealed, oppressed members who remain undelivered, the discouraged who will remain so because we don't believe in prophecy. We have many more small churches than we should and more frustrated leaders than we want. Why would any of us allow the gifts to lie dormant—God's unopened gifts to the church?

One more crucial thought needs to be made, and Wayne Grudem makes it: "The Spirit gives stronger or weaker evidence of the presence and blessing of God according to our response to Him."[11] Samson and Saul are examples of this important reality. They both had the Spirit of God on them. They both turned to other gods and resources, and God withdrew his presence. Ichabod, "the glory has departed," was written over the nation of Israel when the ark of the covenant was taken by the Philistines (see 1 Sam. 4:21). God left his people because of their great sin. The Book of Revelation records Jesus' warning that he might remove the lampstand from the churches that do not remain faithful. The lampstand, of course, is symbolic of the power of the Holy Spirit. We must be careful not to grieve or quench the Holy Spirit's desire to manifest himself among his people. He is God present with us through the exercise of spiritual gifts. I urge you to open yourself to pray, ask God to come, and reveal himself in concrete ways when you gather in his name.

It Started with Me

A terrible truth that I didn't want to accept is that most of what God wants to do in the church begins with the leaders. And the leader among leaders in most churches is the pastor. I wish it were different and that God would normally work through anyone, but when it comes to renewing a community of people, it must begin in the recognized leader. The reason for this dynamic is partly the unspoken belief that the recognized leader's support is crucial to the success of any endeavor. And there is something mysterious about God's calling specific leaders to ministries at specific times.

There is a difference in teaching and practice between Old Testament and New Testament leadership models. Sometimes it seems that Moses is the model and at other times that the team concept is the model. There is truth in both. God does use individuals and give them vision. At the same time it is important to practice some form of accountability, as is stressed in the New Testament.

I had to recognize my role as a blocker to the manifest presence of God. The difficulty in the admission is that I never thought a casual and open attitude was blocking. But then the

Spirit gripped my heart, letting me know that I would need to lead in calling on God to manifest himself in our meetings. This meant teaching the Scriptures and preparing myself through prayer and study. This meant creating forums for the exercise of gifts, such as healing and prophecy, so they could meet needs. So I took one year to prepare our elders and staff through reading and prayer. I gave twelve messages on the theme "Searching for God, a Journey into the Gifts of the Spirit." The main focus was inviting God's presence. I am still in process in my search for his presence, but I have a congregation that has chosen to join me. And that is the key. If you lead, many will follow. I had to confess my sin. I prayed "O, Lord, forgive me for shutting you out. I ask you to come among us and show us your glory. We don't dare go forward without your full blessing and presence."

5

Experiencing the Power of the Spirit

There is a lot of talk on how to get God's power, how to be filled with the Holy Spirit, how to tap into the power and influence of God's chosen resource. Why so much talk? Because we are faced with an impossible task. We are to do greater works than Jesus did. We are to be the witnesses he commanded us to be (Acts 1:8), to love one another as he loves us (John 15:12–13), to be one as he and the Father are one (17:11). And there is more. We are to bear fruit that will last (15:8) and employ our gifts in the service of Christ (1 Peter 4:10–11). Completing these commands and commissions are impossible without God's help. Nevertheless, we are held responsible for nothing less than doing greater works than Jesus.

It is hard for humans to wrap their minds around the Spirit of God. We are told that God lives in us and that he desires to control us. But then the Spirit is likened to wind and fire, things that are hard to control and contain. I live in Southern California where we can experience the wildness and power of wind plus fire. The Santa Ana winds blow from the northeast off the desert and, in hot and dry conditions, create fires. Regardless of where you live, you have seen it on the evening news—the panic in the eyes of the residents of the homes that are threatened, the tears when all is lost. The energy is awesome, and when the winds refuse to relent, the fire is impossible to control. The destructive nature of wind and fire has the power to alter lives. Jesus said that the Spirit like the wind would be hard to describe, but his power is unquestioned (John 3:3–15).

Streams in the Spirit

The various theological traditions, or streams, have sought to explain the ministry of the Holy Spirit. Let's take a look at some major themes.

The "Power" Stream

The "power" stream of the church is commonly referred to as charismatic. The way they would explain the presence of God's power would be through the baptism of the Holy Spirit. This is a second event after conversion when they were filled by the Holy Spirit, an experience that may have been accompanied by speaking in tongues. This stream of the church has its own vocabulary, and there is an emphasis on hearing God's voice through prophecy and other revelatory gifts as part of the regular diet. There is also a strong reliance on Old Testament characters and methods. You would be likely to hear a sermon on Moses or Jacob and how their experience can be our experience.

The "Learning" Stream

The "learning" stream—most evangelical churches—says that the fullness of God has already been provided. There is no separate baptism of the Holy Spirit. The key to experiencing God's fullness is learning the Scriptures. God is not issuing any new material, so learn what he has already provided. This tradition believes that we don't need a lot of external signs anymore. As Jesus said, an evil generation seeks signs. The secret to power is internal. It is the fruit of the Spirit, not the gifts of the Spirit. Quiet power is just as crucial as loud power. The access to God's power, then, is to simply ask to be filled with the Holy Spirit and we will be. We are commanded to be filled and we are promised that God will answer yes to every request that is his will.[1]

The "Holiness" Stream

As a nine-year-old boy I went forward to the altar and "prayed through." It was clear to me that I had "crossed Jordan" and now belonged to God. I was happy about it but was worried about my staying power. I thought being a Christian was like holding your breath—you could do it just so long. It was just a matter of time until you would start sinning again.

My mother was not a believer and she responded to my news with "So what?" My grandmother told me that now I would need to be sanctified. In the holiness tradition, at least in 1955, that meant a second major work of God that makes one more powerful and pure. This just seems like the charismatic baptism of the Spirit without the whistles and horns. I never made it to sanctification the way my grandmother described it. She said I would no longer sin, that I would just make mistakes. She held to this opinion until she entered God's presence, when she truly became holy. I still sin, every day. In fact I enjoy sin. Quick, I need an altar.

The "Liturgy" Stream

The "liturgy" stream is the high church, or as some call it the sacerdotal church—Catholics, Lutherans, Episcopalians, and in some cases Presbyterians. *Sacerdotal* means that grace and power are imparted through the sacraments. Holy Communion in particular is an ongoing means of imparting grace and power. This tradition emphasizes that the power of the Spirit comes through prayer, in the practice of the spiritual disciplines, and by regularly partaking of communion.

Most mid- and low-church groups teach that communion is symbolic. The high church, however, sees the elements of communion as becoming more than mere bread and wine. When Catholics and some Episcopalians partake of communion, they believe that the elements are transformed into the body and blood of Christ. For that reason there is a real sense of impartation that takes place when one engages in communion. There is also a strong role for the priest/rector/pastor as the vicar of Christ to the people.

In the liturgy stream there is an informal, parallel renewal track that runs alongside the formal institutional one described above. It is sort of a highly dignified, "uptown" charismatic movement that is kept at the edges of the church. This is a reaction to the more staid procedural Christianity practiced by the traditional core constituents.

Finding Our Doorway

There is truth to be found in all four streams. All of us are trying to find our way through our own manufactured maze to the throne of God, and each of these traditions offers a different doorway to the power and presence of God. The beautiful thing is that God is not far from each of us (see Acts 17:26–28). He encourages us to keep longing and looking and we will be rewarded. As Tommy Tenney has written, we are God chasers who finally become God catchers.[2] God hides himself from us not so he can't be found but so that he *can* be found. If we are to experience God fully and do the works of Jesus, we must find the doorway to his power. So let's talk about the two primary doors that God has provided to his Spirit, the baptism of or in the Holy Spirit and the filling of the Holy Spirit.

Baptism of the Holy Spirit

There is a lot of cultural froth associated with the experience called "the baptism of the Holy Spirit." It is not unusual for biblical terms to be changed over time from their original meaning. The command to "make disciples" has been changed from the primary task of the church to just another post-conversion activity. People speak of discipleship as a program that is just one of the things a church does, when, in fact, disciple making is not just *one of the things* a church does; it is *what* the church does. Its scope includes evangelism, training, and mobilization of the entire body of Christ. It includes leadership development, counseling, and crisis intervention. Thus the church has made small what God meant to be big.

Originally the phrase "the baptism of the Spirit" identified different ways in which God poured out his Spirit on people. The phrase was extracted from the Scriptures to describe what was happening to people. In the early 1900s there were revivals where people were being empowered by the Spirit with speaking in tongues. The two most talked about were the Azusa Street revival in Los Angeles and a similar manifestation in Topeka, Kansas. Thus the modern charismatic movement began. It has been traditional in the movement to describe its signature experience as the baptism of the Spirit.

By the time I entered the church picture as a college student in the late 1960s, the baptism meant a second work of power in the believer's life. I was taught that it could be experienced by every Christian and that, if I was baptized in the Spirit, I would have more of Jesus, more power, more discernment, more, more, more. What is actually true is that the sincere pursuit of God has many rewards (see Jer. 29:13).

In fact all the people committed to finding God will find him. We can take different routes and name the experience different things, but in the end, if we connect to his presence, we get his power. I do think, however, it is better to use the terms as accurately as possible. I will attempt to clear up the confusion and make a distinction between the once-in-a-lifetime baptism of the Holy Spirit and the ongoing filling of the Holy Spirit.

The phrase "the baptism of the Holy Spirit" is used seven times in the New Testament. In the first four John the Baptist is predicting that Jesus will baptize with fire: "I baptize you with water for repentance. But after me will come one who is more powerful than I, whose sandals I am not fit to carry. He will baptize you with the Holy Spirit and with fire" (Matt. 3:11).[3]

This was a prediction of the great intensity of an encounter with Jesus. It included Pentecost, but fire indicates the impartation of a burning passion. There would be the fire of his healing, his teaching, his truth, his authority, and his divine enablement given to his followers. The ministry of the Holy Spirit was very fluid at this point. It was not fastened down and categorized. It might do us much good to loosen up our present labeling and to loose the power of God among us.

Other uses of "the baptism of the Holy Spirit" refer directly to Pentecost. The first is Jesus' instructing the disciples just prior to his ascension from the Mount of Olives (Acts 1:5). Peter later quotes Jesus in Acts 11:16. The distinguishing words from Jesus to his nervous followers were, "In a few days you will be baptized with the Holy Spirit." The big event would be soon and it would be for a big reason. He diverted their attention from when they would go to heaven and when he might return to what would soon happen to them. He seemed to be saying "I want you to focus on the task," and then issued part of the Great Commission: "You will receive power when the Holy Spirit comes on you; and you will be my witnesses in Jerusalem, and in all Judea and Samaria, and to the ends of the earth" (1:8).

The word *baptized* is used in a variety of ways in the New Testament. Some are wet (in water) and the others are dry (in the Spirit). In Matthew's Great Commission passage, it is clearly wet.[4] All seven uses of the baptism of the Spirit are dry. The word *baptism* means "to be dipped or immersed in a liquid or substance." So it could be said that the believer is dipped in power, in fire, in passion and is plugged into the source of power needed to do the impossible task of reaching the entire globe.

When the 120 highly committed believers spilled out of the upper room into the streets, preaching the gospel, they were on fire. And their passion had impact. Today there seems to be such weakness and vacillation in every stream of Christendom. While we don't seem to have a common way of tapping into

God's power vis-à-vis the four streams earlier described, sadly, we do have the common experience of a lack of power. Whatever we call the experience of the upper room, we want it! We must have it now, or else we Christians will continue to be weak and irrelevant. Our divorce rate will continue to be higher than that of the general population, our work with the weak and poor will continue to be inferior to that of unbelievers, and our reputations will continue to be anal-retentive legalists who lack compassion.

The resurrected Christ appeared to more than five hundred people. Jesus told his disciples to wait in Jerusalem and not to go forward without the power of the Holy Spirit. Some have asked the question, If there were only 120 in the upper room, where were the other 380 to whom Christ had appeared? I am not brave enough to make much of this except to compare those who missed the meeting with the inept majority of the church today, who have not enough humility to ask, not enough patience to wait, not enough passion to persevere, thus not enough power to make an impact.

Paul's Teaching

Pentecost took place around A.D. 31 to 34. Six out of the seven uses of "the baptism of the Holy Spirit," or the idea that Jesus or the Holy Spirit would baptize us, occur during and immediately following the earthly ministry of Jesus. Twenty years passed before the apostle Paul uses the term for the seventh and last time. It is around A.D. 55 when Paul responds to questions and concerns from the Corinthian church. The Corinthian church was divided over the use of spiritual gifts in the worship context. Paul addresses their purpose and use in chapters 12–14 of 1 Corinthians. He strikes at the disunity with his assertion that the things that unite them are bigger than those that divide them. He mentions that spiritual gifts are given for the "common good" of the people. The fulcrum of this commonality is where we find the seventh use of "the baptism of the Spirit": "For we were all baptized by one Spirit into one body—whether Jews or Greeks, slave or free—and we were all given the one Spirit to drink" (12:13).

A fair reading teaches that every believer had been baptized by the Spirit and became a member of the body. It seems to indicate that everyone drank of the Spirit, not just those with a certain gift package. There are some who consider the baptism of the Spirit a second and necessary encounter with the Spirit that separates them in power and access from other Christians. This is usually accompanied by the gift of tongues. One can hardly blame someone who has had a life-changing encounter with God for wanting others to have one too. While I am in great sympathy with those in this stream, Paul's teaching in chapter 12 makes their interpretation impossible.

His argument was to focus and unite around the common experience of the "baptism" and not to divide over different experiences. His classic argument is that a foot should not say because I am not a hand, I am less a part of the body. He goes on to say that every part of the body is equal and important to proper function. He also teaches that God has arranged the parts of the body, every one of them, just as he wanted them to be. Another core truth is that God chooses who gets what gift (v. 11). He closes the chapter with a telling list of negatives.

After listing a series of gifts Paul asks questions that have a clear answer. In fact in the Greek New Testament each question is preceded by the particle *mē*, which is a very strong negative. The negative does not appear in the English text but is clearly implied. "Are all apostles?—no! Are all prophets?—no! Are all teachers?—no! Do all work miracles?—no! Do all have gifts of healing?—no! Do all speak in tongues?—no! Do all interpret?—no! (vv. 29–30).[5]

It is therefore very suspect to teach that every person who is baptized in the Holy Spirit speaks in tongues. There are two simple reasons. First, this passage is not describing being filled with the Holy Spirit. It is describing an event common to every Christian. The only event common to every Christian is conversion. There is really no other time that the baptism of the Spirit could take place that is common to everyone. The "we were all" in verse 13 requires one to believe that every Christian has been filled with the Holy Spirit and speaks in tongues. Given what we have just read this is a bridge too far. The second reason is that Paul says that everyone does not speak in tongues and that this is a God decision, not a human one.[6]

I do not argue this point to diminish the gifts of chapter 12. I believe them to be in full operation and should be a part of the normal Christian experience. My concern is that there is confusion when we mix the terms "baptism of the Holy Spirit" and "the filling of the Holy Spirit," and that confusion diminishes the opportunity many have to realize their full potential in Christ. Those who think that the baptism of the Spirit is a second major event in their lives and then see no lasting change after the experience tend to feel guilty and give up. Others who think the filling of the Spirit is simply an already done deal after a simple prayer also don't see much difference. In both cases they retreat to the lukewarm waters of tepid faith.

In the twenty years between Pentecost and Paul's writing, he had come to teach the concept of the baptism in the way we find it in the Corinthian correspondence. We must remember that during the ministry of Jesus there was great fluidity with regard to both salvation and the role of the Holy Spirit.

Fluidity

It is clear that the disciples were converted prior to Pentecost. They professed Christ, they obeyed Christ, they preached the Good News, and they did works of miracles.[7] They exhibited all the signs required to be followers of Jesus. But their understanding of the ministry of the Holy Spirit was very fuzzy. It would be fair to propose they had no structured thoughts about a third member of the Triune God. In one of his post-resurrection appearances, Jesus breathed on them and they received the Holy Spirit (John 20:22). Jesus gradually introduced the person of the Holy Spirit to them, and they were anything but accepting about this idea. They didn't want Jesus to go; they didn't want to meet the Holy Spirit, whoever that might be.

The church had to deal with who would be accepted in the family. After the day of Pentecost it was clear that the Jews who believed and were baptized were included. The first church in Jerusalem, however, was permeated with many bigoted opinions. There was enough bias among the first believers to block the spread of the message. The biggest barrier was Jewish hubris with regard to race. They were the chosen people and Christ was their Messiah. It would take a clear sign along with a vision or two to get them to obey the Great Commission.

That is why God gave the same experience of tongues to the Samaritans. Peter and John went to check out what had happened among those of mixed ancestry, and they concluded that God's Spirit had been given.[8] Peter required a vision repeated three times to convince him to go preach to Gentiles. Before he even finished his sermon, the people started praising God and speaking in tongues (Acts 10:44–46). Paul met some believers in Ephesus. He explained the Holy Spirit to them and they believed. They also spoke in tongues (19:1–7). Talk about fluidity! At Pentecost you had people who were already believers running out of the upper room with their hair on fire speaking in tongues. In Samaria you have new believers who speak in tongues, but no other phenomena, as happened at Pentecost, occur. At the house of Cornelius you have conversion and the filling of the Spirit with simultaneous tongues. At Ephesus people had believed but they had never heard of the Holy Spirit. They were baptized in water and then filled with the Holy Spirit, then they spoke in tongues and prophesied. Tongues had more than one purpose. Clearly one purpose was to authenticate the coming of salvation to people outside the Jewish covenant. Peter's report to the Jerusalem church was testament to his new belief that all people who believe will be welcomed into the church.

We are not free from the same kind of bias that serves as a barrier to reaching the people around us. A barrier that we don't recognize is our insistence that people clean up their lives before we will spend time with them. We want them to meet us on our turf, but Jesus modeled the opposite. Jesus went to the world. The church is to go to the world. Like Jesus we are called to be the "friend of sinners." That means building relationships with people who live outside the pale of our moral standards. This is not just taking time to evangelize them; it means becoming their friend.

Sometimes I go to a coffee shop that is well-known to be a gay/lesbian hangout. I like to have my coffee and read the paper and talk with the patrons. I know that many of them have strong spiritual beliefs and many consider themselves devoted followers of Christ. I am not going to get anywhere with them if I just pronounce God's disapproval. We are called to love them and with love try to help them understand God's perspective. It is not so easy to dismiss their faith when they agree with me on every point of theology but one. Is homosexuality worse than gossip and slander? If homosexuals have trusted in Christ alone for their salvation, are they Christians? These are the issues that must be discussed if the chasm is going to be bridged. One of the mistakes the church continues to make is to turn up our collective nose at everything from music to alternative lifestyle choices that we don't like. We need more brave and caring souls that will be the friends of sinners. We don't need to change our commitment to truth, but we do need to change our attitudes.

Different Problem, Same Spirit

Paul understood the difference between Pentecost and the spiritual gifts orgy that threatened the Corinthian church. The Holy Spirit's role is to build and unite, that is what he did in his outpouring on all segments of society in the early years of the church. It gave Jews and Gentiles alike a common experience of being empowered by God with a single signature experience. But now the problem that promised to divide a primarily Gentile congregation was a selfish need for many to be prominent, regardless of how rude or wrong it might be.

Corinthian worship was a mess. By reading the remedies, we can discover their problems. They were speaking over one another, there was a lot of tongues speaking without interpretation, and many were giving prophesies without discernment. It is in this environment that Paul urges them to return to their common experience, the baptism in the Holy Spirit. That was common in that they experienced it at spiritual birth. They were twenty years removed from the fluidity of the first years when they were all trying to figure out the role of the Holy Spirit, so I would give this seventh and last mention the most weight in directing our understanding.

Questions That Matter

1. *How do we explain the person who is baptized in the Holy Spirit, in the charismatic usage of the term, and yet there is no change in his or her life?*

Many Christians have a deep desire for a second experience to help them move up to a more acceptable level of spirituality. Each stream of the church has its caste system. There is always a way to work your way up the ladder—the exercise of certain "show stopper" gifts, the accumulation of Bible knowledge, the number of times you witness. The charismatic system honors the baptism experience. But like anything else, its authenticity depends on the repentant heart and yielded will of the person seeking God. When a person has a powerful experience but he or she lacks repentance and a commitment to change, then it was only an experience.

Being baptized in the Spirit as a second event after conversion does not necessarily lead to change. Let me explain. Jane and I were married while attending Oral Roberts University. We love the university and have fond memories of our days there. There must have been something in the food the year we were married because within six months ten other couples from the university were married. Ten years later Jane and I were the only couple still together. All eleven couples had been baptized in the Holy Spirit, with the evidence of speaking in tongues. We were taught that the baptism enabled us to live life on a higher plain and with more power. But what happened to all the couples who could not make life's most basic relationship work?

What happened is that everyone discovered that a single experience subsequent to salvation is not the definitive way to solve problems. The concept that being baptized in the Spirit is the key to making it through life's turbulence is false. This could only be true if the experience laid some kind of ongoing foundation of relationship to the Spirit. No experience alone, whether a salvation-like encounter or a more emotional baptism, is the key to victorious living. Praying a prayer for salvation does not equal salvation. Being baptized in the Spirit does not equal being controlled by the Spirit. So engaging in a subcultural ritual or experience does not always lead to the fullness of the Holy Spirit.

2. *How do we explain someone who is living a powerless life and then receives what they call the baptism of the Spirit, and their life is transformed?*

Hopefully this is a more common experience than the first scenario. The difference is not to be found in the terminology. Every Christian subculture has its ways and means. My grandmother would have called it sanctification; the Baptist pastor might call it surrender; others would consider it revival or break-through. But the answer runs deeper than that. The transformed person came to repentance and confessed his or her sins.

We cannot ask for forgiveness until we see our sin. We will not determine to change our ways until we see our behavior as God sees it. That is called godly sorrow (see 2 Cor. 7:8–10), which leads to salvation when that is the issue at hand. When we experience godly sorrow subsequent to salvation, then it can lead to the awakening of what God has already placed in us. What really happened to the person in question is the filling of the Holy Spirit.

It also should be said that sometimes conversion (the baptism of the Holy Spirit) and the event described above (the filling of the Holy Spirit) can be simultaneous. If there were dormant manifestational gifts resident, then they would be activated. If the gifts were more developmental in nature, the commitment to stir up those gifts would explode within when he or she was filled with the Spirit. An individual's experience depends on his or her faith tradition. When I was seeking more of God, I was surrounded by those who taught the desired outcome was speaking in tongues. Thus I entered into a cultural ritual to gain the skill of tongues. I do not resent this at all. It just happened to be the place I was when I fully committed my way to God. As we like to say in the basketball world, "No harm, no foul." This leads us to a discussion of learned behavior.

3. *How much of what is experienced is Spirit generated versus good intentions or the power of suggestion?*

Let me return to my earlier example of the power of the religious subculture. When you enter a church for worship, the first thing you notice is how it feels. The atmosphere is set by the music, the decor, how much natural light versus artificial light is illuminating the room, the demeanor of the ushers, and whether the people are talking or in silent meditation. We notice if the first person to speak is either somber or slobberingly happy, and when the singing begins, we observe that the congregation raises their hands or is quite controlled, using their hands only to hold a hymnal. Here is a question. Why are they behaving the way they are? Did God instruct a particular church to use hymnals and another not to? Does God look at a group of Christians and say, "Okay, they look like charismatics. I will order everyone to raise his or her hands in worship. They look like Baptists. I will instruct them not to raise their hands except during the invitation." My answer is of course not. It is nearly all learned behavior, based on what that ilk of the church considers the best way to worship.

Another dynamic in our worship is personality type. We have an array of worshipers in our congregation. We have some who fall to their knees when deeply moved in the praise time. We also have some jumpers and dancers. They just can't seem to stand still when the music starts. And there is a large group who raise their hands. The largest group is the quasi-zombie section that shows some expression, but nothing like they would if they were truly in the presence of God.

Four years ago the entire church was quasi-zombie, because the power of the corporate personality overpowered the individual personalities. We set out to establish a more passionate, demonstrative worship, and we lost people over it. We took the hymnals away to free up our hands and put the words on the screens so we could lift up our heads. Uplifted hands and heads do a great deal to encourage expression. We encouraged our worship team members to be themselves, not to be intimidated, to let the true worshiper out.

Change is a lot like mountain climbing. Progress seems slow, but you keep after it and when you look back, you can't believe how far you have come. Our worship has changed dramatically; the personalities of the parishioners have not. But the corporate personality granted permission for the individuals to be more true to themselves. My conclusion is that human personality is powerful, but corporate personality is even more powerful.

At ORU if someone wanted to be filled with the Holy Spirit, we would take him or her to a prayer room for consultation. There we would clarify the need and desire, then lay hands on the person, and pray for God to fill him or her. If it didn't happen quickly, we would encourage the person to praise God with a series of "Praise the Lord!" and "Hallelujah!" until their speech became garbled. As the temperature rose and the speech raced faster, we would reach a crescendo, the person would release his or her spirit, and a new language would flow. Now if every person does not speak in tongues, even Spirit-filled ones, this creates a sticky question. How do we explain that everyone who prayed to be filled at our school did pray in tongues? My answer is that some really did and just as many never did, even though it appeared they did. Many were mimicking a learned behavior. They were thirsty for the experience because it validated their search for God. I think their desire is wonderful. I wish that all believers would cry out to God like those seekers. I have had a prayer language for more than thirty years, but I am still not 100 percent sure it is God or my own flesh. I know my heart is right before God and when it is all sorted out, that is the only thing that really matters.

I am sure that much of what people experience has been designed by God and is authentic, but I am just as sure that there is also a glut of learned behavior in which people engage. It is a reflection of their subculture and there are rewards of acceptance and recognition therein. It seems to me that people simulating tongues are not nearly as troublesome as people who teach a ritualistic prayer that simulates conversion. What is the difference between people grunting and groaning on cue in a prayer circle and people raising their hands in worship at just the right times? None. It is taught by the subculture. I don't want to give learned behavior a bad name. In fact learned behavior is integral to discipleship. In most cases, the reinforcement of the subculture is positive. But we must acknowledge that every pocket of evangelicalism, charismatic or not, has its own simulated behaviors. Sometimes the behavior is a true gift or a real prophecy, but just as often it is a well-intentioned effort of godly people to do what is expected.

Filling of the Holy Spirit

Why is it important to differentiate between the baptism of the Holy Spirit and the filling of the Holy Spirit? When people equate the baptism of the Holy Spirit with the filling of the Holy Spirit, it creates unrealistic expectations and hinders a disciple's relationship to God. People expect that they need a special experience with trumpets blowing in order to get the power, and if they miss it or can't get it, they feel assigned to a lower form of

Christian life. *The importance of this distinction is that the connection to the fullness and power of the Holy Spirit is at the heart of doing what Jesus did.*

I will now put myself at risk and venture into Greek syntax. This is especially daring for a guy who flunked high school English four times. The verbal action in "we were all baptized by one Spirit into one body" (1 Cor. 12:13) is aorist passive in the Greek New Testament. The aorist tense indicates this was a completed action that took place in the past. The passive voice tells us that some force outside the believer did the work. In this case, that force was a person, namely the Holy Spirit. Since the text says "we all," it must mean all believers, and the only single moment that every believer has in common is conversion. That is why, when it comes to the issue of an ongoing relationship to God, the filling of the Spirit is a much better model than the baptism of the Spirit.

Whereas the baptism of the Spirit is presented by John and Jesus as something that was destined to happen to Christ's followers, the filling of the Spirit is a commanded action, one that each Christian is responsible for pursuing. The core passage is found in Paul's letter to the Ephesians. "Do not get drunk on wine, which leads to debauchery. Instead, be filled with the Spirit" (5:18).

The Greek syntax is a double present imperative. Don't get drunk and be filled with the Spirit. The present tense indicates ongoing action, moment by moment. The disciple then is to keep on getting filled with the Holy Spirit. It is not a once-for-all, completed action, but a repeated experience that continues all of our lives. The filling of the Holy Spirit indicates a greater need for intimate interplay between God and his child than does the baptism of the Spirit. So let's talk about the filling and how this interplay works. The phrase "the filling of the Holy Spirit" seems best to describe a second experience, third experience, and a six hundred and forty-eighth experience. Gordon Fee puts this key phrase into context: "This imperative, therefore, is not just another in a long string; rather, it is the key to all the others."[9]

This passage is congruent with the way life is lived. The normal person sins every day, and thus requires regular forgiveness. When I was a child, I thought being good for God was like holding your breath, eventually you relinquished to reality. So you could only be good so long. And I was right, you can only go for so long without committing a sin. Then what do you do? How can one stay in the Spirit, walk in the Spirit, while sinning? I thought that was impossible, but subsequently I have learned that not only is it possible, it is God's design to match the reality of our daily lives.

The command to be continually filled with the Spirit is deeply rooted in reality in two ways. The first is the context of first-century Ephesus; the second way is the four behavioral indicators that follow. The first command—do not get drunk with wine—was a direct warning to avoid pagan worship. A very common temptation for the Ephesian disciple was to engage in the drunken orgies at the temples of pleasure. Drunkenness does lead to an altered state of relating to others, but this is not what God desires, and a temporary altered state does not match life's reality or provide the needed resources to get through one day. God wants us in our right minds.

The four behavioral indicators mentioned above are speaking, singing, giving thanks, and submitting. These behaviors can reveal our internal attitude: speaking to one another with psalms, hymns, and spiritual songs; singing, making a melody in our hearts to God; giving thanks in everything; and, finally, submitting to one another (Eph. 5:19–21). This is life moment by moment, issue by issue, person by person. These activities describe a peaceful person who has a song in his or her heart. This person has reconciled the events in life and has found a way to be thankful. He or she also has a healthy respect for authority and for other people's needs and opinions. This is a person whom God is controlling, not perfect but there are core attitudes that identify him or her as Spirit filled.

The Test Is Relationships

The qualifying exams for the Spirit-filled life center on life's most intimate relationships. Paul first deals with the husband-wife relationship; then he turns to parents and children and finally to employer-employee. Our daily experience in these relationships and the control of our emotions, words, and behavior reveal the Holy Spirit's presence. The command to be filled rules the exegetical roost from Ephesians 4:17 through the middle of chapter 6. It is merely another way, a more powerful way, of repeating Paul's basic imperative found in Galatians 5:16, "live by the Spirit." All truly Christian behavior is the result of being Spirit people, people filled with the Spirit of God who live by the Spirit and walk in the Spirit.

There is loud power and quiet power. The loud power you see on television or highlighted in a public gathering. Quiet power is just as strong but is often not the show-stopper stuff. I have nicknamed my wife "Jane St. Marie." Her real name is Jane Marie, and she has always been a people helper. Needy people and animals are drawn to her. There must be a homing device that directs this kind of person to her. Right now we are baby-sitting two birds, eight cats, and a dog. This is not unusual. Not long ago we had four wild cats living with us along with our three. Because of Jane's generous heart, we loan people money; we provide transportation; I find myself doing favors for people I don't know.

There are plenty of times that I resent helping people because it upsets my schedule. I have a plan of how to reach my world and impact it for Christ. And all these interruptions are frustrating my plan. I also don't like my selfishness being put on display. I will see one of these people coming to the door and blurt out, "Don't answer the door, Jane. We're not home." How inspirational!

Quiet power is performing in the trenches of life; it is holding your tongue when an "I told you so" tells you so. It is loving people who treat others badly because they can get away with it. How we respond to others reveals who controls us.

The Word Filled

Is *filled* the right word when talking about the indwelling of the Holy Spirit? It is the right word because it is the God-chosen word. If you are full of something, the implication is that it will control you. So the issue is who is controlling the will at the moment of decision. For example, I am preparing to order lunch, I have gained ten pounds, and I have committed myself to a one-month diet. I want the cheeseburger with fries, but I should order the sprout sandwich. The battle rages within. Who is in control? Who will win? If I allow the Holy Spirit to control my decision, it is the sprout sandwich with no cheese. Sounds terrible, doesn't it? But this illustrates the real battleground on which we live.

I may be filled with the Holy Spirit when I am driving my car but not when playing golf. I am pleasant and relaxed when sitting in church but a selfish boor when shopping with my wife. We are all filled with the Spirit on a percentage basis. Some of us are filled 25 percent of the time, others 50 percent or 90 percent. But we are filled or controlled moment by moment, issue by issue, temptation by temptation. This is why very spiritual-sounding people can experience divorce or have a hidden life. The human heart is deceitful and it can rationalize just about anything (see Jer. 17:9). So repeated fillings are essential for doing what Jesus did.

Fresh Power

Do you weigh more when filled with the Holy Spirit? Does being filled with Satan have a different weight than being filled with God? These may seem like silly questions, but they help us think about what being filled really means. Often we think of being filled like a glass is filled with liquid, when in actual fact it is an issue of the control of the will.

When Peter addressed the Jewish supreme court, he was filled with the Holy Spirit.[10] I believe that Peter had a fresh encounter with the Holy Spirit just prior to speaking at such a tense and crucial time. It is also very interesting that the entire group who gathered for prayer to celebrate Peter and John's release were freshly filled.[11] We can pray for God's fresh power and anointing even when we have no known sin to confess.

How can we be filled over and over again? Don't think about a glass being filled with liquid, because a glass has limits. Consider the balloon that seems to be filled but has the capacity for even more air until it expands to several times its deflated size. In a similar way, God can give us greater and greater power that raises the percentage of his lordship in us. I think of Luke's description on one occasion during Jesus' ministry that "the power of the Lord was present for him to heal" (5:17). That implies that there were times when it appeared that the Holy Spirit was not as strongly present.

There is both a tendency and desire to figure out the Holy Spirit. We would like to know how to control the Spirit so that his power is always in us. This is reverse thinking, because the Spirit's role is to control us. If we could learn how he works, and draw a few lines, then we could determine when and where he would be strongly present. I don't think the ministry of the Holy Spirit is as tightly organized as we teach. The Spirit is creative and he colors outside the lines and does things that challenge our categories.

Maintaining the Filling

There is a school of thought that goes something like this. When Jesus died on the cross, he paid for all the sin of the world. All sin means sins that were past, present, and future. Ask yourself, *How many of my sins were future when Christ died?* All of them! Therefore, Christ has already paid for our past sins, our present sins, and all the sins in the future. If you are in your twenties, it could be hypothesized that most of your sins are future ones. There is great truth included in the above belief, because everything that Christ had to do to provide eternal life was completed before any reader of this book was born.

It is not the above truth that is the problem, but the wrong application of such truth that strips many of spiritual power. The wrong application is seen in two ways, one more extreme than the other. The most extreme is the extrapolation that since we are already forgiven, we don't need to confess our sin. This is the "one John one niner" group. The verse says: "If we confess our sins, he is faithful and just and will forgive us our sins and purify us from all unrighteousness."

Their take on the verse is that we initially commit to Christ through salvation and then we stand on that forgiven ground from that day forward. We confess by simply acknowledging the truth that we are sinners and then thank God for his forgiveness. This removes any intimacy or interplay between God and the disciple. It is a hyper-positional–truth interpretation that extracts most if not all the passion from our walk with God.

The second application is not as extreme and, therefore, much more common. This interpretation suggests that we confess our sin through prayer, accept God's forgiveness, and go on. To confess, the proponents say, means "to say the same thing" based on the Greek word.[12] This often leads to a rather pedantic or matter-of-fact approach to sin. It is often emphasized that we should not wallow in the guilt and shame of our already forgiven sin. I agree with that. In fact I don't see a lot wrong with this particular application. My objection is the lack of personal emotional investment that often goes along with it. How can we truly be repentant without remorse accompanied by a deeply moving encounter with God?

One of the pathologies of longtime Christians is that we stop confessing. Oh, we still confess the big stuff, the sins that hurt others or will cost us if we don't apologize. But the conscience can be hardened by repeated sins that we no longer see as sin. "See to it, brothers, that none of you has a sinful, unbelieving heart that turns away from the living God. But encourage one another daily, so long as it is called Today, so that none of you may be hardened by sin's deceitfulness" (Heb. 3:12–13).

I can't tell you how many times I have encountered this blindness. A group of people get duped by the devil and begin to slander and gossip. When they are confronted, they immediately morph from attacker to victim. They act like and even claim that what destruction they have done to others isn't that bad. Then they say it, the statement that drives me nearly insane, "We all are sinners." What this means is, You can't hold us accountable for our actions. We were justified in hurting people and destroying reputations, because we were upset.

I'm not sure when my breaking point came, but one day in the wake of this tripe, I shot back, "Name three of the sins you have committed this week." They couldn't think of one! This is what I mean; you can be bullish on the doctrine of everyone is a sinner and at the same time you haven't confessed in months, sometimes years.

If many of us would spend an extended time with God asking him to search our hearts, the dam would break. Numerous times I have gone through a week without confessing any sin to

God. This is due to two things. I don't examine myself in depth daily, and I need some extended time, with fasting, to get underneath the surface. I have found after I peel off the surface in prayer and confess my regular sins that the Spirit begins to speak to me and the sins come pouring out—the fixed and wrong opinions I have developed about people and the way I have ignored staff members' needs, for example. God opens me up and the junk of life is poured out and he fills the hole with forgiveness. I plan to spend more time seeking God for a clean heart. I plan to call my congregation to repentance more often. Know this that there is a lot God desires to clean out of our lives, but we must stay near him and sensitive to his voice. The relationship must be personal in practice, not just in theory.

What if at the wedding altar my Jane had said, "Bill, I know that in the next fifty years or so you will sin a lot. You will offend me, ignore me, forget birthdays and anniversaries. You may even lie to me a few times. So I want to forgive you in advance, right now. So whatever happens, we won't need to talk about it or ask each other to forgive the other one and have all that experience of wounding and healing, of hurt and then forgiveness. I want you to know, I love you and forgive you." What kind of relationship would that be? It wouldn't be a relationship. It sounds like a soulless contract between two entities.

Much of the strength of our marriage is based on a long string of fresh encounters. We have raised two sons, taken care of my elderly mother, moved twenty-four times and lived in seven states. We have rented homes, purchased homes, and built homes. We survived several years of gut-wrenching challenge with one of our sons. We have walked side by side, holding hands, united in our core convictions. More than anything we have talked, argued, negotiated, got upset, stopped talking, asked for forgiveness, and made up.

When we sin against our Father, we can't be cavalier and pretend that nothing is wrong with the relationship, and we won't enjoy the fullness of his Spirit until we have repented and confessed. This is the basis of what I consider the most balanced, workable model for Spirit filling: conviction, repentance, and confession.

CONVICTION

Just recently I was on the phone with a colleague who made a statement that sent me into the emotional stratosphere. My voice took on extra timbre, and I exploded with several tightly reasoned and very hurtful comments. As soon as these cogent words passed over my lips, I knew I had sinned. The good thing is I apologized right then and there before it got worse. The knowledge that I had sinned is a basic work of the Spirit called *conviction*. Jesus told his disciples that the Holy Spirit would convict the world of sin.[13] It is fairly common for a Christian to say, "God convicted me of my bad attitude" or some other behavior.

If the Spirit does not convict, we won't repent, because we are spiritually blind, deaf, and dumb without the illumination that comes via the Spirit. Conviction identifies our sin.

Sometimes conviction will grow because our sin is stubborn or well hidden. My pastoral experience has revealed the hardness of the human heart. A very common problem is holding a grudge. Many won't forgive and live estranged from those they love and from God.

It is common for married couples in crisis to be committed to getting out of the marriage. If they divorce, each may walk away saying, "I am a believer. God will forgive me." Or "God loves me. He wouldn't want me to suffer in this relationship that is not fulfilling to me."

At the time, the divorced couple is not even open to the ministry of the Holy Spirit. They just ignore God and do whatever they want. They say they have peace with God and that they have never been happier. The truth is that God is grieved and they are listening to their flesh—they are not listening to God. Then months or years later, they begin to reap a bitter harvest. They begin to see how they were wrong and then for the first time in years start listening again to God. It is as though they were living in a room that was pitch black and then someone turns on the light. They begin to understand what really happened and how they hurt themselves, the children, their extended family. A godly sorrow enters their spirit. They are filled with anguish. Now they are ready to take the next step.

The point is that we cannot truly repent until we see our sin as God sees it. The whole person is involved. Emotions, intellect, and even the body experience conviction. Conviction is more than cognition, more than an intellectual claim on truth. Conviction penetrates to the deepest part of the soul.

REPENTANCE

The essence of repentance is changing your mind.[14] Conviction tells us we were wrong. Repentance is a heart's desire to change and do what is right. The difference is significant. I can have the conviction that I am doing wrong but not change. The first two years I was in college, I lived wrong. I knew it but I was enjoying myself too much to change. I used to lie awake at night thinking about going to hell. Then the most interesting thing happened, I was recruited by Oral Roberts University to play basketball. A few weekends later I traveled to Tulsa to meet the players and learn about the school. One evening I left campus with a few friends to do some drinking. A few hours and beers later, I was doing the "frug" (a sixties' dance) on the stage of a night club next to the go-go dancer (a sixties' night club dancer in a cage).

Somehow we got back to the campus around 1:00 A.M. I saw an old beater of a car with "Jesus Saves" written in candy stripe script on the back window. I began to scream "Jesus saves! Jesus saves!" as I stumbled toward the dorm. A few lights turned on as people wondered, *Who is that fool?* The next morning I changed my mind about my life and determined to change my ways. That led to my signing with ORU, and early the next fall I committed my life to Christ.

When we confess our sin, repentance is understood. Confession means we have determined to change our behavior. So we are not just sorry that things didn't work out, we are now committed to making behavioral changes. True confession always includes repentance and is proof of repentance. Two times the Scriptures speak of fruit or deeds appropriate to repentance (Luke 3:8 and Acts 26:20).

People come to us with deep needs and ask for prayer. A common prayer request from men is to be delivered from addiction to pornography. I have seen the pain in their eyes and the tears that they can't hold back. I pray for them with all the faith I have. I ask God to restore and forgive them, to make the deliverance instantaneous. Sometimes people are immediately delivered from addictions—I want to make it clear that I think it does happen. More often, however, God chooses to have us work through his principles and methods from his Word. I simply ask these men, "Are you really repentant?" They always say yes or they think they are. The next step then is to restructure their lives in such a way as to establish accountability and protections. I make sure they are set up with a buddy system for accountability. There is also counseling where they can identify the reasons for the behavior. That is repentance. After having changed the mind, there is proof through restructuring the life.

CONFESSION

The classic verse on post-conversion forgiveness is 1 John 1:9: "If we confess our sins, he is faithful and just and will forgive us our sins and purify us from all unrighteousness." I say "post-conversion" because John has been writing about fellowship and he goes on to refer to the recipients of the letter as "my dear children." These references indicate that John is writing to believers.

The promise of forgiveness is conditional on our willingness to confess our sins. It requires us to actually name our sins to God—conversing is part of the relationship.

The distinction I want to draw from the more casual approach to dealing with daily sin is that *confession is power packed with conviction and repentance.* Conviction and repentance are the prerequistists to a satisfying confession. True confession comes from the deepest regions of our spirit. Some of my most emotional moments have been when I was confessing my sin to God. The prayer of confession is a moment of surrender.

There is a sweetness in the moment of forgiveness. It is about acceptance and mercy—I can't get over God's mercy. I know that he has provided it all in the finished work of Christ. But God forbid that I would ever lose my wonder when I think of his mercy and grace. That is why I am opposed to a more detached, theological approach to the forgiveness process.

A Process for Spirit Filling

I have broken down the process for discussion, but this model for Spirit filling is experienced as a seamless process. We become aware of our sin by conviction. When we see it as God sees it, we want to repent, because we have changed our minds and are committed to restructure our behavior. These first two dimensions are awareness issues in our soul. Then we desire to talk to God about it, so we pray our prayer of confession naming our sin to God. We ask for his forgiveness because that is what we do in any meaningful relationship. Then we thank him for that forgiveness and ask for his help in our commitment to change. All these elements are crucial to spiritual growth and Spirit filling. The reason many don't grow is they don't treat their sin seriously; they don't go through the process in a heartfelt way.

I caution you to be on guard against the temptation to feel guilty about the confessed sin. It is a pathology of humanness to wallow in the guilt of already forgiven sin. In forgiveness we must be just as determined to focus on God's mercy and grace as we were determined in repentance to focus on the awfulness of our sin. A negative focus on guilt increases the probability that the sin will be repeated.

Walking in the Spirit

As I said earlier, some people think it is impossible to walk in the Spirit and sin at the same time. What is impossible, however, is sinlessness in this life. When you commit a sin, are you immediately out of fellowship with God? Are you carnal and are you walking in the flesh until you confess? This was a major talking point in the sixties and early seventies as we worked with students on university campuses. To complicate the issue, there is the fact that there is no time when there isn't some sin in our lives.

The psalmist asks God to search him because there are hidden sins (Ps. 139:23–24). There is also a recorded request to God to forgive hidden sins (19:12). This goes back to the fact that many sins are attitudes and wrongly held beliefs. We live and die with sinful beliefs and quite often without ever having dealt with them. But does that mean that we can't experience God's power, share our faith, and live a life that glorifies God?

There is something about the human condition that requires sin to coexist with God's Spirit. We live as forgiven people and with a transformed relationship and status. We are freed from the penalty of sin and can make great gains against the practice of sin. But we still live in a state of sin in that our "flesh" remains.[15] We don't like to talk about this issue because it muddies the water, but I have found it liberating. There really is no time when I am a perfectly clean vessel for God's use. The basic instruction on this point is found in the general letter of 1 John.

John is talking about the basis of fellowship or life together as the people of God. He claims the basis of fellowship is a relationship with God before it is a relationship with anyone else.[16] He then moves to the reality of living daily with God: "If we claim to have fellowship with him yet walk in the darkness, we lie and do not live by the truth. But if we walk in the light, as he is in the light, we have fellowship with one another, and the blood of Jesus, his Son, purifies us from all sin" (1 John 1:6–7).

Another way of saying it is, as our hearts are in tune with God, we will live with the intention of not sinning, but when we sin, God will keep forgiving us and keep us in fellowship with him. This is confirmed by the already discussed ninth verse. Walking in the Spirit or the light is about an open, honest relationship with God.[17] It is not pretending that we no longer sin. We are warned against such a position in verses 8 and 10. In fact, as chapter 2 opens, it continues to tell us that our intention is not to sin, but when we do, and we will, God will forgive us. This is not permissiveness slipping into the New Testament. It is a practical theology that matches the way life is, given the reality of our flesh.

Think of driving down the middle of the road, where the white line in the middle represents the ideal—no known sin in my life right now. As I drive down the road, because I am human, I begin to drift and find myself nearing the edge of the blacktop, which is marked with a yellow line. That yellow line represents a "conviction point." That is the Spirit of God telling me that I have sinned. If I cross over the yellow line and start wandering into places that should be avoided, I lose fellowship with God because I ignore the Holy Spirit's promptings. But if I respond to the prompting of the Spirit at that point and repent, then I start back toward the middle line. I confess my sin and enjoy God's mercy and start driving in the middle of the road again. Then I have not broken fellowship with God. I have continued to walk in the Spirit or the light. Staying in fellowship with God is not about perfection; it is about heart intent and responsiveness to God's Spirit.

This understanding liberates us from the catastrophic ups and downs that come with the idea that one sin sends us over the edge into carnality. It also provides a means for measured growth. As one matures in faith, the yellow lines start moving slowly toward the middle line. This is the process of sinning less and knowing more about what sin is. In the end, the mature believer is walking a greatly narrowed path developed through a lifetime of walking in the light.

This chapter's mission has been to sort out what it really means to be filled and empowered by the Spirit. A major part of that mission has been to grasp the theological mechanics of walking in the Spirit. Now I would like to ask a question that will draw a perspective on the power needed to do the works Jesus did.

Spiritual Power

Do charismatic disciples have more spiritual power than non-charismatics? By power I mean God's intervention in a visible way that changes behavior, heals the body, or provides a financial miracle. The question could seem divisive or even frivolous. Why draw another line between two evangelical movements that are beginning to blend? The answer is, if charismatics have more power, then noncharismatics need to admit it and figure out what went wrong.

It is not frivolous to discern why many a ministry seems saturated with power while others are dead in the water. A challenge steeper than the question is how does one measure such a thing? The biblical measuring sticks are fruitfulness (Matt. 7:15–20), godliness (1 Tim. 4:7–8), and even size (Acts 2:41, 47).[18] Jesus taught that "by their fruit you will know them." It is very difficult to measure the love, joy, kindness, and self-control of a congregation. The pollsters would need to be as numerous as the objects of measurement. A 24/7 "big brother" observation would be fundamental to any accurate data. For that reason the true measurement of spiritual greatness is humanly impossible. Not only would a person's actions need to be rated, so also would his or her motives and most private thoughts. There is no computer or mathematical construct that could figure out how to measure what really counts. That is the reason God claims that measuring greatness is his private purview.[19]

So we humans measure the two tangible signs of "success," size and money. Our society still worships at the altar of bigger is better. The world's richest man or greatest athlete is a celebrity. We ask for his autograph, we listen to what she has to say, and people grapple to be near the power. I must tell you I see very little difference in the Christian community. Yes, it is true we cloak it and try not to break out into a full worship mode, but our admiration of money and power is there anyway. The largest churches have the most famous pastors. Christian leaders flock to their seminars on "how to do what we did."

You may be protesting saying it isn't that bad. "Who wants to spend money to see how a pastor kept his church at two hundred for ten years?" That is a fair and very pragmatic point, but consider mine. Because a ministry is big, is that really a sign of greater spiritual power? Or is it evidence of better talent? I believe it is the latter, but that does not mean the megachurch has less spiritual power. The church of three thousand could have equal spiritual power to the church of three hundred. The difference is not necessarily spiritual power. It is more often a measure of giftedness.

It appears worldwide that the fastest-growing churches are charismatic. The United States, however, has a pretty even megachurch distribution between charismatic and mainstream evangelical. There is no evidence that charismatics have more spiritual power as measured by church size in the United States. The most important elements in the creation of the megachurch are the personality and skill of the leader, the growth of the community, and the timing of the church's birth. The last factor has to do with God's sovereignty and what he entrusts to a church.

To repeat my question: Do charismatics have more spiritual power than noncharismatics? The answer? Spiritual power is a matter of faith, not a matter of giftedness. The amount of spiritual power one has boils down to the individual's application of faith to life's challenges. How much power is enough? Jesus said that faith as little as a mustard seed is enough to move a mountain. His use of hyperbole was to point out that faith directed specifically is serious power. If I have the faith to believe God will meet my financial needs, then I will experience inner peace, which will enable me to concentrate on my work. Thus I am content and productive. That is the difference spiritual power makes—you see needs met. God seems to work just as powerfully in all evangelical streams, but there is one thing that charismatics have over the rest.

The Charismatic Advantage

Charismatic congregations have potentially greater power because they have more options. They expect God to speak to individuals and groups through visions, words of prophecy, and other means. They look for him to do miracles. Those who believe these gifts have ceased have removed at least one third of the spiritual gifts arsenal from their ministry toolbox. If you remove discernment of spirits, working of miracles, gifts of healing, tongues, and prophecy from your ministry, you have limited your options. You may still pray for healing and some people will be healed, but you don't encourage and develop the gifts of healing. When your family or church faces an impossible challenge, where are those with the gift of faith or the workers of miracles to give leadership? Where are those through whom God will deliver a timely prophetic message? My conclusion is a simple one. If you have the use of more tools, you will see God meet more needs.

When God speaks personally through a prophetic word, people receive a deep sense of God's love and care. That gives them an increased hunger to know God and the faith to take on greater challenges. Experiencing God begets the desire to experience him again and again. This breeds an atmosphere of optimism that encourages faith, and that is why God does more. Can this happen without the gifts of 1 Corinthians? Yes, it can and does, but why operate with one hand tied behind your back? The *charismatic advantage* is not "charismatic" at all. It is the *Christian advantage* that is available to all who would dare believe it to be true.

If we are to do the works that Jesus did, we must have access to his power. Many days I feel so inept and powerless. Our church has just completed a building project. We are two Sundays past grand opening; the new hasn't worn off yet. I found myself thinking, *What if we don't grow numerically and financially? Then I will get pressured, the leadership will feel that pressure, and things will get rough. I will resign, sell my home, and live off the money.* That is what God has to overcome with me some days. I shake it off. *I can't allow myself to think that way.* I require divine intervention daily. I deeply desire to experience all his fullness, because I want to do the works of Jesus, not what my weakness dictates. How about you?

6

Understanding the Purpose of Spiritual Gifts

Discussion of spiritual gifts is largely the preserve of the apostle Paul. His letters to the Romans, the Ephesians, and the Corinthians are the magnum opus for the what and why of gifts. I think he would be both appalled and puzzled by the way we have interpreted his teaching. He might even laugh at our lists and categories, but he would really let out a hoot if he could read one of our spiritual gifts tests. The idea that one could discover their gift by answering multiple choice questions would scandalize the scholar from Tarsus. "No, no, no," he would cry. "That is not what I meant."

Paul taught us to accept the gifts we were given, that they would emerge from our spiritual passion.[1] For many of us discovering our spiritual gift is in the same realm as tracing our family tree and learning our personality type. It is all about the fun of me. It is part of the psychologized society in which we live. And this is par for the human condition. In the first century, disciples were selfishly pursuing gifts in order to impress. In the twenty-first century, disciples are pursuing gifts in order to reach their full potential for maximum enjoyment.

What are spiritual gifts? I believe they are God present with us through another person. That is why it is so crucial to help people discover them. If you are at church and the others present don't know their gifts, you might as well have stayed home. The idea of getting together is for mutual encouragement, so not only do the gifts need to be known, they must be exercised, and not only exercised, but exercised with the right people in the right context. Gifts must be developed, and there needs to be a forum with permission for their exercise. So knowledge of the gifts, self-awareness, and opportunity create the environment in which gifts flourish. Before we get into the reasons for spiritual gifts, allow me to present a short primer.

A Primer on Spiritual Gifts

1. Every Christian has at least one gift (1 Cor. 12:7).
2. The gifts can vary in strength (Rom. 12:6).
3. They are strong enough to help others (1 Peter 4:11).
4. Most are permanent (1 Cor. 12:11).[2]
5. They can go dormant (1 Tim. 4:14).
6. They can be rekindled (2 Tim. 1:6).
7. God chooses who gets what (1 Cor. 12:11).
8. Everyone needs to use his or her gift (Eph. 4:16).
9. We should earnestly desire them (1 Cor. 12:31).
10. The gift of prophecy is mentioned the most (12 times).

When Christ ascended, the plan was to empower the church and then to provide the tools to meet needs. The raw power was the Holy Spirit coming to live in each believer. That would be a fixed reality for every disciple. The use of the power would be contingent on each believer's faith and obedience, i.e., his or her receptivity to the filling of the Holy Spirit. The Spirit provides tools or gifts to meet three crucial needs: to show God's care, reveal his power, and deliver his message. These three needs explain the purpose for spiritual gifts. God becomes present with us through others to meet these three basic needs.

To Show God's Care

Peter put it well: "Therefore be clear minded and self-controlled so that you can pray. Above all, love each other deeply, because love covers over a multitude of sins" (1 Peter 4:8). Love each other deeply sounds really good, but what does it mean and what do gifts have to do with it? It sounds very important because that kind of love makes up for the way we hurt and irritate one another.

I used to have an assistant who was difficult to work with. Or, I should say, it was difficult for her to work before her daily counseling session. She would come to work distraught over a conflict with her husband or one of her children. I would say, "Good morning," and she would burst into tears. This was routinely followed by a few minutes of conversation and prayer. Sometimes she would need to return home. This was very irritating, especially when we had a lot of work to get done. I was struggling with where to draw the line. Yes, it is a church. Yes, I am a pastor. Yes, she is a parishioner, but at some point she also is an employee paid to do necessary work.

Then something happened. My wife had a gall bladder attack and was in the hospital for two weeks. My assistant-counselee came over and cleaned my house, did the laundry, and cooked some meals. She cared for my two preschool boys and helped me survive those fourteen days. She was exceedingly strong and helpful; she was exercising her gift of showing mercy. This erased all the anger I felt over her weakness at work. She had the gift to love our family deeply. It made all the difference.

We can love deeply through our gifts. Peter goes on: "Each one should use whatever gift he has received to serve others, faithfully administering God's grace in its various forms. . . . so that in all things God may be praised through Jesus Christ" (vv. 10–11).

The remarkable truth is that God's grace is issued to others through our use of spiritual gifts. Conversely, if people are not unleashed to minister to one another, the church becomes a wasteland of unrealized potential and unmet needs. The various forms that show God's care are what some of us call *serving gifts*. They are gifts of healing, service, helps, encouragement, mercy, and giving. This cluster when exercised gives people a sense of a personal touch from God.

Jane St. Marie, my wife if you didn't catch it the first time, was at it again this week. A woman who lives nearby is down on her luck. She is an unbeliever who has come to a couple of fun events at our church. In fact she came to an Alpha Course introduction but made it clear she had no intention of being converted. She had one back surgery that didn't take and so last month had a redo. She has one of those personalities that irritates those around her. The nurses were happy to see her go after two weeks in the hospital. But Jane, being a saint, actually gets along with her and has been very helpful. (This makes me wonder if I am a good husband or simply an object of Jane's mercy.)

The two men who own the two-room house Jane's friend lives in forced her to move. It took them over a year to get her to comply to their sixty-day notice. She asked Jane if we could keep a couple of things in our garage until she found a permanent place. I came home and there were old dog houses, kitty scratching platforms, dilapidated lawn furniture, and piles of unidentified junk surrounding my house. I'm not kidding, it starts on one side and forms the letter U around my home. I blew my stack; Jane listened patiently and agreed with me. Don't you hate it when someone returns good for evil—when you're giving the evil? It makes you feel like a dirt clod.

But Jane has loved this woman deeply. If she ever comes to Christ, Jane's loving her deeply will be the reason. It certainly won't be my putting her number on the caller I.D. reject mode. A couple of days ago the woman came to our house in tears and Jane gave her comfort. The way I figure it, pretty soon this lady will be a member of our church and I won't be able to ignore her anymore.

The caring gifts are God's personal touch. They are his "hands on" way to say "I love you; I know your name; I haven't lost track of you."

To Reveal God's Power

The nature of the nine gifts in 1 Corinthians 12 is manifestational. "Now to each one the manifestation of the Spirit is given for the common good" (v. 7). To manifest is to reveal. These gifts stand out. They are the show-stopper gifts. This is one of the basic ways God has chosen to have an impact on the watching world. Jesus taught that everyone would know by the church's unity and love for one another that he had been sent (see John 13:35; 17:20–21). Another way he said the whole world would know is through the preaching of the Good News.[3]

The gifts of message of wisdom, knowledge, faith, healing, miraculous powers, distinguishing between spirits, speaking in tongues, and interpretation of tongues are the demonstrative power package, *the manifestational gifts*. These show-stopper gifts are designed to create a sense of awe among the church and then among those watching the church. Needy people need God's care, and God gets their attention through pain and loss. At any given time needy people are in the minority. For the vast majority of people only a supernatural demonstration will get their attention. They need to see God's power.

This is what is meant by "common good." The gifts don't focus on one kind of person or type of need. The gifts address the full range of human need. God meets us in our pain with the caring gifts. With his power gifts he creates a sense of awe and worship.

THE CONTEXT IS WORSHIP

Gordon Fee makes the point:

> The worshipping community includes several extraordinary phenomena, which Paul variously calls charismata ["gracious gifting," 1 Cor. 12:4], pneumatika ["things of the Spirit," 1 Cor. 12:1; 14:1], or "manifestations of the Spirit" [1 Cor. 12:7]. Such phenomena are especially the activity of the Spirit in the gathered community, as 1 Corinthians 14 makes abundantly clear.[4]

How 1 Corinthians 14 makes this abundantly clear is Paul's teaching about managing the manifestations when the church is gathered. The early church didn't gather in open public meetings like contemporary congregations. They met in homes and other facilities. As we know, church buildings didn't come into being until the third century. Their gatherings would be closer to what we call adult Sunday school class, numbering between ten and fifty people. The entire church might be several hundred or, as in Jerusalem's case, thousands, but there was no worship center.[5] It took many years for Jewish Christians to extract themselves from attending synagogue and practicing cultural customs. Then the persecution of the Jews and Romans made it impossible for the church to build and maintain houses of worship. So they preached in the streets, in the marketplaces, on mountains, in ships at sea, in caves, and in desert retreats. Wherever they gathered, they expected something to happen.

THE NATURE OF THE GATHERING

Think of twenty people crammed into a home's central meeting space. Here are Paul's instructions: "When you come together, everyone has a hymn, or a word of instruction, a revelation, a tongue or an interpretation. All of these must be done for the strengthening of the church" (1 Cor. 14:26). This setting is radically different from twenty-first-century church meetings. I say *radically* because it is different at its root. The setting was intimate, the method interactive, and the members were to come prepared. The kind of depth described by Paul is vital to building healthy disciples, and it requires a special environment that is fundamentally different from our normal public meeting. The interactive environment brings new meaning to "And let us consider how we may spur one another on toward love and good deeds. Let us not give up meeting together, as some are in the habit of doing, but let us encourage one another" (Heb. 10:24–25).

In the early church it was important for each member to be there because he or she was called as a worshiper to make a contribution. Today's contribution is usually monetary, as we are expected to be semi–pew potatoes.

Today's worship is impersonal, the method is one-way communication, and people come in a passive mode. This does not mean, however, that our public worship services are bad. Let me be clear. The early church did not hold public meetings in the same way we do. We desire "walk in" business; we advertise in local newspapers and invite strangers to be present in our meetings. The public services we call worship are designed to appeal to the widest audience possible. The more urbanized and impersonal our society becomes, it is crucial for our public meetings to appeal to a wide spectrum. But still the focus of worship is God and the meeting should primarily address the needs and responsibilities of the believer.

Back to the central living space in the first-century home. The meeting's purpose was to strengthen the people present. The worshiper would arrive prepared, with an insight from the Scripture readings of the previous week, a direct word of revelation, or even a message in tongues.[6] I am sure there was a leader, but the focus was interactive, ministering to one another. We already know from 1 Corinthians 14:24–25 that sometimes an unbeliever would come into the gathering. Paul was strongly convinced that the greatest need of all the worshipers was for the teaching to be understood. That teaching, however, arose out of a prepared and gifted congregation.

So much is missed when the church doesn't understand the different worship contexts. There is a certain kind of worship that takes place in a public gathering dominated by group singing, prayer, and a sermon. If that is the only way the church worships, then some of the most powerful ministry—interactive ministry—is impossible. Through interactive ministry, God's personal touch and his power are applied to specific needs. When we think the essence of worship is learning more Bible and having an enjoyable musical experience, then we aren't expecting what Paul is advocating. His desired result is that believer and unbeliever alike will reach the same conclusion: "God is really among you!" (v. 25).[7] To minister without all the tools is like swimming with one arm. It can be done but it can never be what it should be. Therefore, we must create new worship contexts.

CREATE DIFFERENT WORSHIP CONTEXTS

After one year of preparation I preached a series of sermons based on the thesis that all God's gifts are present in his church. The follow-up has been slow but steady. We have slowly built adult fellowships of twenty-five to fifty people, with a more interactive form of worship and learning. People are asked to come prepared with a hymn (any form of music), a word of encouragement from Scripture, or even a tongue or revelation. The first thing we learned was that people rarely think about worship before they arrive at church. The second thing we learned was that when it gets this personal, many begin to back off. The interactive worship context is highly threatening and when people are confronted with it, many run for cover. They run with a variety of defense mechanisms: "I want more verse-by-verse teaching. This is too touchy-feely for me."

In our genre of church, the desire to be lectured to, even in smaller settings, dies hard. Our commitment is to learning, to a deeper experience through application. We've found that the road to deeper ministry is one of change and it can be bumpy. As they have led the fellowship groups, the pastoral staff has been seriously challenged and has experienced significant emotional turmoil before reaching a point of acceptance by their groups. One of our pastors went through six months of people leaving his class, then returning, leaving, then returning, and some leaving for good. There would be side meetings that would go on for hours—we call them agony sessions. After six months, breakthrough came. Now the groups are on their way and have reached the "buy in" stage with the majority of people. Isn't it ironic that we must go through so much agony to create an environment in which God's power can work?

Our next challenge is to build this interactive model into our small groups. You may question why the interactive model of worship is not already in our small groups. By nature small groups are interactive, but not in the way Paul meant when he spoke of the people contributing to one another's lives. Small groups interact over the Scripture, members share their prayer needs, they talk of the pressures of daily life, but rarely do they employ the supernatural gifts. So how do we teach this, especially if we are novices ourselves? The next section will answer this question.

EXPERIENCING GOD'S POWER

One of the most disappointing parts of my quest for personal and public revival has been the sparse numbers at prayer gatherings. It is difficult for me to say this but I know it to be true. Many more will attend a meeting centered on controversy than one focused on prayer. It occurred to me that I needed to seek God's insight on what would motivate people to want to pray. At the same time I was flailing about seeking a door through which I could minister with power. A number of people in our congregation are afflicted with serious illness. We have the full range of human suffering—cancer, ALS, diabetes, stroke victims, and the panoply of bad backs, migraines, arthritis, and the like. God impressed me to call the people to pray for those they care about. There is great affection for those who are suffering, so I called on the congregation to unite in prayer for God's power to heal those we love.

I was not sure what I would do and how I would do it. I just had a wonderful peace that God would be faithful. My confidence was a deep-seated belief that going out on a limb pleases him. Several people asked me how I was going to proceed. "What if no one gets healed?" was the common question. I determined that I was willing to fail and look foolish. "Pastor overboard. He's lost at sea, grasping at straws, trying to find something that will work." Some even thought I was watching too much Christian television. (I will have you know I watch very little Christian television. I enjoy non-Christian television much more.)

God gave me a simple agenda:

1. Invoke his presence with worship.
2. Remind them of his power and mercy.
3. Follow the flow of the Spirit; keep my spiritual ears open.

God gave me a sense of what worship should be—simple and reflective. After the first two lines of the first song, I knew something was different. God's presence began to fill the place. You're asking, "What do you mean? How did you know?" Several people went to their knees. Some normally unresponsive worshipers lifted their hands. There was a deep reverence; there was a sweetness to it. It was like God sucked all the pride out of the room. I must admit that I was feeling a bit fearful, but I was reminded that God had not given me a spirit of fear, but of love, power, and a sound mind. Twenty minutes into the worship we were ready. I was ready. I mounted the pulpit and turned to Isaiah 53 and delivered the message of the suffering servant who brought victory and healing to his people. Then I walked down into the aisle and began to wander among the largest group that had ever attended such an event.

I asked who had a physical need and wanted prayer. I had planned to start with a man who had a strange blood disease that will require a bone marrow transplant. Instead, another person raised his hand, I stuck the microphone in his face and asked him what he wanted God to do. While the man was speaking, I didn't know what I would do next. I knew I would pray, but would it be me alone or somebody else? The teaching of Paul flooded my mind. "When you come together, everyone has a hymn, or a word of instruction, a revelation, a tongue" (1 Cor. 14:26).

"Who feels like they have the faith to pray for this man's healing?" I heard myself asking. Immediately two people stood and came over. I gave them the microphone. As they prayed, many of the people stood and lifted their hands toward the man.

Then I started moving to the young man who had the mysterious blood disease. I had Heather with me, the one person I know for sure who has the prophetic gift. She is almost always right in what God tells her. She walked near me. As I approached the man, she whispered in my ear, "I see a spirit of depression over his head." I wondered, *Do I pass this on to the congregation?* It witnessed with my spirit; it did not violate Scripture; it was general enough that I sensed liberty. I told everyone, and we prayed against that spirit of depression and discouragement. There was a stronghold over the man. The congregation rose as one and prayed in great faith.

What happened in the next ninety minutes transformed some lives. After watching me, the people began to do the same thing and pray the same way. We prayed for fifty people, and then some of them began to speak. A man who had cancer in his leg and brain said his leg looked and felt normal. Recently doctors have given him a clean bill of health. One woman was fighting depression and she is now much better; another suffering from scoliosis was healed. There have been a number of sustained healings from that evening.

At one point I asked, "Who thinks they may have the gift of healing?" There were two hundred people in the room. No one raised his or her hand. "What does this tell us?" I asked. Everyone got it. We have a room packed with needy people, and the gift they need the most is absent. The conviction of the Holy Spirit fell on us. We realized our sin. How can the body of Christ meet needs when we have banned a third of our tools? How many of the suffering continue to hurt because of our theology and fear? How many never have God's personalized word because we don't believe the gift of prophecy is valid? How many churches languish for a lack of power and work of miracles? We have even accused those who seek miracles as weak in faith and much like the Pharisees.[8]

It is the very hunger for God and his manifest presence that has been the impetus for revival. It is not seeking a sign for the sign's sake. If I am driving from Seattle to Los Angeles and see a sign that reads, "Los Angeles, 400 miles," I don't pull over and sit under the sign. The sign points me to my goal. Signs of God's manifest presence point me to Christ.

After we had prayed for many, I asked for those who desired prayer but couldn't bring themselves to talk about it to raise their hands. Again after two hours of wandering among the people, listening to them and the voice of the Spirit, God gave me words and phrases to say that met the needs of the moment. I would often start a sentence, "I'm not sure how to say this, but I am impressed that we should pray for a broken relationship in someone here." People would raise their hands or quietly nod their heads. Twenty-plus people had their hands raised. I asked others to move to those close to them and begin to pray. The scene was beautiful. What I saw before me were clusters of people caring for people. That night we went to a new level in mutual ministry. It was powerful and it changed those of us present.

The next such service is in a few days of this writing. Its focus will be to pray for our children and grandchildren. Recently I preached a sermon on raising normal children and then another on the hard-to-parent child. I left a prayer box at the front of the church, and hundreds of parents wrote their children's names on slips of paper and placed them in the box. The staff has been praying for several weeks for the names in the box.

Pray for what people care about. It will build their faith and give them a positive experience. Then they will develop a thirst for prayer and intimacy with God and for those around them.

Oh, by the way, since I asked the question about gifts of healing, two people with the gift of healing have been identified. I am now prepared to ask about some other gifts so they can be manifest.

I salivate when I read Luke's account of the early church. Everyone was filled with a sense of awe as they witnessed the leadership of the ministry of the apostles. But it didn't stop there, through the entire Book of the Acts of the Apostles, the church had the world's attention. Sometimes that attention was negative, manifested in persecution, but even so the world was seeing the power of God and couldn't ignore it.[9]

The secular world has no problem ignoring the contemporary church. There is no manifestation of power that intersects with everyone's inner desire for spiritual reality. In his book *Virtual Faith*, Tom Beaudoin draws an interesting conclusion as to why Generation X is not captured by the church.

> This turn to experience has particular implications for Christian Xers in regard to experiencing Jesus. A new sort of GenX liberation theology is emerging, but it is not primarily about the poor, who are normally the focus of liberation theology. Instead, it begins with *the liberation of Jesus from the clutches of the Church.* Jesus himself needs to be liberated so that Xers can experience the power of his words and deeds, the blessing of his bodily and spiritual presence."[10]

The "turn to experience" Beaudoin mentions is the need of Xers in a postmodern environment to experience the presence and power of God. In fact Beaudoin begins this same chapter, "Experience Is the Key," by describing a personal encounter with a charismatic worship service. He says "I was awed by such an intimate religious experience. . . . thereafter, personal religious experience has a ring of authenticity that remains for me to this day."[11]

Jesus is a prisoner of our theological and cultural prejudices. We have him in our clutches, but we are afraid to turn him loose among us. Jesus comes to us and desires so much to give us that sense of awe in his presence. Our familiarity with spiritual things perhaps does not breed contempt, but it breeds domestication of Christ among us. Our churches have become little Nazareths, unwilling to let him be fully who he is. Like the frightened people of the Gerasenes, we ask him to go away, and he does (Luke 8:37). He doesn't go away in a theological sense, but he is history with regard to his manifest presence and power. The risk is to figure this all out from a kneeling position.

There is one more reason for gifts among us that completes the package.

To Deliver God's Message

A church that experienced only God's care would be self-indulgent. A church with just God's power would be full of itself. A church with both God's care and God's power could operate like a superstore that opens its doors and waits for people to come. The satisfied customers would then by word of mouth encourage others to try it out. This is how most of the superchurches in the world have grown. People sense both the love and power of God at work and so they bring others. That is what I want for our church. That is what happened in the early church, and I only wish it would take place in all churches.

Even as good as some churches have become, there is a dimension missing. It is easy to be satisfied with numerical success. In fact success can cloud over the issue that continues to plague world evangelization. That plague is our waiting for the world to come to us. It is our lack of commitment to deliver the message to where the needy reside. The missing link is revealed in that church attendance overall has been in decline, even with the emergence of larger churches. Even more revealing is that 75 percent or more of people are not attending church at all. Those people are not going to seek out a church. They are not going to try out the superstore; they will need to be sought after.

This is the reason for the third set of spiritual gifts. The first church in Jerusalem was attractive and it grew rapidly. The caring and power gifts were clearly on display. The believers were slow, however, to go to the world and deliver the message. A persecution was required to ignite the multiplication.[12]

What will it take to spring us into action? It will take the combination of all three dimensions of God's giftedness applied to the ministry. The third grouping of gifts are *leadership gifts*.

GIFTED OFFICES

I am not going to get into a fight over this, but I believe Paul's listing in Ephesians 4:11 is a list of gifted offices, not spiritual gifts themselves. "It was he who gave some to be apostles, some to be prophets, some to be evangelists, and some to be pastors and teachers."

There is a clear distinction between prophets, such as Moses, Isaiah, and Micah, and those who exercise the gift of prophecy in today's church. Old Testament prophets held a special office and position with regard to the nation of Israel. They were held to a higher standard. If a prophet was wrong in Israel, he was stoned to death.[13] If a person misses the mark in the church today, he or he is simply disregarded.[14]

The church was built on the foundation of the apostles and prophets (see Eph. 2:20). The historic interpretation of this statement is that the foundational revelation that established God's redemptive initiative was delivered by those chosen men. This draws a distinction between a special office of apostle and prophet and actual spiritual gifts. The right gifts for an apostle today could be the gift of faith, working of miracles, leadership, and any gifts that assist in starting new things. The role of prophet could be filled by someone with the gift of teaching or writing or by someone calling the nation to repentance. The same is true of evangelist. God has called certain people to give their full attention to teaching and preaching the Good News. The evangelist has the right spiritual gifts to match the function of evangelist. But every Christian has the responsibility to evangelize. Some are better than others, but I don't think there is a gift of evangelism. There is a calling to evangelism, and there is a communication ability that goes with the calling.

There have been an awful lot of Christians who have used the idea of not having the gift to take a pass on their responsibility to be a witness.

The final office is that of pastor and teacher. For many years this was considered one person because of the Grandville Sharp rule. The rule is simple, "When two nouns are connected by *kai* [the Greek word for *and*] and the article precedes only the first noun, there is a close connection between the two. That connection always indicates at least some sort of unity. The best research indicates that elders are teachers, and pastors are also teachers. But it would not be accurate to strongly hold that this is one person. It could very well be two different functions that are similar in nature."[15] I have always thought that if there is a gift of pastor-teacher, we should find out who has it and allow only those people to pastor churches. But there seem to be so many of us who can shepherd but can't teach all that well and those who can teach great but can't seem to make it with people on the relational side. This is probably an unintentional argument against the one-person interpretation. It makes sense that all pastors are to be teachers, though not all teachers are to be pastors.

Another way to view the list of gifted offices or abilities is to think of it as God's provision of needed leadership to the developmental process. In fact I often teach the passage by saying, just write *leadership* in capital letters across the verse. God has left us with marching orders to seek and save the lost. We are on a mission called the Great Commission and special leaders will be required. God matches gifts with the functions. The gift of faith or working of miracles may be given to the sending or apostolic position. The present-day apostle is in somewhat the same category as the contemporary prophet. Neither has the station and absolute authority of the apostles and prophets of the Bible, but the functions remain vital to the spreading of the gospel.

Gordon Fee gives some perspective:

In light of Ephesians 2:20 and 3:5 and the fact that Paul himself functioned as both apostle and prophet, the first three designations refer primarily, though in the case of prophets and evangelist not exclusively, to itinerant ministries among the early churches. Itinerant workers founded churches by evangelizing and built them up through prophetic utterances. There can be little question that this is the understanding of the term "apostle" in Paul's letters.[16]

The position of prophet is a bit more cloudy because prophesying is a churchwide ministry experienced by very ordinary believers. There are many who prophesy, providing warning and preaching to the church. There are prophets in the church today, mostly recognized in the charismatic branch. Paul's mention of them probably is connected to the role of his coworkers and the increased need for prophetic ministry in the absence of a New Testament.

Consider the problem we have, a third of the gifts have lain dormant in many of our churches for decades. I lament the lost ministry and the lack of power and progress. There are people with prophetic gifts that are needed by the church who may never know it or practice their gift unless we do something.

Thinking Mission

The gifts related to delivering God's message are prophecy, tongues in a cross-cultural mission expression, teaching, leadership, and administration. The most misunderstood gift is prophecy. People know what tongues is and are very familiar with teaching, leadership, and administration. I like Wayne Grudem's definition of prophecy the best: "telling something that God has spontaneously brought to mind."[17] The definition looks like a formula for disaster. But later we will discuss in detail how following scriptural guidelines can protect us from the malpractice of this gift.

This third dimension of Christ's being present with his church is to ensure the mission doesn't die. Without these gifts the church would sit around a collective campfire with s'mores, singing "Kum Ba Ya" until Jesus returns. Conversely, if the leadership gifts were the only ones we had, the church would wear battle fatigues, and goose-step behind a battalion of tanks. The caring gifts are God present with us like a mother. The leadership gifts are God present with us like a father. Their context and purpose are to *prepare* the body's members to be *ministers* (Eph. 4:12). It is well-known that most of us would rather not undergo the discipline that is required for effective ministry. Winston Churchill said that some people grow; others just swell. Here is a vote for growth.

I never met my father. I was blessed to have a wonderful grandfather and two uncles. But once we moved away from them, there was no father figure in my home. I was tall and loved basketball, and by the end of my freshman year in high school, I had met the new basketball coach. His name was Gene Ring. He grew up in the rough-and-tumble neighborhoods of South Bend, Indiana. He went to Indiana University on a basketball scholarship and was a Big Ten boxing champion in his spare time. To say he was competitive would be a vast understatement. When he was a senior at Indiana, a highly touted sophomore was positioned to replace Ring on Indiana's starting five. The first day of practice Ring confronted the diaper dandy. "The only way you will start, boy, is over my dead body, my dead body." That year Ring played and the wonder boy sat the bench. He was intimidating, and we all were a little afraid of him.

The first time I met him was at a meeting for all those interested in trying out for the basketball team. He paced back and forth in front of thirty boys. His use of language was captivating. "We are going to run up and down that floor; we're going to get up on those boards; we're going to wear them down; we're going to take them down; we won't back off anyone." By this time he was yelling and I felt a spark of passion ignite down deep within me as I caught his vision.

I was talented as a player but I was a poor student. As the passion burned within me, I sat there academically ineligible. After a summer course I was declared eligible and was ready to try out. I was placed on the reserve team with the other sophomores, but I was still under the influence of Ring. The first time I remember him smiling was at the end of the first quarter of a reserve squad game. The score was Bill Hull 12, the opponent 6, not bad for an eight-minute quarter. The reserve squad had a good year but it ended early because there was no state tournament for us. Ring considered both the varsity and reserves to be a part of the Indiana State tournament. Ring gave us his now famous "It's tournament time" talk.

"It's state tournament time, boys, state tournament. I want you to focus and think of nothing else, nothing else." He had a staccato cadence, often repeating a portion of his previous sentence. "I want you to throw those books out the window, out the window." This could have been hyperbole, but probably not, knowing Ring. Most of us didn't do it. Somehow we all managed to remain academically eligible. But it was a great idea and I gave it my best shot. He went on, "No chasing skirts. I don't want you dating a girl. I don't want you to think about girls. I don't even want to see you talking to one in the hallways. If I see you holding hands or playing kissy face, it's Katie barred the door, Katie barred the door." I still don't know what "Katie barred the door" means, but I didn't want to find out.

A couple of days later I am walking down the hallway with the love of my life, Linda Stevens. We were in love; we were going to marry; together we were thirty. I looked up and I saw Ring. He came toward me and said, "Get in here, boy. Get in here." I followed him into the gym and then to a janitor's closet. His face was red and his body was in the attack mode. All I could remember was this must be Katie barred the door, Katie barred the door.

"Boy, you think you're in love, don't you? Well, you don't know about love. You're just a big puppy, a big puppy. You're not going to marry that girl. I want you to break up with her. You have too many other things to do with your life." Linda, wherever you are, we can thank Gene Ring that we are not married.

Coach Ring was a Catholic. I am not sure if he was a good one. We didn't talk spiritual stuff in those days. He was concerned about me and came to visit my mother a few weeks later. He recommended I attend a Fellowship of Christian Athletes camp in Henderson Harbor, New York. The week I was there, Linda Stevens took up with another guy and broke my heart. I still think Ring had something to do with that, probably set them up on a date.

Coach Ring became that male figure in my life that demanded more of me than anyone else. My grandfather and uncles loved me and were wonderful men, but Coach Ring inspired me to achieve. I practiced basketball 365 days a year, at least one hour a day for the next two years.

Two years later I was six foot seven and the center on the varsity basketball team. Since I was the biggest player, I got the traditional nickname of "Hoss." This was 1964 and Hoss was one of the stars of *Bonanza,* a very popular television series at the time. Before the season Coach Ring called me into his office. "Hoss," he started as he paced back and forth in front of me. "We're going to have a great year and as you go, so goes the team. Whenever we lose a game this year, whenever we lose a game, it's your fault, your fault." This is what you call giving a person responsibility; others would call it unfair pressure. I counted it an honor to be spoken to that way and I would do anything for Coach Ring. He never said it, but I knew this man loved me. He cared about me and what happened to me.

I will never forget the night we were losing to our arch rivals, and I had played poorly in the first half. The team was seated in folding chairs in the locker room. It was tense because we were waiting for Ring to enter the room. He was highly unpredictable. He was wild on the bench and on some occasions had to be restrained from going after officials, opposing coaches, and even players. He burst through the door and lunged toward me, the force of his body knocked me backward out of my chair. The wrestling coach pulled him away into a back room. The players were stunned because it was rare that he would attack a player. I didn't file a complaint; I didn't fight back; I went out and scored twenty-five points in the second half. Some people would call that effective coaching. I wanted his approval and I interpreted his actions to be motivational in nature. It didn't offend me in the least. In those days such antics by coaches were normal.

The day came for my last game. I didn't want it to be my last, but in the Indiana State Tournament it is single elimination. We were playing a team we had beaten the previous week. The game took place in historic Hinkle Fieldhouse on the campus of Butler University. It is the same arena that the final game in *Hoosiers* was filmed. We started out poorly but in the second half we caught them and took a lead. At every time-out Ring would yell over the din of the bands and fans, "Don't make this your last game; don't make this your last game."

In the end, we lost by a point on some highly controversial calls. As the game ended, Ring chased an official into his locker room and they nearly came to blows. Meanwhile I was seated in front of my locker in tears. I was remembering those words, "If we lose a game, Hoss, it's your fault, your fault." Just then Coach Ring walked in, sat down beside me, and put his arm around me. "Hoss, that wasn't your fault, son. It wasn't your fault." He had released me from the burden when that burden no longer served a productive purpose.

Coach Ring loved me like a father. He built into me characteristics that to this day serve me well. When I get discouraged, when I face a tough challenge, when I feel sorry for myself, I hear those words, "Get up in there, Hoss. Come on, boy. You can do it." My mother cared for me, but Gene Ring taught me how to set a goal, to focus, to practice self-discipline, and then to persevere. He loved me like a father.

Leadership gifts are resident in flawed men and women who are called to lead the church. They are the ones who prepare us and that preparation is demanding. What would we be like without these gifts? I played on several basketball teams in my day. And without exception we needed leadership in our coach. Even the Athletes in Action teams that were composed of college stars needed coaching. If the coach was late for practice, we could be found doing various unproductive things. Some players would shoot half-court shots; others would fool around playing "horse" or other games. No one was running the offense, doing defensive drills, running conditioning drills. We were doing the easy and fun stuff. This is typical of Christian basketball players, and it is normal for Christians in general with regard to the mission of the church. As soon as the coach walked onto the court and blew the whistle, the entire environment completely changed.

The purpose of the leadership gifts is to deliver the message of the gospel to the world. This requires strategic thinking. People need the challenge to give and also the discipline to prepare themselves for the mission. The leadership gifts stretch us, challenge us, and irritate us, but without them we wouldn't take the message of God's love to the world. As much as the caring gifts care, they won't get the word out as soon and as powerfully as is needed. As glorious as is the power of God in the church, most people who need Christ are outside the church. They aren't even looking through the window at us. They just aren't interested. The caring and power gifts, however, are vital to outreach if the leadership gifts motivate and mobilize that marvelous thing called body life. That is why at the end of Ephesians 4:11–16 we are told, "From him the whole body, joined and held together by every supporting ligament, grows and builds itself up in love, *as each part does its work."*

The gifts of the Spirit make the church a symphony. The leadership gifts are charged with the responsibility to coordinate the direction of the church. We become world changers because through the gifts we are Christ present in the world. Christ is present in his care, in his power, and in a trained and well-organized team that is effectively penetrating the world around us. God has equipped us to love God, love one another, and love the world. That is what spiritual gifts are for, so eagerly seek them and especially those that minister to the most in the deepest way.[18]

7

Accepting the Challenge of Unleashing the Miraculous

The Corinthians were at war in worship. And it wasn't about music or the gifts of leadership or administration. No one fights about the serving or mercy gifts. There is always applause for the kitchen workers at the annual dinner. The conflict is about the unusual, the works that draw attention, that create confusion, envy, and controversy. Paul wrote the letter in response to the SOS sent by the few clearheaded members. The Corinthians had splintered into four groups, their worship was out of control, and their unity was only a memory. This is the challenge of the miraculous. It is often misused and abused and brings out the worst in us.

A Word about Miracles and Dissension

If we define *miracle* as a direct activity of God in the world, then all spiritual gifts are miraculous because they come from God. But by this definition everything that God does would be miraculous. Therefore, the word *miracle* loses its usefulness. Under this definition it would be difficult to eliminate anything from the miraculous. So I will use another definition: *A miracle is an uncommon work that arouses people's awe and gives strong witness to God.* To embrace the miraculous then is to wait on God to express himself in ways that are the expected unexpected. We expect miracles and we are awestruck when he delivers.

The moment you start teaching that miracles are to be a regular part of discipleship, duck! I am a little faster on my philosophical feet than I use to be. That is why recently I did something for the first time in twenty years of pastoring. I submitted a proposed sermon series to the elders for their approval. My custom was to announce to the elders my sermon topic for their information. This time I told them that we had been teaching for years that all the gifts of the Spirit are available to the church, but we ignored them and didn't help people learn if they possessed them and how they might exercise them.

I am an idealist with a few dents here and there, but my head remains in the clouds. I expected a few questions followed by, "You're right. Let's go with it." One year, eight meetings, and a retreat later, I began the series. Even among the elders and pastoral staff, there was concern that people would start running the aisles and rolling around the church speaking in tongues with foam dripping from their mouths.

Once the series began, there were some furrowed brows. The concerned gathered in hallways and whispered their fears to elders or pastoral staff. "Are we going charismatic?" It didn't take long for the word to get out among the local busybody church network that we were charismatic. The busybody network was around before networking was cool.[1] It was spoken in hushed tones as though some heinous crime had been committed. One group identified six heresies that I was teaching. They took their dispensational study Bibles and left the church. I told them they should always begin reading the text itself from the top of the page, before consulting the notes at the bottom of the page. Many Christians don't believe what they dig out of Scripture for themselves. They believe only what they have been taught.

The first challenge of inserting the miraculous into normal Christian experience is to overcome the fear of a fully revealed Jesus that exists in the church. I told them what I was *not* doing and what I *was* doing. I was not trying to create a cultural charismatic church. I had no plans to copy very fine charismatic churches in our community. I wanted our worship and culture to match who we are and how God has gifted us. On the other hand, I was trying to develop a church that believed and practiced all that Christ taught, and I was committed to doing the works that Jesus did.

The two most important qualities in seeing anything through are patience and process. In this case, patience to allow elders to get to the point where they believed that there would be no dancing around the golden calf and time for people to process the newer teachings and assimilate them into their theology.

There is much to learn from the Corinthians. It would be easy to draw the wrong conclusion about the nature of their conflict, to think that they were not fighting tradition like many of you reading this book. They were at least fifteen years old as a church when Paul wrote them. They had plenty of tradition, what they were short on was definitive teaching. What most of you are facing is a long tradition of both practice and teaching. The theological barriers are at least as big as methodological barriers. Paul's strategy then was to take the Corinthians to the higher theological ground so they could see the grandeur of God's love.

The only thing that unites people is a common commitment to the same goal. The gifts of the Spirit were given for the common good; their purpose is to meet needs in worship, to build up and encourage. What went wrong with this group? The desire was not for the common good. The church was driven by a lust for private religious experience. They wanted to choose their own gifts, the ones that drew the most attention and made them feel special and more needed. When gifted disciples start behaving as actors on the stage, comparisons are inevitable. No one likes to be upstaged.

The Corinthians took precious gifts that were meant to unite and used them to divide. The reason Paul wrote chapters 12–14 was to teach them how to love one another, a lesson that remains difficult at best whenever attention and achievement are on the line. The option of "everyone who wants to dance in the spirit and go yabba dabba doo" starting a new church was not present in the first century. So they had to stay together and work it out.

Go do whatever you want, have a nice divorce, call it a church plant. This is a contemporary Christian trait. But what kind of message does that send? The watching world thinks, *If you can't get along and love one another, why should we be interested?* God gives gifts to unite us and we self-destruct because we can't control our need for attention. You may have noticed that the church landscape is dotted with some churches built around a certain package of gifts and others built around the absence of those gifts. The sad result is the lost ministry and the lack of churches that have both a commitment to the Word and an equal commitment to spiritual power.[2] This is Romans 8:28 in reverse. "In all things God works for the good of those who love him, who have been called according to his purpose." God takes the bad and turns it into good. The church has the gift of taking the good and turning it into the bad.

All my life I have heard that the charismatic gifts are divisive, but there is no way I can accept that. God gave them for the common good to unite (see 1 Cor. 12:7, 12, 18, 25), so they are not divisive. It has to be something else that divides. Paul identifies the culprit:

> Brothers, I could not address you as spiritual but as worldly—mere infants in Christ. I gave you milk, not solid food, for you were not yet ready for it. Indeed, you are still not ready. You are still worldly. For since there is jealousy and quarreling among you, are you not worldly? Are you not acting like mere men?
>
> 1 Corinthians 3:1–3

Paul's use of "worldly—mere infants" is from *sarkos* or the "flesh." All attempts to call it low self-esteem or a struggle for self-actualization are futile. In fact studies demonstrate that the group of Americans with the highest tested self-esteem are serial killers. The "flesh" represents the negative part of man's immaterial nature that is selfish and corrupt. One only has to read Paul's lists of the flesh to understand its devilish potential.[3] The Corinthians were divided into four camps, the followers of Apollos for those who loved eloquence, the Peter party for those who were attached to the big fisherman's ways, the holier-than-thou club who followed Christ and would submit themselves to no man, and finally those who followed Paul because he started their church.

The above conflict was centered in one congregation. As I said earlier, they were the only church in town, so they were stuck. They stayed and fought. As the church has developed, we have divided into several streams that have weakened us—the holiness stream, the charismatic stream, the evangelical stream, the liturgical stream, and the separatist/fundamentalist stream. This is our reality but overall is proof that we have had trouble with balance.

We Christians are very adept at camouflaging our malice and hiding behind righteous-sounding rationale. So Paul directly challenges their and our pseudo-spirituality with a dissertation on love. Chapter 12 expresses the need for love, chapter 13 is on the way of love, and chapter 14 deals with the practice of love. I intend for us to focus on the gestalt or center of the passage. The center of Paul's thought is a commitment to fight the four enemies of unity that plagued the Corinthians then and many of us now: fragmentation, ineffectiveness, arrogance, and emotional distance.

Fight Fragmentation with Belonging

> Now the body is not made up of one part but of many. If the foot should say, "Because I am not a hand, I do not belong to the body," it would not for that reason cease to be part of the body. And if the ear should say, "Because I am not an eye, I do not belong to the body," it would not for that reason cease to be part of the body.
>
> 1 Corinthians 12:14–16

You are a member even if you don't feel like it. This is a message geared as much to the twenty-first century as to the first century. People then were told this so they would show consideration for others. It was for those who didn't feel important to the body as well. In present-day culture we would need to add the application to those who don't feel any connection to the local body and stand apart from its life and work.

When I turned fifty, I received my AARP card in the mail. It informed me that I was now a member of the American Association of Retired Persons. I am American, and I am a person, but I am not retired. I didn't like being a member and I don't consider myself a member.

It makes sense that the AARP would have a fragmented membership with people like me who say, "I don't belong!" But how is it that the church would have a fragmented membership? Why would a Christian who has chosen Christ declare, "I don't belong"? The context of the passage indicates that it is someone who believes he or she has an inferior gift. This person's view of his or her contribution has been communicated either by other Christians' behavior or by the competitive nature of culture. Christians don't communicate a hierarchy of gifts by discounting the less interesting gifts but by the homage paid to the more spectacular gifts.

I have a close friend who periodically says things that lead to an unintentional insult. Whenever we talk about a mutual friend, he will say, "What a wordsmith he is!" He *is* an articulate guy, but I always think, *Hey, I'm the guy with nine books. I'm the writer; words are my life. What am I, chopped liver?* This reveals my insecurities and my flesh. Others feel discounted when they feel their spiritual gift is unappreciated.

It takes a lot of good teaching and reinforcement for everyone in a church to feel valued and equal in importance. It is a challenge for us all to overcome the powerful forces of culture and the human condition. It is still so common to hear, "I'm just a helper; I'm just a prayer; I'm just an usher." My first response is, "Wash your mouth out with soap and scrub the barnacles off your theological brain." Paul wants us to believe that everyone counts.

Paul is swimming upstream against the human condition with his analogy that one member should never think of himself or herself as less valuable because of his or her role. He advocates thinking of oneself as needed, as much a part of what God wants to do as the most prominent member. Only two things are needed to create fragmentation. The first is people swooning over the show-stopper gifts, such as prophecy, tongues, working of miracles, discerning of spirits, and teaching. The second thing needed for fragmentation is people sensing that the show-stopper gifts are more valued.

When my wife was in college and a dorm counselor, she encountered many a strange event. One night a girl was running up and down the hallway crying, "I have all nine gifts. I have all nine gifts." She was referring to the nine listed in 1 Corinthians 12. The women on that wing of the dorm were incredulous. Their disbelief was both rational and emotional. Many of them possessed enough biblical data to reject the idea that anyone is supposed to have all nine gifts. On another level it was shocking that someone would be that emotionally immature to gush out such a lusty thought. But there was a narcissistic honesty about it that just for a moment allowed all to see her unbridled desire for prominence. And all the young women there either laughed it off or resented it.

The words of 1 Corinthians 13 should have been echoing down the hallway of the dormitory. Paul jumped from the need for love to the way of love as it related to this problem. If you can speak in the tongues of men and angels, if you would give all you own to the poor, but there is no love in it, you might as well be beating a kettle with a hammer. Love means focusing on other people's needs. That young lady and many of us get locked up in our own needs, become selfish, and hurt others. Paul puts it so well in just a few paragraphs. Gifts of the spirit will go away, tongues, prophecy, and knowledge itself will pass. But someday we will all see Jesus face-to-face. That is the perfect state. Until then, we are like children. Until then, we see through a glass darkly. We all look forward to the second coming and the eternal state. Until then however, we must love one another and admit to our limitations. So any exercise of gifts must be governed by love, meaning that everyone is ministered to, and worship includes the widest group possible.

In my experience people function on an emotional level at least as much as on a cognitive level. A person can be told that the gift of helps is as vital to the church as preaching, but when we look at the behavior of the church, none of us really believes it. Preaching gets top billing and in many cases the church tends to grow or not grow because of it. Preaching is prominent, and at least 50 percent of the Sunday meeting is focused on that gift. It is very difficult to be in the kitchen making coffee and think that it is just as crucial as the "main event." Can this change? Should it change?

The prominence of preaching should not change. The person exercising the gift of helps, however, must have a change in perspective, change from the natural feeling of being a minor player to feeling just as needed as the pastor. It is a matter of gifting and role, not of importance. This requires a supernatural perspective that must be repeatedly taught and affirmed. The teacher is charged with communicating that the essence of belonging is perspective and being able to freely exercise your gift in an environment that honors it is belonging.

There is a second reason that people sense they don't belong when in fact they do. Fragmented lives and schedules have taken their toll. The most natural flow of urban life is to have hundreds of acquaintances and no serious friends. For many years I lived a disconnected life, because my work required a great deal of travel. I didn't stay long or go deep with the people in my life, and I found that it was easy to have work associations and think of them as friendships.

The most interesting thing happened when I changed jobs, almost all those people went away. I must have more than one hundred e-mail addresses in my address book that I haven't used in three years. They don't contact me and I don't contact them. There was not a deep connection. Since I have become more stationary geographically, I am going much deeper with those around me.

Many Christians are living the way I used to and thinking that it is normal. If it is not normal, it certainly is a necessary evil. Necessary evil implies a benign evil, but evil always hurts us and fragmentation is far from benign. People won't sense they belong until fragmentation ends.

To counteract cultural fragmentation, two things are needed. The first is proximity and the second is permission. Proximity is taking time to be with people, to be in the same place with the same people at the same time long enough to get permission to drop your guard and consider it safe to let others know your needs.

The single most effective step to end fragmentation is to reach out to others and invite them to join a group. Start harvesting your mailing list and target the disconnected. Invite them to a party or in some way try to befriend them. Ask connected members to name and pray for a few they know who are not in any way presently in a group. People need to live belonging before they will feel it.

Fight Ineffectiveness with Cooperation

Paul reaches into the theater of the absurd to make his point.

> If the whole body were an eye, where would the sense of hearing be? If the whole body were an ear, where would the sense of smell be? But in fact God has arranged the parts in the body, every one of them, *just as he wanted them to be.* If they were all one part, where would the body be? As it is, there are many parts, but one body.
>
> 1 Corinthians 12:17–20

What an appealing idea! Every obedient person is strategically placed in the church just as God wanted him or her to be. Not only do we belong, we have a clear mission as well. That is why Paul encourages us to eagerly pursue our gifts. They are vital to the proper functioning of God's plan.[4]

Actors want to sing; singers want to act; comedians want to be thought of as serious actors. Nonfiction writers want to be novelists; Kathie Lee Gifford wanted to play a slut; Michael Jordan wanted to play baseball. So many successful people want to be someone else, not fundamentally but professionally. In the long run this is a punishing part of our personalities. As we watch Kathie Lee try to be a bad girl, we keep asking, *Where is Regis?* Every time Michael struck out, the public would collectively wince and say, "Get back on the court!" Trying to be what we're not usually ends up in rejection. Our feelings get hurt, and we retreat to lick our wounds.

Accepting Your Role

When people in the Corinthian church wanted to be first and were not willing to accept a lesser role, it ripped the church apart. (To be fair, it could be true that until Paul wrote them, they had no teaching on the subject.) Accepting our role really comes down to our confidence in God. If he placed us in the body in a support role, then accepting it is a battle with our ego.

This reminds me of when I took that teaching assignment in the United Kingdom. I had been told that several key leaders in England would be spending time with me and that in addition to my daily speaking assignments, I would be able to speak in the evening sessions. It was clear after a few days that key leaders were not really interested in talking to me and that I would be given no part in teaching in the evening plenary sessions.

Each evening there were five venues for worship. Over two weeks time there were sixty worship services, and I was not asked to clear my throat. At first I was frustrated because I was there to get national exposure to promote our ministry. I felt isolated and as I listened to some speakers that were mediocre at best, deflation of ego was added to my feelings.

The crowning blow came one day when I walked into the lounge and there was a large banner that read "HAPPY 60th BIRTH-DAY, BILL." Some of the team started congratulating me. I was forty-nine.

God was teaching me humility. I had to laugh and I really enjoyed my talks with God during that time. Sometimes God asks us to take a backseat or a support role and it doesn't make any sense. But if we simply erase our pride from the situation, everything is easier.

Recognizing Gifts

Putting the wrong person in the wrong role can be both disastrous and funny. Think of Dennis Rodman as a youth pastor, Madonna as the school nurse, or Dr. Jack Kevorkian as the "go-to guy" at your local HMO. Having the wrong person in a position is part of life, not only in the general culture but in the body of Christ as well.

Many years ago a parishioner dedicated himself to exposing me for the louse he said I was. He determined to destroy my credibility by weaving a fabrication that made me look like a deceiver. He finally decided to write a letter to the former pastor of the church, the president of my denomination, and several leaders who knew me. The letter was false in almost every detail. He did get the spelling of my name right. He connected the dots between events in a way that would make a kangaroo court seem honorable.

The church leadership decided to confront my accuser. The leaders were to meet with him and ask him to retract his letter. The leadership meeting that preceded this action just so happened to be the one in which a new board chairman was selected. Everyone knew what lay ahead and no one wanted the job. You have heard stories about someone who missed the meeting and they were elected chairman. This was almost that bad. Several key candidates missed the meeting, so the board appointed Paul, a kind and godly man, as chairman.

Paul was not a leader; his personality was passive. That is one of the reasons he was so well liked. The evening finally came when my nemesis was to be voted from membership. I talked with Paul before the meeting and explained how important it was to tell the full story. The man in question had been so bitter that he put all the evidence of his wrongdoing in writing. "Paul," I told him, "regardless of your feelings, you must show them the sin, all of it." I went on to explain that if the congregation could not see the depth of the man's sin, they would feel sorry for him. "They will erect a monument in the church parking lot for him."

The meeting began, and Paul presented the case for expelling the member. I couldn't hear him. He was mumbling, "All in favor of the motion say aye." And it was over. I was in shock; he hadn't done any of the things I had asked him to do. In the end the man was expelled, but Paul had glossed over the entire matter. Yes, the man had threatened to sue, but we had all the evidence. Whatever happened to standing up for the truth?

There was another leader absent from the meeting when Paul was selected the chairman. His name was Tom. Tom approached me a couple of days after the debacle. "Bill, I must tell you. I love to go after sin. God help me; I love it." Now Tom should have been the leader that night. He was properly gifted for the role. It is just another example of putting a godly man in the wrong position.

How dramatic! you may be thinking. *Isn't that a bit overdone for Paul's point?* Not really. There are so many stories like this, many of them worse, where people have been placed in the wrong position and needs remain unmet, people get hurt, and the kingdom doesn't advance.

Find the right gift and put it to work in the right place meeting the right needs. This is the cure for the curse of selfishness and promoting self. The model for cooperation is Paul's other body analogy passage: "From him the whole body, joined and held together by every supporting ligament, grows and builds itself up in love, as each part does its work" (Eph. 4:16).

I love what Philip Yancey and Paul Brand write:

> In exchange for its self-sacrifice, the individual cell can share in what I call the ecstasy of community. No scientist can yet measure how a sense of security or pleasure is communicated to the cells of the body, but individual cells certainly participate in our emotional reactions. Hormones and enzymes bathe them, bringing on a quickened breathing, a trembling of muscles, a flapping in the stomach. If you look for a pleasure nerve in the human body, you will come away disappointed; there is none. There are nerves for pain and cold and heat and touch, but no nerve gives a sensation of pleasure. Pleasure appears as a by-product of cooperation by many cells.[5]

I'm still a dreamer. My heart's desire is to see this kind of cooperation happen.

Fight Arrogance with "I Need You"

How do you say, "I don't need you?" Actually, you don't have to say it. People can feel the condescension. They sense that they are dispensable. It is so easy for those with the more honored gifts to consider others their supporting cast. Paul goes for the throat of pride when he writes, "The eye cannot say to the hand, 'I don't need you!' And the head cannot say to the feet, 'I don't need you!' On the contrary, those parts of the body that seem to be weaker are indispensable" (1 Cor. 12:21–22).

Pride thinks, *I don't need them. I can get along just fine.* The problem is that often the prophets, preachers, and healers live for themselves, and their admirers encourage them to do it. Christian personality cults have always been around. I have ran into people who ask speakers, authors, and other luminaries to sign their Bibles. I have signed a few and have always felt uncomfortable doing it. The very structure of a church meeting illustrates the point. Those with the more splashy gifts are on the platform, and everyone else sits in the audience. This creates a performance-audience environment. The up-fronters get the green room, the hors d'oeuvres, and the limos. They have the agents, the personal trainers, and the aura of being busy and important. The celebrity culture in which we live has corrupted the kind of interdependence advocated by Paul. The luminaries shuffle the supporting cast around to meet their needs and to enhance their performance.

There is something buried deep in our immaterial natures that desires to be first, to be noticed, to seem special. Since the Corinthians had little instruction on the matter, it was a spiritual gifts free-for-all in their church. There was a competitive spirit—people trying real hard to outdo one another in worship. There was way too much spiritual pride and very little humility. There was a serious shortage of "How can I serve you?" or "What would be best for everyone?"

What causes a prominent member of the body to show honor for a less honorable member, indeed to see him or her as indispensable? It only happens when the humility of Christ changes our minds and subdues our flesh.[6] Paul's metaphor asks, If the whole body were an eye, where would the hearing be? His use of the absurd reminds us that each part of the human body is vital to health and function. There are vital parts of the body that are hidden, but the parts you can see are not more vital. His point is an obvious one. The people in the background, the supporting cast, are a necessary part of the whole. If we really believed such a thing, then there wouldn't be the scramble for prominence.

I have to think only of how people with serving gifts have helped me. There are times in pastoral work when discouragement moves in like a fog. There is a woman in our church dying of cancer. By the time this book is released she may be in heaven. She is aptly named Sunny. Ever since I met her, she has always said, "I just love you, the way you talk and what you have to say." At first I thought she was one of those new people who tend to be exuberant: when she got used to me, the enthusiasm would diminish. She had been experiencing problems with her treatments and was in a lot of pain. I would go to her house and pray with her and serve communion. I can't count how many times she cheered me up and helped me draw a perspective on the eternal.

Recently there was a group of people who told me they didn't think I was teaching the Word. What they really mean is, you're not teaching it the way we want it taught. Or they may be saying that it's really me, not my preaching, that they don't like. I had undergone two weeks of getting hammered. I was physically and emotionally tired. I stopped by Sunny's to serve communion. She greeted me with her usual cheer and asked me how I was doing. One thing I don't do is share my problems with a person who has far greater ones. I smiled and said okay.

Sunny launched into a glowing summary of how much she loved me and how much she loved my sermons. She pointed to a pile of used tapes in the corner. "See those tapes, Pastor Hull?" I nodded. "I have listened to those so many times the sound is gone. I have worn them out. I can't wait until your sermon tape arrives each week. I listen to them over and over again. I can't tell you how much they minister to me and give me the strength to go on."

The tears are coming as I write. Sunny may be weak but she is an indispensable member of the body. Her encouragement helped me remember that the effort to preach and the criticism that inevitably comes are worth it. I drove away knowing that a suffering servant had once again given me what I needed.

Fight Emotional Distance with Empathy

A sociopath is someone with an underdeveloped conscience. This person can't feel empathy and has very little sympathy.

Some scholars have opined that the root of evil is the absence of empathy. The shutting down of empathy is the secular explanation for the Holocaust. The Christian viewpoint would trace evil to the mystery of Lucifer's will. That will plus opportunity led to his and to all of creation's fall. Our culture is creating many semisociopaths, those who shut down emotions when it comes to others. The avalanche of negative information through the media makes many of us want to turn our back to the world. One only has to channel surf to see the horror of it all—bodies burned in fires, little boys drowning, babies beaten, pedophiles going free. We erect defenses so we won't have to feel all that pain and frustration.

We Christians, however, cannot turn our backs, not if we are going to close the distance between ourselves and those around us. God has taught me to go toward the pain, to dive in headfirst, because there is great peace and sweetness on the other side of pain and conflict. Move toward the pain. Close the distance between them and us, between you and me. Unless we do that, the competitive spirit, the superior spirit, the apathetic spirit will not leave us. These are the spirits that allowed the Corinthians to engage in such selfish worship.

Paul counters: "There should be no division in the body, but . . . its parts should have equal concern for each other. If one part suffers, every part suffers with it; if one part is honored, every part rejoices with it" (1 Cor. 12:25–26).

The new, and I hope short-lived, quiz show rage is *Weakest Link.* It features several contestants who compete for one million dollars. After each round the weakest link is voted off the program by fellow contestants. The show's host is one Anne Robinson who has come over from the UK to get it right. She has a constipated face with chiseled features and wire-rimmed glasses perched on a narrow nose. She comes on like forty acres of horseradish and dismisses contestants with derisive comments, such as, "All beauty, no brains. Good-bye." Or "So you're first in your class. Some class! Back to school for you." Or "Cheerio and don't bother to write." The dismissed contestants then spew their disappointment and explain why they were treated unfairly. The program promotes survival of the smartest. Everyone else is considered weak and unworthy.

Paul's teaching on human relationships couldn't be more different. When someone fails or is hurt, the rest of the body should rush to help. The entire body hurts with the sufferer. When I stub my toe on the bed frame at 3:00 A.M., my entire body hurts. When one member is wounded, the body doesn't function right until healing takes place. There are weak links in the body, but they are indispensable. "Paul stresses connectivity and linkage. Paul warns against continually tugging and pulling to see which link will snap under pressure. The church is one place where the weak link can be strong, where the littlest can be big, where the powerless can be empowered."[7]

I know my defense mechanisms are in working order. I don't want to feel others' pain. I don't want to spend time with the weakest link. There is a man who has a lot of problems who hangs around the church. He just shows up and wants to meet with a pastor. When he is spotted, we tend to hide in our offices, because we know that it will take a lot of time and it will be draining.

We all want to switch off others' pain, and even our own. Why do you think God gave us a remote control? So we can change the channel. When I see starving children, murder, and mayhem, I say, "I don't need to suffer with the whole world," so I change the channel. Didn't someone write a book about boundaries? It was about protecting yourself from the people who would suck the life out of you. It is wise to know where to draw the line; otherwise we will have nothing to give.

The paradox is that when we do enter into another's pain, we gain strength. It changes our hearts. It deepens our ability to feel, to connect with people and with God on a deeper level. The actor Richard Dreyfuss, who has a child with a disability, has had more than his share of challenges. He said a most interesting thing during a television interview: "Other people's problems cheer me up." What he meant was that hearing about others' concerns tells him that he is not alone. There are others who suffer and they form a fraternity of encouragement. He doesn't have to carry his burden alone.

There is a difference between having empathy for a person in pain and allowing the takers of the world to drain you. People in pain can be givers, giving us what no one else ever can—a greater capacity to love, accept, and reach out.

You will get hurt, it is the law of humanoids. If you lay your heart on the altar, someone will come and jump up and down on it. There is something very small in all of us that enjoys it when others fail and becomes angry when others succeed. A couple of years ago a display of my eight published books was placed in a showcase at the entrance to our church. The idea was to inform the congregation of another part of my ministry that they knew very little about. Within days there were complaints, "What's he trying to do, puff himself up?" That hurt me. It wasn't even my idea. Why wouldn't people rejoice with me? Where did that resentment come from? I can understand a few hypersensitive souls who don't believe in advertising or any kind of display of one's work. I started thinking of how when singers in the church or other writers release their work, the church stands as one and applauds. We would promote their work and even sell it for them. I promised myself that I would never become that petty. I committed myself to rejoicing when others succeed and crying when others cry.

So there it is, the challenge of unleashing the miraculous. You must be prepared to fight. It begins by fighting fragmentation created by those who desire to be prominent. That results in the ineffectiveness of a fragmented body that doesn't work together. Then a competitive spirit and arrogance build walls between people. Finally empathy goes missing and emotional distance is created. These are not superficial divides that can be easily closed. They are deep and debilitating to the body. The only hope is love, the kind applied in the context of 1 Corinthians 13 that connects our capacity to love with our capacity to worship.

8

Employing the Miraculous in Worship

The consummate showman P. T. Barnum called California a circus without a tent. The Corinthian church did not have a tent, but they were a circus without a ringmaster. You've heard of a three-ring circus; the Corinthians had many more than three rings. Each ring was a small group of people meeting in a home. They were self-governing and they were out of control. The Corinthians were competitive and passionate about their personal worship experience. They had very little love for others or interest in what they were experiencing in worship. This is the zenith of arrogance when we detach ourselves from other people's experience. I am sure the Corinthians would protest my accusation, but their behavior has spoken.

The Way of Love

People were being selfish in worship. They would speak in tongues all at once, out loud! They would prophesy out of turn and not take the time to determine its validity. Everyone reported to Jesus; authority meant very little. This might remind you of the church you attend and a person you know when you look into a mirror. We can underestimate the challenge it is for leadership to try to bring all activity under one authoritative tent.

It is almost certain the Corinthian church met in several locations. The Jerusalem church numbered ten thousand. They must have met at hundreds of sites. The chances are quite high that the Corinthian church had several hundred members, possibly more. You can only imagine how hard it would have been to teach and bring to accountability such a large and separated group. The closest contemporary parallel would be large churches with small groups that meet in homes during the week. A small-group network requires agreed-on guidelines and a commitment by the leader to the larger group. Even with leaders' meetings, manuals, and one-on-one interaction, it is dicey at best to say there is control.

Not only did the Corinthian leaders face the normal dilution of vision over time, but they had to deal with the four factions mentioned earlier.[1] There is no way to monitor every behavior. That is why Paul appealed to love and an agreement that everyone had something to contribute to the body.

Paul's first letter to the Corinthians is a response to what is called the lost letter. Concerned members had written him with a list of questions and concerns. Paul's answers are tailored to the precise problems and, therefore, cannot be considered a total treatment of the subject. This is not everything you will ever need to know about worship. It is specific to the immediate needs of the Corinthian church.

Paul has drawn a perspective by teaching them that they are one body, and each person is a gift to the others in worship. His insertion of chapter 13 was a master stroke. All the temporary aspects of this life, the exercise of spiritual gifts, the understanding of profound mysteries of the universe, the study of the Bible, all will go away. One day the Perfect will come and they will see him face-to-face. But until then, they must fight for unity so they can experience all that God has for them. Instead of fighting with each other, fight *for* each other. Love is not withdrawing; it is giving to others and commitment to the other's experience.

Jesus was committed to our experience when he fought through his humanity and determined to die. Paul is asking the Corinthians to do the same. Fight through your sinful desires to withdraw or dominate. There is a better way—the way of love. The way of love is a commitment to building the body and sharing oneself with others. Paul shows the way of love in two major areas. The first is through interaction with others in worship. The second is through practicing the gifts in worship.

Interacting with Others in Worship

Have you ever worked with people who don't speak your language? It is pretty frustrating when you cannot communicate. A few months ago I was teaching at a seminary in Kiev, Ukraine. At one point I was left in a room with four Russian-speaking Ukrainians and no translator. We just sat and stared at each other, occasionally there would be a smile, but we couldn't begin our discussions until the translator returned. Even with the translator present, a good deal of nuance was missed in the translated communication. Paul makes the point that if there is no effective communication in worship, there is no building up of the body. If the body is not being built up, then worship has been ineffective.

Worship is what worship does, not what people believe it does. Many people hope that worship will help them, but it doesn't. This had led to a conspiracy of silence, everyone pretending that he or she likes worship, but in fact it has become something to be endured. This is caused primarily by the misleading training of the church subculture that worship is something done to us. That's what we have come to expect. It becomes the pastor's job or the choir's job or somebody's job to take us to the throne of God and provide a motivating experience. In reality, though, worship is not passive; it is meant to be active. That is why attitude and behavior in worship matter. We must bring ourselves to worship. We bring our story of how God is working out our salvation. "When you come together, everyone has a hymn, or a word of instruction, a revelation, a tongue or an interpretation. All of these must be done for the strengthening of the church" (1 Cor. 14:26).

Jesus has promised to be present in a special way when two or more are gathered in his name (Matt. 18:20). When we gather for worship, we believe that God is present in a special way to minister to us. One of the reasons Jesus made the promise in Matthew 18:20 was the necessity of believers to meet in small groups. He was addressing a small group of disciples when he made the promise. It has been very helpful for all believers to know that we don't need a cathedral and a robed choir to worship.

The picture Paul paints of worship is intimate rather than public. It portrays disciples coming together with something to offer. I contend that our going to church unprepared is a curse that has destroyed much of what God would like to do among us. It may be true that visitors or the unchurched don't want to be noticed. That is all about natural fears and defensive shields we employ to protect ourselves from commitment. But it should be different for believers. Paul expects us to come to church prepared to minister to others. Come prepared with a song, a word from God out of his Word, a revelation or impression that God has given you, even a tongue if you know that there is an interpreter.

God has promised to "show up" when we gather, but what about *our* promise to show up? Are we committed to showing up? God said, "There I am in the middle of you." God shows up to give of himself, but do you show up to give of yourself? I am not talking about your body; I am speaking of your soul. Have you prayed and prepared to enter into other people's lives? Are you committed to making a difference?

For years I have heard about the responsibility to prepare oneself for worship. That however is not what I am talking about. That was about taking a few minutes to clear one's head of the secular and clear one's soul of sin—a silent pause during the prelude or on your way to church. That kind of preparation is still passive. It is not the worshiper taking responsibility for what happens.

The way of love is going to church with a commitment to minister to others. This commitment begins during the week as we pray, read the Scripture, but most important, as we live out the faith in a hostile environment. This cannot happen without a commitment to others, a commitment that overrides many other activities and obstacles. It means when we walk through the doors of the church on Sunday, we expect to interact on a deep spiritual level with others, encouraging them and strengthening them as we share ourselves.

We don't know much about true community. True *koinonia* is experienced only among the company of the committed. And what are they committed to? They are committed to each other, to reaching each other in authentic interaction based on trust.

The reason so many are stuck in their lives is they have no place in the structure of their church to live authentically. The public worship experience leaves them wanting something more. Don't confuse the exhortation to gather together with a public church service. Sitting in pews with an order of service is one manifestation of worship, but if done alone, it misses the mark. That is why attending a public service once a week is inadequate to accomplish meaningful discipleship.[2]

Life-impacting worship occurs when we enter God's already promised presence and are prepared to be involved. Some of us withhold ourselves from others and from worship. That means we are living a life of regret and of missed opportunity.

Practicing the Gifts in Worship

I have written a great deal about the value of structure.[3] Structure dictates to a great degree what is allowed to happen in worship. We must know the purpose of each gathering. If worship is an open forum and there are hundreds of people present, then limits need to be placed on what can happen. The public meeting will have a few who have come to give of themselves, but they are in the minority. The majority are passive and can be run off by certain worship practices.

Paul exhorted "everyone" to come ready to extend him- or herself.[4] A room with five hundred precludes the "everyone" standard. This means that a separate forum must be chosen. I suggest that groups of fifty or fewer can have a meaningful interchange of hearts. Small groups of fourteen or fewer can also accomplish this. For people to give themselves to one another, there must be a means of enrolling their commitment. That is where covenant comes in. The people agree to a set of guidelines and then demonstrate their commitment to each other by living by those guidelines. They allow others in the group to help them keep their commitments to God.

If you want to grow your groups, you must understand the dynamics of each type. The large group of more than seventy-five is built around common beliefs. Middle-size groups of twenty to seventy-four are built around fellowship. People want to know names and needs. Yet if it gets too personal, or the group assumes that newcomers will fit right in, the group will behave as a closed group and shut down growth. Small groups of three to sixteen are designed for serious accountability and intimacy. They can become closed groups for the purpose of teaching and training.

A group of twenty to fifty in size must be careful not to get too personal. If, for example, a man tells a group of forty he is trying to stop abusing drugs, has he given permission for forty people to hold him accountable? I would guess not. He has expressed a problem but has not granted permission to be monitored. When a group assumes they have the right to hold people accountable, it creates too much intimacy for many; then they will stop attending. When new people walk into a group that is talking about personal issues, the group intimacy will spit them out. Intimacy creates a closed group.

Loving as Christ loved is a commitment to give oneself fully to others. Jesus held nothing back. He gave himself fully for our sin. His love for us overpowered his desire to get out of the crucifixion, out of becoming sin.[5] Part of group discipline, however, is to limit your self-expression so others can participate. This on the surface may seem like contradiction, holding nothing back yet disciplining oneself not to dominate. The way of love is to wait for the right opportunity and then to give yourself fully. Being present in a group, listening carefully, and sensing the right moment to exercise your gift is fully giving yourself. It combines maturity and consideration for others, which is integral to love. Every group has a covenant. It may be written or unwritten. It is obvious that people will be clearer and better able to live by it if it is written. When there is a commitment on the part of the members to keep the rules, the group will work.

The promise you make in a typical covenant is to attend all meetings, be on time, call the leader if you cannot make it, to follow the ground rules once you are there, and prepare your-self before arrival to contribute to others. So the mind-set is to come to the gathering to give to others. The divine paradox is that those who give the most receive the most. This is a very hard lesson for us to learn, and it takes a lot of living for it to become our experience.

This kind of covenant works best in small groups. The middle-size–group covenants need to be more loosely strung. They should stay on the intent level rather than the behavorial level. It won't work for a Sunday morning class of forty to sixty adults to commit to calling ahead if you're not going to be there, or that you must do homework or you will be called on the carpet by the whole class. Again, that will close the group and reject new people. By "intent level" I mean that people are encouraged to come on time, do homework, and let others know if they can't attend. And then there can be no mention of it at the class itself. Class members writing postcards to people who haven't been in a couple of weeks would be much more effective. It feels like concern rather than a police action.

Let's say you have joined a subgroup of your church called an adult fellowship. You have agreed to a written covenant that sets the ground rules. You as a group have, therefore, committed yourselves to causing something to happen when you gather. If you don't come prepared, then you have broken a promise, but in most cases the group tolerates violating one of the group rules. We have been breaking promises for most of our lives, and our consciences are callused over by years of not having integrity. That is why you are protesting even as you read this paragraph. You might think of it as nitpicking and unreason-able. "Stuff comes up," you might indignantly say.

Promise keeping is the foundation of community. When peo-ple break commitments, others see it and slowly the group morale breaks down. Then group members begin to withdraw their hearts from the community and everyone returns to being their own little gods. I have seen many small groups and medium-size groups fall apart because there were no clear prom-ises to one another they were committed to keep.

Now think of it this way. The Corinthians had very little instruction, and what promises were made were broken repeat-edly. People came prepared to experience the thrill of express-ing their own gifts with no regard for others. They were all loudly speaking in tongues at the same time, there were no limits on prophecy, and very seldom did anyone determine the authen-ticity of prophetic statements. Everyone was forced to give some credence to the most bazaar and twisted prophecies.

During my college years in the late 1960s, I spent a lot of time in late-night discussions. I regularly went down the hall and spent time with my two friends, whom I affectionately called the minor prophets. Eugene and Roy—sounds like they should be taming lions in Las Vegas—always had something special for me. They promised me that California was going to break off and become an island. I'm sure the residents in Blythe, Califor-nia, and Bull Head City, Arizona, would love it—they would have beachfront property. I heard a lot of things like that, which gave me pause, but I didn't take them seriously. The fact that I now live in Long Beach, California, is proof enough that I didn't con-sider the prophecies from God. Paul, in his letter to the Cor-inthians, dives in headfirst to present ground rules that would protect them, and even us, from the fanciful creations some peo-ple call prophecy.

Prophecy and Tongues

I was taught that prophecy was two things—forth telling, or proclaiming the truth of Scripture, and foretelling, the predict-ing of future events. The caveat was that forth telling is preach-ing and foretelling is no longer needed. It passed away with other unnecessary gifts. Clearly I do not agree with the above expla-nation. I agree with Dr. Wayne Grudem, who writes, "A fresh examination of the New Testament teaching on this gift will show that it should be defined not as 'predicting the future,' nor as 'proclaiming a word from the Lord,' but rather as 'telling something that God has spontaneously brought to mind.'"[6] Grudem goes on to give four reasons that support his conclusion. I highly recommend reading his work on this crucial matter.[7]

If prophecy is what God has spontaneously brought to mind, it can be prompting, impulses, scriptural statements, principles, comments, and revelations. All can fall under the general category of prophecy. "Whoa, Nellie," as my grandfather used to say. This opens Pandora's box and all the other ones I have in my garage. Any whacked-out charisaholic can claim to have heard from God.

Prophecy and tongues were a part of the early gathered church. The main focus of the gathering was the review and teaching of Scripture. This was true in the synagogue and it was also central to first-century Christian worship. They used the Old Testament, the written and oral teachings of Christ, and the letters written by the apostles as they were distributed among the churches. Paul's instructions to Timothy indicate that the reading and teaching of the Word of God were at the center of the gathered assembly.[8]

Before the written record was complete, there was more of a need to supplement Scripture. A case can be made today for less prophecy, because we have the complete written Word of God, but it cannot be made for the elimination of prophecy. Special and specific words from God to his children will always be needed. God has gifted certain people to deliver these messages, which reveal his love and give a personal touch. We are needy; we crave his attention. The teaching of God's Word is the foundation of our instruction, but periodic special words nourish the soul.

When a person prophesied over me and told me that some people's rejection of my teaching was not a rejection of me but of God, that gave me comfort. The prophecy also said that soon those people would be able to receive my teaching. It gave me a new sense of determination to continue, as a dead man preaching with nothing to lose.

I want to say it again and again—to close ourselves off from an entire dimension of ministry is a tragic missed opportunity. I feel haunted by the many years I lived without the gifts of the Spirit. I am committed to never hold back again from their exercise. Paul compared the gift of tongues and the gift of prophecy.

Basically he said that tongues edify the individual, while prophecy edifies the church.

Tongues Edify the Individual

We can glean understanding about the gift of tongues from 1 Corinthians 14.

1. *No one understands the one who speaks in tongues (v. 2).* The passage says that the speaker speaks to God. This is not entirely a bad thing to speak to God in prayer. The person praying speaks mysteries and I believe nourishes his or her intimacy with God.

2. *He edifies himself (v. 4).* In my theological circles this always was presented in such a way as to imply that anyone who spoke in tongues was really selfish. Since when has it been selfish to desire edification? The same people who ridicule the selfish tongues-person go to church every week and desire to be edified via the Word or music. How is that any different? There is nothing wrong with legitimate edification. That is why God gives gifts so the body can help one another.

3. *Speaking in tongues is of no value in public if no one understands (v. 6).* I have been in several situations where most of the people around me were speaking in tongues. I was edified only in thinking that they were expressing their hearts to God. It really didn't bother me but it also didn't build me up.

4. *Pray that you can interpret so there will be understanding (vv. 12–19).* There are some who believe that before you can speak in tongues, you must know that there is someone present who has the gift of interpretation. I don't believe the text comes right out and says that. The person must first give the message and then wait to see if God gives the interpretation. The gift of interpretation doesn't work perfectly all the time any more than the gift of teaching works right every time. In a small-group context you may already know the gifting of those there, which would provide more freedom and security.

5. *Tongues are a sign to unbelievers (vv. 20–23).* Verse 22 has always confused me. On one hand Paul tells us that if we all pray in tongues without interpretation that unbelievers will be repelled and think, *They are out of their minds* (v. 23). Yet, on the other

hand, he tells us that tongues are for the unbeliever. Commentators have consumed reams of paper trying to explain it. The way I understand it is that in verse 23 he is speaking of uninterpreted tongues. He connects the statement to an Old Testament prophecy that predicted that Israel would have the gospel preached to them in foreign languages (v. 20). This was to be a judgment for rejecting Jesus as Messiah and took place on Pentecost when 120 men and women spilled out of the upper room onto the streets below and preached in sixteen dialects, and three thousand turned to Christ.

The prophecy taken from Isaiah 28:11–12 was changed substantially by Paul.[9] He tailored the Isaiah passage to apply it to the Corinthians, with the purpose of demonstrating that tongues have a very specific role. They must be interpreted or they confuse and alienate. Uninterpreted tongues can edify the individual but not the group. Prophecy is more valued because it can be understood, and this is always preferred in worship.

Positives about the Gift of Tongues

1. *Tongues edify the person who prays (v. 4).* Paul stated that he prayed in tongues more than all the rest (v. 18) and he wished that all could experience it (v. 5). He knew the value of this gift. If the gift is not exercised in public worship, then it should be exercised in the private prayer life.

2. *Tongues can edify the body when interpreted (v. 5).* Often when a message in tongues is interpreted, it is general in nature. It is usually uplifting language that promises God's comfort, blessing, and faithfulness. Prophecy, on the other hand, is generally specific to situations and persons.

3. *The spirit prays and sings (vv. 14–15).* There are times when words don't work. One of the benefits of "praying in the Spirit" is the total release of pain or joy. Releasing our total being from the heart is therapeutic. One of my consistent obstacles to intimacy with God and others is being stuck in my head. Relating to God on a deep emotional level has given me a new intimacy with God.

4. *I would like you all to speak in tongues (v. 5).* This statement is both an authentic wish and a teaching tool. It is obvi-

ous that Paul doesn't believe that everyone has the gift of tongues (see 12:30), but he had found praying in the Spirit a helpful experience and, because he loves them, he wishes only the best for them.

At the same time there is a touch of sarcasm here that is instructive. Paul seems to be saying that everyone can't speak in tongues, but everyone is trying. We desire the spectacular; we want others to think of us as being special; we want to be in the elite realm. We think that if only we could speak in tongues we would be happy, that our life would be more meaningful. But that is not the way it is and we wouldn't be happy trying to get what God doesn't want for us. Paul is crying out to the church: Love one another, then you will have everything God wants for you and everything you need.

5. *Paul thanked God that he spoke in tongues (v. 18)*. And in verse 39 he says the church should not forbid tongues. This does not require us to allow the expression of this gift all the time and in every venue. It does mean, however, we need to craft a place for it so that God can give his personal touch to his children.

Tongues have their place in the private prayer life of those so gifted. There is a benefit in worship if there is an interpreter. The gift is to be exercised with love and with the caveat that it will be used to build up. Otherwise it can confuse and offend and then it is not done in love.

Prophecy Edifies the Church

Paul explains the gift of prophecy in 1 Corinthians 14.

1. *Its purpose is to strengthen, encourage, and comfort the believer (v. 3)*. This is the heart of being edified or built up. Paul's point is simple. Prophecy can be understood, and people must understand if they are to be helped. Here are other facts about prophecy:

1. The person who prophesies is greater than one who speaks in tongues, unless there is an interpreter for a message in tongues (v. 5).
2. Prophecy can be a revelation, message of knowledge, or word of instruction (v. 6). (A lot of this will be based in the

written record. The more you are in the Word, the more
God can speak to and through you.)
3. Prophecy is for the believer (v. 22).
4. Do not treat prophecy with contempt (1 Thess. 5:19–20).

Prophecy is one of the greater gifts because it can be understood by others. It operates at the epicenter of need. I have
already mentioned in a period of discouragement for me, a person gave me the encouragement that the "dough would rise." I
was also comforted by the prophecy of two shoes. The picture
was that I had on one shoe in preparation to take a stand, but
the second shoe remained unused. The word of prophecy told
me that I would be putting on the other shoe very soon. I believed
that the image referred to the limited way in which I had
preached the series on the gifts and the way I had related my
experience. I revealed a lot of my heart and I held nothing back
doctrinally from the church, but at some point I would need to
create a new venue in which the gifts could operate. That second shoe meant the establishment of that venue and my willingness to look foolish. What if I gave people a chance to speak
what God was telling them and no one said anything? What if I
thought God might be giving me a word or picture and I spoke
it and it was not confirmed. What if it were rejected as not coming from God?
I have now donned the second shoe. I am taking my stand.
And the results have been very sweet. People are ministering to
one another on a different level, and gifts are emerging.
A third word I received recently was a great comfort to me.
It was a picture of a great waterfall pouring its unlimited sup-
ply on the ground. That waterfall was God and his endless
resources of the Spirit being poured out. As one looked to the
ground, the water was running off hard, dry ground. There was
no penetration. That represented my heart and the hearts of our
congregation. But then the ground began to crack. That single
crack was me and my brokenness before God. When I cracked,
other parts of the ground also cracked, and the water began to
penetrate the ground. That picture was personal and gave me
strength to continue to be broken and humble before God. I was
undergoing significant pain, seeing my sin and arrogance, and
it gave me the courage to move toward the pain and dive in head-

first. These are three prophetic words that met my specific need at the moment. They continue to provide hope and the endurance to keep going.

The prophetic word continues to minister to me, but I don't count on it like Scripture. If some of these prophecies turn out to be wrong, I will be disappointed but not shaken. As of this writing I have received only one that predicted trouble. I expect as I grow in the prophetic that I will hear many a squirrelly thing. That is why Paul advises a serious evaluation of any prophetic word. I know this, though. When you open yourself up to it, God delivers. Yes, you open yourself up to every person's opinion as well, but it is worth it. You can sort it out.

Prophecy is not equal to Scripture and that is why people should preface their remarks with, "I think the Lord is putting on my mind that . . ." or "It seems to me that the Lord is showing us . . ." If prophecy does not contain God's very words, then what is it?

PROPHECY AND TEACHING—THE DIFFERENCE

There has been a tendency by noncharismatic evangelicals to equate the ancient gift of prophecy and the contemporary gift of preaching. This of course reveals a theological prejudice that dismisses the supernatural aspect of contemporary prophecy.

Preaching is talked about in Scripture, and it seems that preaching and teaching have a symbiotic relationship.[10] They are closely linked. There is significant overlap, and the distinctions are real but not deep. Preaching or *kerygma* was primarily used in an evangelistic sense. Teaching or *didache* was instruction, the kind of ministry Paul modeled for two years in the lecture hall of Tyrannus (Acts 19:9–10). The tradition of distinction between preaching and teaching has been experience based. Preaching is addressed primarily to the heart and calls for a decision. Teaching is focused primarily on the head and edifies, based on information. Preaching is a passionate address that seeks to stir the heart and penetrate a person's defenses. Teaching is less passionate and may use graphs and charts. This traditional distinction is superficial and doesn't deal with the biblical record. Michael Green's *Evangelism in the Early Church* provides an excellent treatment of the similarities and differ-ences between the *kerygma* and the *didache*.[11]

Preaching may be considered a spiritual gift by some. It is not listed with the gifts in the New Testament, unless we allow preaching to become prophecy. If prophecy is "telling some-thing that God has spontaneously brought to mind" (as I quoted Grudem earlier), then it is unlikely that what we call preaching can be the same thing. Preaching today has become an encul-turated function of the local church. It has been turned into a hybrid of the art of communication, used to explain the Scrip-tures. It is crucial to the church, and I give my best time to it. I think it has more impact on the church than any other single function. But that doesn't change the fact that what we call preaching is an expression of the gift of teaching.

Prophecy is generated by a spontaneous prompting from the Holy Spirit[12] and may come in the form of a revelation, message of knowledge, or word of instruction and may be expressed in a couple of words, a sentence, or a body of knowl-edge. Teaching is not based on a revelation; it is the explana-tion of *the* revelation.

> As far as we can tell, all New Testament "prophecy" was based on this kind of spontaneous prompting from the Holy Spirit [Acts 11:28; 21:4, 10–11]. And note the ideas of prophecy represented in Scripture [Luke 7:39; 22:63–64; John 4:19; 11:51]. Unless a per-son receives a spontaneous "revelation" from God, there is no prophecy. By contrast, no human speech act that is called a "teaching" or done by a "teacher," or described by the verb "teach," is ever said to be based on a "revelation" in the New Tes-tament. [Grudem goes on to draw a conclusion.] Rather "teach-ing" is often simply an explanation or application of Scripture.[13]

Teaching is an exposition of Scripture that requires extensive preparation. Prophecy's preparation is a heart and ear tuned to God's voice.

I have the gift of teaching but up to this point have never received a prophecy. God has seen fit to deliver prophetic words to me through the members of the body. This may be due to God's estimation of the limits that should be placed on my flesh. I have noticed how most television ministers have a direct line to God. He tells them special stuff that no one watching knows. This gives him or her a position of power that keeps the person on TV. Some pastors operate as prophets. It is tough for the congregation to argue with "words from God." I am not satisfied to be sitting with my nose pressed against the prophetic window. But for now I am willing to let other members of the body teach me. The beauty of my lack of personal experience in prophecy is that it forces me to stay in a position of humility.

Prophecy in the Future

The closer we get to the second coming, the more supernatural expressions we should expect. I base this on Peter's explanation to the curious crowd at Pentecost.

> This is what was spoken by the prophet Joel:
> "In the last days, God says,
> I will pour out my Spirit on all people.
> Your sons and daughters will prophesy,
> your young men will see visions,
> your old men will dream dreams.
> Even on my servants, both men and women,
> I will pour out my Spirit in those days,
> and they will prophesy.
>
> Acts 2:16–18

The last days are the period of the church and as it draws to a close. At that time God will increase the outpouring of his Spirit. It began at Pentecost and should increase as the second coming draws closer. This is opposite to much of the teaching I received and gave to others. Some of us have taught that God's intervention or the miraculous would decrease until the tribulation, then the floodgates would open. Now, with my theological systems stripped away, I can see that the plain teaching of Scripture indicates that the supernatural will gradually increase and naturally flow into the tribulation.

I sense a calling to pray that God will restore the supernatural to our church. I have confessed my sin of pride and theological bias and asked God for a merciful outpouring of his power. I pray for an outpouring of prophecies, dreams, and visions without regard to the gender, age, or economic position of the person receiving them. I want people to hear about what God is doing and be drawn to our campus. I yearn for them to enter the sanctuary, the various groupings large and small, and say, "God is really here. I have a sense of awe that makes me want to worship."

God Present through Me

I have now covered the distinctions between tongues and prophecy and between teaching and prophecy. Additionally I have proposed that the church should expect more prophecy and supernatural communication, not less.

My vision for prophecy is that it will become common, that it will be as normal to receive encouragement from someone with a word as it is to sing in worship or be stimulated by a sermon. At the same time, there must be the continuing caveat that prophetic messages be evaluated and not considered equal with Scripture. The reason I consider this an important goal is the impact it can have on those nearby.

> But if an unbeliever or someone who does not understand comes in while everybody is prophesying, he will be convinced by all that he is a sinner and will be judged by all, and the secrets of his heart will be laid bare. So he will fall down and worship God, exclaiming, "God is really among you!"
>
> 1 Corinthians 14:24–25

This is the goal of worship. Believer and unbeliever alike with humility will repent and turn to God. The greatest church-growth tool is God's presence. If people experience God's presence in worship, they will come back, they will tell their friends, they will long for it. It's all here—conviction of sin, a dissection of the heart, and awareness of God's presence.

I was a pastor twenty years before I started seeking God's presence. Oh, I talked about it all the time. I taught it and claimed it whenever two or three of us were gathered in his name. I owned it theologically, but I didn't seek to experience it. I didn't even know that it was to be expected. I knew God revealed himself on special occasions, but I never expected that one of those special occasions might include me.

I have avoided the responsibility for making things happen in worship. It makes me feel uncomfortable when worship leaders shape events to create an effect. My understanding of theology and cultural conditioning have been a high wall to scale. The first barrier was my belief that leadership is *teamwork*. The authority and power should not rest in one person. So what happens in worship should be a team effort. As I have said before, spiritual gifts are God present with us through another person. The insight God has given me is that taking responsibility for worship leadership does not violate my principles. It just means that when I spend forty minutes every Sunday leading people, it is okay in that context for me to take charge.

A second fear was that taking risks to create a favorable environment for God to manifest himself would make me look like a *manipulator*. If I took the microphone and ran down the aisle asking people to declare how they need God's power, it might not work out.

There is a third barrier that is the most important. I did not want the *personal pressure* of making things happen every week. If you do it one week, then you have to match it or top it the next week. And to be frank, I don't have that many good ideas or stories.

I have been praying for God to manifest his presence each week for over three years. And the awful truth is that whenever it has happened, I played a major role. That means that I must be spiritually present and prepared so that God's presence will show up through my gifts, because, through my gifts, I am God present to others.

What does God's presence look like? I say "look like" because I am referring to his manifest presence. I am ashamed of what I have settled for in my many years of leadership. People thought the sermon was good and a couple of songs were good too. "Keep up the good work, pastor. We might come back again." Dedication and duty have their place, but I want more. I am ready to stand up and scream, "Wait a minute. There must be more." I am talking about *awe,* my friends. I want people to be drawn to worship because of its deep impact. While organization and talent play a part, it is really about the spiritual preparation of the gifted in the moment.

When people come forward for prayer in great numbers, when they are moved to ask for help, when people spend extra time praying in little groups throughout the sanctuary because they just have to, when there is exuberance in worship and tears in the eyes and joy on the faces, when the pride is sucked out of the room, you can walk in and immediately know that God is here. A few weeks ago many of us stood around the prayer steps at the foot of our platform. A man kept saying, "It's a miracle, a flat out miracle." He was talking about being reconciled to another person that morning during our ministry time. Virtually every time we experience a sense of awe, it has been when I broke through to them on a deep emotional level. My greatest single challenge is to connect with others on a deep emotional level. It doesn't come easily to me. It takes extra prayer and meditation. I mentioned earlier how frightened I was when people started coming forward for prayer, when the response was beyond my control. *How can I keep this going?* has been my fear.

It is painful for me to struggle every week, to think how much things depend on me. I don't mean that I do it myself, but that I must prepare to hear God's voice. I can't just go through the motions. There is a weekly accountability of the most important kind. Then I get immediate feedback on Sunday. I know when God has manifested himself. Almost always it is in a two-punch combo of exposition of Scripture and passion that gets through.

Since I have made a commitment to being God present with others through my gifts, I have seen the following changes. People who opposed my new philosophical architecture have moved to agreement with me. The resistance was not philosophic; it was a lack of emotional bond. I have seen young leaders come to my defense when some have been critical. I have seen small-group leaders willing to learn instead of resisting spiritual authority. As I have become more honest and forthcoming with my problems and emotions, others have opened up. This also has given me a new freedom to speak my mind in a way that leads to breakthroughs and changes hearts. God's presence is about breaking down our resistance so that our hearts long for change and desire to become more like Christ. This is discipleship with power!

Tools and Rules

The first priority in employing the miraculous in worship is the importance of being understood. We now address how to practice the gifts in worship.

The *worship toolbox* contains guidelines on how to manage the supernatural in worship. The following are our governing principles:

1. The context of the principles is worship.
2. The purpose is the building up of the members.
3. The way of love is to limit the flesh and contribute to the common good.
4. The people must understand to be helped.

The *participant toolbox* is for the worshiper who is to come prepared. It is not exhaustive but representative of being ready to worship. It includes:

1. A hymn. A song or poem the participant has created, a praise, or a song to be sung to or with others.
2. A word of instruction. Teaching based on Scripture or an application of Scripture.
3. A revelation. A revelation is necessary for a prophecy. It is what God brings spontaneously to mind. The more one is in the Word, the more likely one is to be a candidate to minister in this way. Long periods of meditation on Scripture and listening to God's voice are required.
4. A tongue with interpretation. Paul encourages using this gift to minister to others. Pray that you may interpret what you say (1 Cor. 14:13).

If we are committed to being spiritually engaged and present when we worship, then the full panoply of spiritual gifts are in play. Smaller settings are more friendly to participation and should be considered when a ministry time is planned. A ministry time is unstructured time when we listen to God and reach out to others. This seems to work best in a small group environment where high trust relationships already exist.

I did a series on the gifts and I asked people not to give a message in tongues in our public meetings. This was really funny in that most didn't think there would be anyone in our church who would speak in tongues. I didn't have the heart to tell them that several of our pastoral staff did. I explained how our meetings were very different in nature from first-century meetings. Their meetings were smaller and people knew each other. When you know people, you are usually aware of their gifting. You would know if there was someone present who could interpret.

Our services are much larger and are open to the public and there is no shared understanding of what is to take place. We want our public meetings to reach the widest audience possible. Our highest value is for the truth of Scripture to penetrate the souls of those present. Therefore, we want to avoid events that would confuse and alienate.

There are people present in our services with preconceived ideas about tongues and all the baggage that goes with them. We have people of every persuasion, and we don't insist on complete agreement to our doctrinal statement among attenders. In fact we hope that nonmembers will feel free to hang around the edges and sort it all out. They can believe that God is three pounds of feta cheese and we are saltine crackers. We just want them there to hear and interact with God's Word.

Paul's Rules on Tongues

Rule 1: Limit speaking in tongues to two or three speakers, one at a time.
Rule 2: There must be an interpreter.
For Paul's rules on tongues, see 1 Corinthians 14:27–28.

Our Rules on Tongues

Rule 1: There will be no audible tongues in public church meetings. This goes back to the problem of uninterpreted tongues and their inability to build up or help worship.
Rule 2: In small groups or adult fellowships, ask permission and consider who is present. If there is no interpretation, then

the leader should graciously state, "The Lord has no word for us at this time, but we encourage you to exercise your gifts. We know that he will speak at another time."

There is a tendency to worry about disappointment when people give a message and there is no interpretation. It is not a problem if people will encourage instead of make judgments or become critical spirits.

Paul's Rules on Prophecy

Rule 1: Limit prophesying to two or three speakers.

Rule 2: Weigh carefully what is said (1 Cor. 14:29). The word used here is *diakrino,* meaning "serious scrutiny." Sometimes this could take days. A prophecy might be controversial, and the elders may need some time of prayer to determine its validity.

Rule 3: One prophecy at a time. Prophesying is to be done in turn. If one person desires to speak, he or she should be given the floor. Paul made clear that there was to be no speaking over another person's words. If this control is lost, the prophecy is not of God. Paul declares that people can control themselves and that a sign of the Holy Spirit's presence is order and courtesy. The entire purpose of prophecy is to strengthen, encourage, and comfort.

For Paul's rules on prophecy, see 1 Corinthians 14:29–32.

Our Rules on Prophecy

Rule 1: If you think God has given you a word for someone, go to that person rather than to others. Many experienced leaders estimate that 80 percent of prophecies are for one other person; therefore, rarely are they a message for the entire body.

Rule 2: Introduce what you have to say with, "It seems to me" or "I feel impressed to say." Then end the comment with, "Does that make any sense to you?" or "I don't know what it means, but I believe it is for you."

Rule 3: If the message is for the church:

1. In an open public meeting, if a message is received, deliver it to the pastor in private. If the pastor believes it is of God,

he will deliver it. If he cannot decide, then the elders will need to hear it. This rule exists to cull out the wide variety of things that could happen in a public meeting where there is no common basis of understanding.

2. If you are in a believers only meeting that is closed by its nature, then feel free to deliver the message. Then it can be evaluated by those present.

An Interview with a Prophet

I am acquainted with a proven prophet. I sat down to ask her about her faith journey and how the gift developed.

Bill Hull: When did you know you had something special?

Prophet: I was raised in a missionary home and became a follower of Jesus at a very young age. When I was twenty-two years old, I was filled with the Holy Spirit and prayed in tongues. That is when I learned about the gifts of the Spirit.

Bill Hull: Did you have a vision or hear a voice? What happened?

Prophet: I was being taught by a mentor, a seasoned veteran. I saw him in operation and by watching him I learned how gifts ministered to people's specific needs.

Bill Hull: How many words, revelations, whatever have you experienced?

Prophet: I have been getting them for thirty years and there have been hundreds, possibly thousands.

Bill Hull: How do they come to you?

Prophet: Mostly I see pictures. I will see a great waterfall running off hard dry ground, a fortress over a person's head, ground eroding under a family, a person running through fire.

Bill Hull: How do you know they are from God? Are you always right?

Prophet: Sometimes I know what they mean. Often, however, I do not. I just deliver the message to whom I think it is for. Sometimes people receive it with thanks, and it is rare that I don't get feedback. But 90 percent of the time the feedback is positive and affirming that God has spoken.

Bill Hull: What do you do when you see images that don't seem to be from God?

Prophet: I discard silly pictures that are clearly nonsensical. But I deliver what I think is from God. I don't ever tell people that I am speaking for God. I will tell them what I saw and I thought it might be for them. It is like when I told you I saw you making bread and looking in the oven door to see if the dough would rise. In my vision you seemed worried about it by your repeated trips to the oven window.

Bill Hull: Yes, and I understood immediately that God was giving me what I had prayed for, encouragement. How does one develop such a gifting?

Prophet: It is all about seeking God. When you seek God, your gifts will be manifested. As I spent time with God, he started giving me words and pictures for his people. It is also imperative that you find a mentor, someone who has been through the fire before you. I was introduced to many pastors, and my ministry was reviewed by them. They helped me learn how to listen to God's voice, how to understand the role of pastoral authority, and how to help rather than hinder with my gift.

Bill Hull: What is the first priority to your gift?

Prophet: I spend several hours every day reading the Scriptures and praying. I find in those hours of listening to God that he speaks to me. My personal devotional life is the single most important factor. That is how I prepare to minister. I don't go looking for opportunities. God presents them to me every day.

Bill Hull: What advice would you give to those seeking the unveiling of their gifting, especially if they believe they are being led into the area of prophecy?

Prophet: I would advise them to find a seasoned veteran and ask him or her to evaluate what they are seeing or hearing. There is an informal school of prophets that network and help each other. But it should always be done under the authority of a pastor of a local church.

Inviting the miraculous into a noncharismatic environment is a gradual process. I would not recommend it unless you are fully committed and patient. Make sure it is your calling and not just another attempt to create church growth. The curse of Americans is that we use everything, even the hot pursuit of God, as a means to our own success. The first step to seeking the miraculous is the personal pursuit of God and asking him for direction. Until that takes place, every book and conference on the subject will be like jumping into deep water before you have learned to swim. Let God take you by the hand and walk you in. He will tell you what to do.

9

Becoming a Healing
Community

The feeling was surreal as I watched the first man land on the moon. I looked out the window at that bright ball called the moon and then back to the television. It took all my capacity for wonder to capture the moment, to embrace the fact that man was walking out there in space. It was a moment of awe, the beginning of who knew what. Man would go even farther and make more discoveries.

"That's not happening. It's fake!" spewed an old man. "The government just wants to spend the money. It is a setup."

About that time a nurse said, "Henry, it's time to go to your room." She unlocked the brakes on Henry's wheelchair and rolled him down the hall. But not before several more patients confirmed Henry's analysis. "It's a government conspiracy." "No one can fly to the moon." "They're on a sound stage in Hollywood." "What bunk!" The vote was in at the Dry Ridge, Kentucky, Convalescent Center and it was unanimous.

Jane and I smiled at each other and rolled our eyes, but we were there on more important business. When I was the twenty-five-dollar-a-week pastor at the Mount Pisgah United Methodist Church in Dry Ridge, part of my weekend duties was to visit the Methodist folk at the center. I've already described the misery of that place. What I saw there indelibly marked me for life. People who were once lawyers, teachers, or executives were now talking all day and saying nothing, walking for hours but going nowhere. Children whose development had been inexplicably halted spent their lives lying in beds behind bars, like little caged animals.

I've already written about how I prayed for Kenny, not a child but a young man whose paralysis had sealed his fate. I also prayed for the babies. I asked God to heal them. I never saw any change in them, even though I prayed in faith. I was a graduate of Oral Roberts University and believed that if you have enough faith, God will heal you. I was greatly troubled by God's lack of action. I just didn't get it.

I once visited a friend who suffered from lymphoma. He had been flat on his back for six weeks and it looked like he would remain in the hospital for another two months. I asked him if he had given up on a miraculous healing. He confidently said, "No! I am trusting God."

As I drove home, I had to face my own faith. *Have I given up on God's healing him?* It has been thirty-two years since my unanswered prayers in that Kentucky convalescent home. I have seen people healed, I've been healed, but it is so easy to get weary in prayer. Sometimes it feels like I am riding a wave of faith and I see many answers to prayer. Then it seems as though I find myself in the doldrums of faith, with no wind for my sails. Will God do anything about our frustration as we live between power and pain?

I walked into that hospital determined to do the works of Jesus. I left there wondering if I could ever do the works of Jesus. I knew what Jesus did, I wasn't sure how he did it, and I was a long way from knowing how to do it myself. That is why the questions addressed earlier in the book—What did Jesus do? How did he do it? And how can we do it? are so crucial to those who really want to try. The two questions I now ask are, Why does God heal? and Why does God not heal? I expect to take these questions to heaven with me, but the following is what I have learned. (I will answer the first question in this chapter and the second in chapter 10.)

On September 11, 2001, my friend died. I went to his home as soon as I heard he was gone. That day we knew grief upon grief, for as I stood over his body, mourning my loss, my attention was caught by the television that was on just across the room. There, to everyone's horror, planes were crashing into the World Trade Center towers.

Why Does God Heal?

The basis for healing is not found in the physical realm. Physical healing is the application of spiritual healing. They actually are closely linked, but we must start with the core issue of sin and forgiveness.

It is obvious that the only source of the provision for healing is the finished work of Christ. There has been an ongoing debate over how far we can take the core passage:

> Surely he took up our infirmities
>   and carried our sorrows,
> yet we considered him stricken by God,
>   smitten by him, and afflicted.
> But he was pierced for our transgressions,
>   he was crushed for our iniquities;
> the punishment that brought us peace was upon him,
>   and *by his wounds we are healed.*

Isaiah 53:4–5

The classic evangelical interpretation is that this is primarily a spiritual healing from sin and secondarily has a physical application. I have no problem with that, but some people go too far and say that there is no healing in the atonement. What I think they mean is that there is no guarantee of physical healing as there is a spiritual healing. The atonement is a way of saying that God provided through the sacrifice of Christ a means of again making one God and his creation (at-one-ment). If there is not physical healing in the atonement, then where does it come from? Of course it has to be there. The debate is really about whether physical healing is guaranteed as is spiritual healing.

Peter's Interpretation

I assume that most of us believe Peter would be much more qualified to interpret the Isaiah passage than any of us. He wrote: "He himself bore our sins in his body on the tree, so that we might die to sins and live for righteousness; by his wounds you have been healed" (1 Peter 2:24). Here Peter interprets the Isaiah passage as primarily a spiritual healing. I support the idea that sin is the primary issue and physical healing is secondary. I do not, however, support those who would like to stop there and limit the work of Christ to sin alone. When you really get down to it, the issue is how willing is God to heal now as an intermediate solution to the inevitability of physical death? How much intervention should we expect? A healing now delays the ultimate healing. God heals a person of cancer now; the person dies later of other causes and only then receives the eternal healing. There must be reasons. How much is faith and how much is sovereignty?—good fodder for our consideration.

Some contend that Peter took a side in the debate when he interpreted the Isaiah passage for us in the above text. Peter himself knew better, and so did Matthew, who records Jesus' healing Peter's mother-in-law.

> When Jesus came into Peter's house, he saw Peter's mother-in-law lying in bed with a fever. He touched her hand and the fever left her, and she got up and began to wait on him.
> When evening came, many who were demon-possessed were brought to him, and he drove out the spirits with a word and healed all the sick. This was to fulfill what was spoken through the prophet Isaiah:
> "He took up our infirmities and carried our diseases."
>
> Matthew 8:14–17

I would be shocked if Matthew and Peter had different understandings of the Isaiah passage. Under the guidance of the Holy Spirit both writers have helped the reader see that the healing promised in Isaiah applies to both spiritual and physical maladies.

The basis of healing is the finished work of Christ on the cross. The primary work is not only about sin, it is also about the body. It is the work of Christ that provides eternal life with a new body. There is also an important role for physical healing now to demonstrate God's mercy, love, and power. But Timothy still had stomach problems, Paul was troubled by his thorn in the side, and people of faith take multiple prescriptions every day. What is God's purpose in healing some of us temporarily on our way to an eternal healing?

God's Purpose in Healing

To Authenticate the Message

Aren't you tired of society's collective yawn when they think church? Many writers and consultants propose from their research that people are yawning because of music style and predictability in the services. Recently my sons were in town and visited our church. Later while we were enjoying our dessert, I asked them what they thought about our service. They are both graphic designers and the first thing they critiqued was our use of media. We discussed music, preaching, the whole thing. I am very confident that I got an honest response from these two twenty-somethings.

I asked my oldest son whether any of his friends went to church. He assured me that none of them did, so I asked why not. His answer really stung, "Because nothing ever happens."

"Nothing?" I protested.

"Yeah, there is the singing, the prayers, the sermon, the offering, and then it's over." What he went on to say was that nothing miraculous or special seems to take place. God doesn't seem to be present. There is no movement of the Spirit. Now that is a real challenge to ol' Dad. My son's unbelieving friends can discern what is missing in our worship better than we can.

Their critique was about spiritual anemia. It is the lack of spiritual power that causes them to find the Sunday paper more exciting than the standard church's encounter with God. An example from the first church makes the point.

> Philip went down to a city in Samaria and proclaimed the Christ there. When the crowds *heard* Philip and *saw* the miraculous signs he did, *they all paid close attention to what he said.* With shrieks, evil spirits came out of many, and many paralytics and cripples were healed. So there was great joy in that city.
>
> Acts 8:5–8

Philip was one of the preachers without portfolio. He had some status as a deacon, but that would have meant nothing to the rabble in Samaria. Yet his impact was to create joy in the city, and not just joy but *great* joy. This was not because of his well-illustrated three-point message. It wasn't because of his ability to tell a story and provide cool background on his Power Point program. It wasn't because his agent did a great job with publicity, and the room was packed with fans. It was because the people did more than hear; they saw God's power.

I have a recurring dream in which I cast a demon out of a person in the worship service. It's usually someone that is giving me trouble—it's called the demon of disagreement with Bill. My dream goes on to include many healings, the kind that are dramatic where withered hands are restored and the paralyzed get up and walk. The congregation starts celebrating. They burst into uncontrolled praise, dancing before God. Don't you have that same dream? I hope you do, because it doesn't need to stay a dream trapped in our heart's desire. I long for that kind of impact, and I don't care how messy it gets.

The beauty of it all is that Philip had a powerful citywide impact through simple preaching and faith. One of our members is Jewish, believing in Jesus as Messiah in his late teens. His family responded as expected and were disappointed and hurt. One day his father called him and told him his grandmother was dying of cancer. Would he go and pray with her? He went to his grandmother's bedside, but before he prayed, he told her about his faith in Christ. He asked if he could pray for her in the name of Jesus, and she agreed. She was seriously ill and was expected to live only a few more days, but after her grandson prayed for her, within a few days she started improving. Soon she was able to leave the hospital. The cancer left her body and she lived twenty more years. She also lived those twenty years as a Christian along with the young man's father. There is no way his grandmother and father would have committed themselves to Christ apart from the work of power.

This is what drives me to pursue God, to experience his power, and to see great joy come to those touched by him. Our dreams can become reality if we are willing to risk. I am not sure how God will do it in our church, but I am ready and am looking for the pathway.

To Show Mercy to the Ill

"When Jesus landed and saw a large crowd, he had compassion on them and healed their sick" (Matt. 14:14). Don't ask me to explain the following statement. Sometimes God heals because he chooses to display his mercy. Conversely, there are times when he chooses not to heal. There are a number of times Jesus heals because his heart is moved. See, for example, Matthew 9:35–38.

For God to Be Glorified

When Jesus raised Lazarus, he gave the reason: "This sickness will not end in death. No, it is for God's glory so that God's Son may be glorified through it" (John 11:4). The same purpose is stated concerning the man born blind. The disciples questioned Jesus as to what sin the man or his parents had committed to bring on such a terrible malady. "'Neither this man nor his parents sinned,' said Jesus, 'but this happened so that the work of God might be displayed in his life'" (9:3).

Healing works on several levels. There is the sheer mercy of it, and there is a natural human response, which is to praise God and thank him. There is the strategic element that propels the message forward with such force that it penetrates hearts and minds. And there is a way in which it cuts through all the reasons people give for not believing. That is to glorify God. *God's glory is all that God is and all that God has.* When

God is glorified, who he is and what he has is revealed. God is glorified on his own terms. He determines what glorifies himself, and it happens even if not one person on earth knows it. God is glorified in all ten lepers that Jesus healed, even if only one thanked him (see Luke 17:11–19). Isn't it true that God is glorified daily in our lives, even if we don't recognize it or give thanks? Often we take the responsibility to glorify God and to determine when that happens. God is sometimes glorified based on our behavior. This is clear from Jesus' teaching in the upper room: "This is to my Father's glory, that you bear much fruit, showing yourselves to be my disciples" (John 15:8). But he is not limited to our obedience or response before he is glorified. He was glorified in his creative work, even before it included the human response, because it revealed who he is and what he has. God heals the human body to glorify himself, and, as a bonus, we praise him and that glorifies him as well.

Medicine and Divine Healing

The Oral Roberts University School of Medicine can be considered either an oxymoron or a metaphor. It is no longer open but for years it was a legitimate medical school. It can be scoffed at as a cultural oxymoron in that Oral Roberts's healing crusades through prayer seem to contradict the need for medical science.

I choose to see the school of medicine as a metaphor, a picture of what God does, bringing balance to the healing question.

How does God heal? In a variety of ways is the right answer. The body's ability to heal itself is evidence that God heals through the design of the body. The finger is cut and over time it heals itself. Surgery is performed and the body heals itself of the incisions and intrusions of the process. The surgeon removes a growth or repairs internal damage. That is a form of healing. I want to delve into this a bit further by addressing three issues: Is it okay to take medication to treat an illness? Should we seek God's healing for every illness? What should be the relationship between prayer and medicine?

Jesus' Stand

When Satan took Jesus to the top of the temple—some 150 feet off the ground—he dared Jesus to jump. He even quoted Scripture to Jesus as a justification. Jesus responded with his own quote, "It is also written: 'Do not put the Lord your God to the test'" (see Matt. 4:5–7). Jesus in effect is saying, Why jump when I can take the stairs? This gets into questions such as, If I have a headache, do I pray and believe God to take it away or do I pop an aspirin? I have experienced heart palpitations in the last eighteen months. I have prayed many times that God would heal me, take them away. God has chosen not to heal me, but I haven't given up on a healing. I also went to the doctor and am now on medication. There are now medications that can treat arrhythmia that were not around fifty years ago. So this leads to the natural question, Is there a difference between praying now for medical needs and praying in the first century?

The obvious answer is yes. God hasn't changed but, through man's creative ability, he has provided a means for people to be healthy that didn't exist during his earthly ministry. So a lot of the people pursuing Jesus for healing would not be sick in the twenty-first century. Many of the crippled and paralyzed would be fine because of the polio vaccine. The black death from the Middle Ages is not a problem today because of medications, clean water, and good sanitation. The discovery of penicillin means that many problems that once were a threat to life can be controlled.

I presently take several medications for a variety of ailments. I have prayed about them, but I am also thankful that God has provided the medications. I am not healed, but I am living well because of them. To refuse medication would be foolish. It would be like jumping off the top of the temple when I could walk down the stairs.

There are people who will quote Scripture to us like Satan did to Jesus. They will take a verse out of context and present it as the full teaching of Scripture on the issue. Someone may say, "Jesus said all things are possible to him that believes. Whatever you ask in prayer believing shall be done." Those are real Scriptures, but Scripture also records people being sick after prayer. Paul himself was not healed of a physical ailment. The full theology of healing should be taken into consideration.

Asa's Mistake

"In the thirty-ninth year of his reign Asa was afflicted with a disease in his feet. Though his disease was severe, even in his illness he did not seek help from the LORD, but only from the physicians" (2 Chron. 16:12). Asa died. The implication from the text is that his death was premature. It may not be normal for Christians to exclude God from the healing equation, but it is common for the unbeliever to do so. Oh, they pray but they are not sure to what or to whom. Certainly believers must be careful to seek God for healing and not trust only in the doctors. Doing so is an insult to the Great Physician.

Hezekiah's Healing

In 2 Kings 20:1–7, we read that Hezekiah was at the point of death. Isaiah had delivered the bad news: Put your house in order. You are going to die. Hezekiah appealed to God, pointed out his faithful service, and wept bitterly. God tells Isaiah that he has heard Hezekiah's prayer and has seen his tears. He gives him fifteen more years. "Then Isaiah said, 'Prepare a poultice of figs.' They did so and applied it to the boil, and he recovered" (v. 7). For those who are asking, "What is a poultice?" It is a hot dressing in a compress, applied to the skin.

This episode reveals a right partnership between prayer and medicine. There are times when we are in immediate danger—we pray on the way to the emergency room. There are other times when there is time to prayerfully consider what approach to take. God's yes to our healing could include medical means. What I don't mean is that we pray and God says no, then we turn to medicine and it works. Hezekiah was about to die. God intervened and agreed to heal him, using medicine as the means of healing. We must believe that hundreds of poultices of figs would have been useless without the prayer of Hezekiah and the intervention of God. This should encourage us to pray with passion and then accept any means God chooses to restore health.

Kinds of Healing

We generally think of healing as it relates to the physical or the spiritual.[1] There are two other areas however, that have been seriously neglected, inner healing and deliverance.

Inner Healing

There are many people who are stuck in the past. The psalmist describes their plight: "For I am poor and needy, and my heart is wounded within me" (109:22). "The Lord is close to the brokenhearted and saves those who are crushed in spirit" (34:18). There is a sickness of heart in many people that prevents them from growing spiritually. They cannot seem to get unstuck to make positive steps forward. After being stuck for a long time, you take on a defeatist posture. Because of other people and circumstances, you become convinced there is no hope for change. A common term in contemporary vernacular is *victim*. A victim allows his or her life to be governed by external circumstances, people, or events. Victims believe they have no choices, that they are powerless.

BEING A VICTIM

I am not challenging the reality of victimhood. People are victims of armed robbery, various kinds of accidents, and many forms of abuse. I am not talking about a person who can't walk because of a broken leg or a rape victim who won't go out at night from fear or a person who is on disability for a variety of reasons. These people truly need time for healing and recovery. What I am saying is that there comes a day when one must stop acting like a victim.

The rape victim acts like a victim when she never tries to trust others again. The person on disability is content in his victimhood when he stays on disability and doesn't need to. When a person with a disease won't try to be independent or make a contribution to society, she is embracing her victim role. The worst victims are Christians who give up on overcoming sin in their lives or who won't try to reconcile with others because it is too hard. They say, "I've been hurt, so I can't try. It hurts too much to try."

What if Jesus had given up on us because we rejected him? What about when he stood over Jerusalem and wept over the Jews' rejection (Matt. 23:37–39)? Yet he was committed to loving us. He went to the cross and paid the ultimate price. So where do we get off saying "God can't help me. It requires too much change, too much humility. I can't take it"? It's always somebody else's fault. How tragic when we won't take responsibility.

FILLING IN THE HOLES

There is a wound in the human heart. It's a hole that needs to be drained of poison and filled with God's love. This doesn't change the past, but the wounds of disease, poverty, natural disasters, even wrong choices and destructive patterns can be healed. They need to be healed so Christians can take their place and contribute to the cause of Christ (see Eph. 4:16). Many wounds are from childhood when we were the most vulnerable. Satan doesn't play fair, and there are many horrific stories to be told. For this reason God heals memories and restores souls and reconciles enemies. He wants his children happy and productive. God doesn't change the past, but he does transform our response to the past. Inner healing is a crucial part of discipleship.

Deliverance

Deliverance is a distinct form of healing that has two dimensions. The first is deliverance from demonic influence. The second is deliverance from patterns and thoughts, lies of the enemy if you will, that prevent us from breaking through to others.

DEMONIC INFLUENCE

It is clear from examples in the New Testament that demons are real and that they play a part in the warfare that is being waged for the souls of humankind.[2] Jesus demonstrated his dominance over Satan in his ministry, at the cross, and in the resurrection.[3] Paul made it clear that our fight is not with flesh and blood, but with the unseen enemy that wants to steal everything that is good in life. Every time I get at odds with someone I

remind myself that the flesh and blood person across the table
is not my real enemy. What complicates matters is that just about
every Christian lives with lies and deceit in his or her life, so it's
hard to know if someone's behavior is being influenced by
demons. How can we know and are there times when we really
should confront a demon that is resident in a person? This is
not a book on demons. There are many good books on the subject.[4] The only way I know to deal with demonic influence is in
the natural flow of life. Here is what I look for and how I
approach it.

A person may be under the influence of a demonic power if
he or she has

- invited a spirit into his or her life through worship, music,
  or a séance
- had an occultic background, with family members or rel-
  atives who were witches or warlocks
- had a wrong reaction to emotional hurts that turned to
  bitterness
- a persistent pattern of sin that leads to addiction and dom-
  ination, such as pornography, drugs, gossip, sex, money

When you go beyond just the Word and desire God's power,
you will enter new and unknown realms of spiritual warfare.
Prophetically gifted people begin to identify strongholds in
people's lives. During our prayer and healing services someone will see erosion over a family or the stronghold of despair
over someone.

When I pray with people, I routinely ask about their background in an attempt to find a leading of how to pray. If a person tells me anything about the four areas above, it becomes
something to probe.

Recently after service a member came to me with a new person who was under attack by demonic forces. Before I had time
to be afraid, I told the member to bring the person into a nearby
room. A few people came along, and the next forty minutes were
eye openers for many of us. He was pulling at his skin and claw-
ing himself. His voice was deeper than usual as he was rejecting the help of those in the room. We spoke directly with the

demon and also with the man. It was exciting to see a room filled with novices challenging the demonic force and doing the right things. At the end of the very intense session, there was definitely a peace and release. I could identify when the spirit departed. It fled in the face of Jesus.

There are far too many people in our churches who are dominated by demonic forces. When we take doing the works of Jesus seriously, we can begin to help them. If we shy away and shrink from the task, they will continue in defeat. How might it change your church if no one in leadership or in the body were dominated by destructive habits, thoughts, and even physical maladies? I think you already know the answer to that question.

STRONGHOLDS IN THE MIND

For many years I believed that there are always a certain number of people you can't reach. There are many a management seminar and personality analysis that have confirmed my belief. The exceptions to the rule, I thought, are leaders who excel beyond the rest of us and are somehow able to communicate warmth and acceptance to nearly everyone. So I figured I would have trouble relating to 25 percent of the population, while the superstars had trouble with only 3 percent. God has shown me that my belief was a devilish stronghold that limited my ministry. There are many lies, such as this, that hold Christians captive and diminish our effectiveness.

> For though we live in the world, we do not wage war as the world does. The weapons we fight with are not the weapons of the world. On the contrary, they have divine power to *demolish strongholds*. We demolish *arguments* and every pretension that sets itself up against the knowledge of God, and we take captive every thought to make it obedient to Christ.
>
> 2 Corinthians 10:3–5

The word *stronghold* is derived from a word meaning "fortress" or "prison." A stronghold is an ideology, argument, or thought pattern that the enemy puts in place to challenge the truth of God. And these strongholds are calculated. They are erected by the enemy to imprison us all. If you can picture an ancient city surrounded by walls and punctuated with towers, then you have grasped Paul's warlike metaphor.

I encounter people who are trapped in a world of lies and deceit. They can't get a job because nobody wants someone over fifty. They can't be reconciled to their estranged parent because it hurts too much. They give up on friends because people never change. They give up on themselves because *they* can't change. Paul claims that we Christians have the weapons to bring down the walls of deceit and the towering lies that challenge the truth and sovereignty of God.

God showed me the lie that had imprisoned me, that I could reach only a limited number of people, that my personality plus their refusal to trust me were too much to overcome. But then I realized that Jesus loved me with a full commitment, that he didn't allow resistance and even rejection to stop him. He was willing to pay the ultimate price to love the world. Then I saw that he expected me to love others as he had loved me (John 13:34–35).

I had believed a lie. God tore down that stronghold and now I understand how to commit myself to love others until they experience God's love through me. Are there people that won't be reached? Sadly there are, but not because I wrote them off or gave up on them. When I am faced with a person who is upset with me, I take it as a challenge. My commitment is for that person to experience God's love through me, and I am willing to pay the price for that to happen. What happened to me is called deliverance.

Praying for Healing

How should we pray for healing? There are several things we must take into consideration. The clearest call to pray for the sick is found in James, the first New Testament book that was written. "Is any one of you sick? He should call the elders of the church to pray over him and anoint him with oil in the name of the Lord" (5:14). So many these days think that calling for the elders of the church is an officially sanctioned prayer that has more power than other's prayers. At least this is implied in that usually the elder prayer is one of last resort. The context is much more practical. If you aren't well enough to go to church, then ask the elders or their representatives to come to you. Elders are to be an example to the flock. Therefore, they should lead the charge in praying for the sick.

Preparing to Pray

When preparing to pray for someone, the first order of business is to talk with the person who has requested prayer. Are there sin issues, problems, and attitudes that could be the key to healing?

I think of the woman who had been crippled by a spirit for eighteen years. Jesus knew the problem and freed her. Immediately she stood straight (Luke 13:10–13).

On another occasion Jesus was able to heal because "the power of the Lord was present for him to heal the sick" (5:17). Already two issues are surfaced for prayer. Is there a demonic influence that must be confronted as the key to the healing? Is God present in a special way to heal?

When Jesus went into an ancient version of a hospital at the pool in Bethesda (John 5:1–9), he chose to heal one rather than many. Why? We can only speculate. We honestly don't know. This is the mystery of his will and presence. I can hear your protest. "What use is it? It's just too subjective, too uncertain." I agree, but we don't stop pursuing because we don't have it figured out. The more we seek his direction in how to pray, the more we will find his answers for each case.

The Prayer of Faith

James states the results of a prayer of faith. "And the prayer offered in faith will make the sick person well; the Lord will raise him up" (5:15). Is this an ironclad guarantee? I don't think so for a couple of reasons. There are some who say no because the guarantee applies only to those who are sick because of sin. This is built around the attempt to connect the thought of verse 15 with the next statement. "If he has sinned, he will be forgiven. Therefore confess your sins to each other and pray for each other so that you may be healed. The prayer of a righteous man is powerful and effective" (15–16).

Trying to explain the promise of verse 15 with the call to confess the sin in verse 16 is flawed. There is no direct connection with the promise to heal. The promise to heal is based on a prayer of faith by elders when they anoint with oil. The issue of sin is a reminder that very often people are sick because of an evil spirit or a pattern of sin. And in those cases, when the Holy Spirit reveals it, then healing can take place.

But we also know that many come for prayer who are not sick because of sin, and they are calling out in faith for healing. The calling of the elders is a significant sign of faith on the part of the sick. The promise for elders and righteous people who pray in faith is that their prayer will be powerful and effective. I take the prayer of faith to be one of complete confidence that God will heal.

Sometimes the elders will need to seek a direction from God as to how to pray. Through the discernment of the Spirit, revelation, or a word of prophecy, God often reveals a problem and how to pray about it. That would lead to a much stronger confidence level on the part of the people praying.

I believe this promise concerning the prayer of a righteous person must be taken into the larger context of the promises of prayer. There are conditions that go with prayer, such as faith, commandment keeping, obedience, praying according to God's will, and praying persistently, with humility, with fasting, and in agreement with others.[5] I would rather face the mystery of God when prayers for healing are not answered than try to wiggle out of praying for healing on illegitimate exegetical grounds. The prayer promise should stand alone as valid. When we get a no under these conditions, it is either because of a lack of faith or the mystery of God's own counsel. I can live with that for now, as I look through a glass darkly.

Who Prays?

Any believer who has faith can pray for the sick. This is what James indicates in 5:16 where he encourages people to pray for each other so they may be healed. A person doesn't need to be an elder to be "righteous and effective" in prayer. In verse 17 James uses Elijah as an example. He claims that Elijah was "a man just like us."

When I was a student at Oral Roberts University, people would come from all over the world to have Oral Roberts pray for them. Most of them made no appointment. They didn't even know if O. R. would be on campus. They were so determined to have him pray for their illness that the obstacles of distance and money were overcome.

People still do this. They want a certain person to pray over them. Why is that? People want results, and when it's a life-and-death issue, many of the restraints of life are released. People who would never darken the door of a charismatic church and have been critics of faith healers will discard their theology and criticism to get a healing. I understand this very human tendency that arises in a time of desperation.

I would want a person of faith to pray for me, but I don't think it needs to be an ordained clergy person. Elijah was a person just like any of us. He believed God and that made him a favorite for people's prayer requests. James's point is that any person can pray in faith, with powerful results.

In our prayer and healing services I simply call on people who feel called to pray for others. I find that compassion overpowers shyness; people take the microphone and start praying. After a few of these meetings, I have trouble getting the microphone back. So many are now confident about praying for healing.

Elders and Pastors

The titles elder and pastor have the same meaning in Scripture. Various traditions have renamed elders deacons and pastors ministers. For our discussion I refer to the teaching and managing elders defined by Paul in 1 Timothy 5:17. The church now often has paid elders called pastors. Are the prayers of elders/pastors special or more powerful? It depends on their faith and maturity level like anyone else. It is important that elders/pastors be good examples in prayer. Both Testaments give a special place to their prayers for the people they are to oversee. "Woe to the shepherds . . . who only take care of themselves!

. . . You have not strengthened the weak or healed the sick or bound up the injured" (Ezek. 34:2, 4).

The New Testament example is of course James and it seems clear that elders/pastors have a special authority to pray for those in the community of faith. When they pray for you, however, it does not increase the likelihood of your being healed. Rather, their prayers are special in that they represent the force of the entire community of believers, and by nature of who they are, their prayers should be stronger. The implication of the James passage is that the elders' prayer would be one that is coming from righteous men. The idea of righteousness is more than a positional standing by faith. It means evidence in their life that causes others to think of them as righteous. It does not necessarily mean that they have more faith than other believers.

The Gift of Healing

You may recall that at our first prayer and healing service I asked if anyone had the gift of healing. No one raised a hand. I could have but didn't want to encourage the stereotype that only clergy have the show-stopper gifts. *No one* raised his or her hand—quite a statement in a room of hundreds. Many of those present had been Christians for a long time; they knew the Bible very well; they knew all the Christian lingo. They listened to the acceptable Christian radio station; they had been to all the important conferences; they had read the right books. But there was an entire dimension of ministry about which they knew nothing. What a tragedy! All the physical needs in the room and no one gifted to address them.

Now in our church we have several who sense the gift of healing. I encourage them to exercise their gift, to take risks, to pray in faith. Those with the gift of healing operate in the four realms where healing is needed: spiritual, physical, inner or damaged emotions, and deliverance from demonic influences and destructive thought patterns. I yearn for a church populated with people who can minister with healing, where people can be delivered from the devilish maladies that the enemy has cast on us. It is part of Lucifer's plan to keep in storage the divinely powerful weapons God has made available to the church. My heart hurts for the unhealed, the undelivered, and the unrealized dreams of victory and peace.

The issues and answers in this chapter form a theological platform concerning healing on which we can stand. The platform provides a foundation on which to build a healing community. But we can't leave this subject without confronting the complexity and confusion that swirls around our second question, Why does God sometimes choose not to heal?

10

Discovering Obstacles
to Healing

Why did my mother suffer so long before she died? Why won't God heal my son of drug addiction? Lord, why won't you take away the nightmares. Lord, I'm afraid, and you haven't given me peace. Why not? I'm in pain. Don't you care? Won't you help me? These are questions wrapped in pain. Many people never seem to get over the suffering of loved ones and they become hostile toward God. Most bitterness has to do with someone dying, but there are other experiences that hurt just as much.

I am again dealing with the four types of malady defined in the last chapter. Healing does not always come in these areas: *spiritual*—why didn't my son accept Christ before he was killed in an automobile accident? *physical*—my father lost his mind and wore a diaper the last year of his life; *inner*—I've prayed, sought counsel, and am still riddled with anxiety; *deliverance*—my husband, the father of five, can't shake the cocaine habit that is destroying our family. These cases are real people I know who trust God, pray in faith, and have seen no results. What are some possible reasons why prayers aren't answered? When you look at a faith community filled with sick people and no one seems to be getting healed, what is going on? It should make us frustrated, angry, and in hot pursuit of some answers. Don't be passive on this. It is too important. Pursue answers and that means pursuing God. Some reasons that healing doesn't come include carnality, unbelief, and God's sovereign design.

Carnality

> Brothers, I could not address you as spiritual but as *worldly*[1]—mere infants in Christ. I gave you milk, not solid food, for you were not yet ready for it. Indeed, you are still not ready. You are still *worldly*. For since there is jealousy and quarreling among you, are you not *worldly?* Are you not acting like mere men?
>
> 1 Corinthians 3:1–3

Christians being driven by the flesh is old news. The premise is that a disciple who should be a teacher has allowed sin to retard his or her growth. This means the person has not believed God in several areas of life. He or she chooses not to submit to God and lets ego drive his or her appetites. As a result prayers are ineffective. A lot is wrong and part of that wrong is no healing.

There are three realms where carnality is manifested—behavior, doctrine, and attitude.

Behavior

"If we claim to have fellowship with him yet walk in the darkness, we lie and do not live by the truth" (1 John 1:6). Walking in the light is willingness to see our sin. It is a commitment to confess our wrongs when the Holy Spirit points them out. It is humbly accepting God's forgiveness. When we walk in the light, we are not afraid of any change God wants to make in our lives. We live a life of giving, not taking, of loving, not holding grudges, of a sweet interchange of intimacy with God.

Carnality is the opposite. It's about living a lie, living week after week and finding nothing to confess. It is being dominated by patterns of thought that don't permit an admission of weakness. The carnal Christian does not consciously ignore the voice of the Holy Spirit but has developed a state of mind that no longer hears his voice. In fact this person lives outside any ongoing communication with God. When the "ears to hear" are gone, patterns of disobedience become deeply ingrained.

The carnal father no longer sees his neglect of his children; the carnal husband slowly retreats from the nurture and care of his wife; the carnal wife starts having "business luncheons" with a male counterpart. They start sharing their disappointments in their marriages and begin looking to each other to meet emotional needs. You know the rest of the story.

Now picture 50 percent of your congregation living lives based on deeply ingrained lies. The damage is incalculable when the loss of spiritual insight and power are considered. This is why our battles are not against flesh and blood, but against principalities and powers and spiritual wickedness in high places.[2] Satan's strategy is to get disciples in comfortable ruts that turn discipleship into a safe journey insulated from the world by the Christian subculture. But more important, Satan wants to get Christians to live in comfort zones insulated from God himself and the movement of his Holy Spirit. It is subtle and sinister in every way and is how Satan robs the church of its power and potential. I assert that the reason the evangelical church is in decline in the West is that carnality is standard operating procedure. And we don't even know it! We have accepted it! May God forgive us. God can't heal those who think they are well (Matt. 9:12–13).

There are other aspects of sinful behavior that keep people from being healed:

1. Sin leading to death (1 Cor. 5:1–5.) This is when God turns a person over to the destruction of the body to save the soul. This is necessary when a Christian refuses to repent and turn away from shameful behavior.

2. Destructive habits (Gal. 6:7–9). This is the sowing and reaping principle. A person who damages his or her body through habits that are abusive and self-destructive will reap the consequences.

Doctrine

"Some have rejected these and so have shipwrecked their faith. Among them are Hymenaeus and Alexander, whom I have handed over to Satan to be taught not to blaspheme" (1 Tim. 1:19–20). To blaspheme is to do more than disagree on the periphery of scriptural understanding. Blasphemy is any teaching that challenges the deity of the Triune Godhead, the inspiration of Scripture, the reality of one's need for Christ, and the final judgment.

Many have selected a path outside the healing power of God. There have been the classic departures from the power of God via standard cults.[3] New doctrinal departures in the twentieth century have been liberal Christianity fueled by neoorthodoxy and contemporary theologians. There has been a gradual erosion of confidence in the fidelity of Scripture, the deity of Christ, the reality of a physical resurrection, and a literal second coming. This has drained mainline Christianity of its power and relevance. What once was the heart and soul of God's power in America is now a dying giant.

There are newer trends that now threaten evangelicals, such as the acceptance of homosexuality manifested in ordination of ministers and same-sex marriages performed in the church. The role of women and other issues are pressuring evangelicals to reinterpret the biblical text to satisfy the appetite for acceptance by one's culture. There continues to be a human need in the church for recognition on one hand and the avoidance of labeling on the other. No one wants to be hated for the sake of Christ (see John 16:33).

The propensity to go with the flow of culture is weakening the church and separating us from the power of God. There are many churches that have reasoned themselves out of the script of God's plan. They have sold their birthright for the cheap transitory price of cultural acceptance.

It is so sad to see theologians with marvelous intellectual gifts sit around and discount the truth of Scriptures. The Jesus Seminar is the best-known manifestation of this intellectual hubris. Those who have been called to study God have decided he was wrong and they are right. He no longer is the final judge. God is in the dock. The intelligentsia have prosecuted him and found him guilty. No one in this camp will be healed.

Attitude

"So, because you are lukewarm—neither hot nor cold—I am about to spit you out of my mouth" (Rev. 3:16). Laodicea was located halfway between Hierapolis and Colosse. The hot waters of Hierapolis would flow down from the elevated falls and meet the cold waters of Colosse at Laodicea. The mixture of the hot water loaded with minerals and the clear, cold water from Colosse created a terrible tasting, tepid water that one would immediately spit out. Christ drew on this very graphic and local experience to exhort the church to be of some use. The hot springs of Hierapolis were good for healing, the clear, cold waters of Colosse were good for drinking, but the mineral-laden, tepid waters of Laodicea were good for nothing. So be good for something, but don't stay lukewarm. Living with a tepid spirituality is good for nothing.

I used to think that the U.S. church was most like the church at Philadelphia, faithful to Christ with an open door of opportunity before it. I now think we are more like Laodicea, proud, thinking we are rich, but we are really naked and poor. We live in a spiritual slumber and are making very little difference. It is like we are asleep and the alarm is going off. We hit the snooze button a few times—we listen to the Word—but we finally turn the alarm off. We ask, "Why should I get up?" And God is shaking us. "Get up. It's time to go, to make an impact."

Historically, parents have been challenged in finding ways to get their teenagers out of bed. One of our sons was a very deep sleeper. He would sleep through alarms, turning them off without waking; he would sit up and talk to you in complete sentences and later not remember doing it. There were times when he would get up and walk to the bathroom and go back to bed,

never awake. In our efforts to wake him up, we got very creative. We tried loud music, coffee, food. Nothing worked. Then
we discovered the spray bottle. Take any ordinary pump spray
bottle, fill it with water, and do the following. Pump the spray
three times over the sleeping child, then run. If it doesn't work
the first time, repeat until it does. This worked on our son. It
made him so mad, he would get up and look for the culprit.

What will it take to wake up the church? It may require problems that force us to our knees, a challenge to our faith, sickness. How sad that it would take tragedy, persecution, or illness
to pull us out of our stupor! God loves us so much he might even
send problems to wake us. Then and only then can we be use-
ful, not something God wants to spit out. People will go to great
lengths to please self. We can become very creative in our doctrine and attitudes to justify our behavior. Lukewarm Christians
will remain in the company of the unhealed.

Unbelief

Jesus returned to his hometown. It is a lesson in how familiarity breeds spiritual blindness. Jesus couldn't do many miracles in Nazareth because of their lack of faith (Mark 6:5–6). The
locals were amazed at his teaching in the local synagogue; they
wondered how he became so wise. But then they started to size
him up. It is obvious from the text that Jesus was the oldest of
at least seven children.[4] Believing he couldn't possibly be authentic, they began to take offense at him. Their cynicism manifested
itself in unbelief, and Jesus couldn't do much there. What the
biblical writer considered not much would be revival in most
churches. "He could not do any miracles there, except lay his
hands on a few sick people and heal them." Tonight people will
gather in our sanctuary for a prayer and healing service. If I
thought there would be a few sick people healed, I would be
ecstatic. But we are led to believe from this encounter that a few
healings isn't much. The implication is that Jesus would like to
do much more if we would believe him.

If Jesus came to your church to minister, what would amaze
him? I can only speak for my genre of church, but I think he would

be amazed that we have tied his hands theologically. How can mortals tie the hands of God? Just as in Nazareth, Jesus could not heal much, and he chose not to violate his own rules and over-power unbelief. God's hands are tied by his own promises and integrity. He requires faith to be present before he takes action to heal (Heb. 11:6). *We have rendered Christ helpless by saying we are open to his work but then not committing ourselves in faith.*

Jesus never said, "Blessed are the open" or "According to your openness, be it done unto you" or "If you have openness the size of the grain of a mustard seed, you can move a mountain." Openness is shrinking from faith; it is unbelief. When someone says, "I believe God can heal. I am open to it," it only means they do not yet believe. I don't want to impugn the motives or heart of the openhearted. Openness just doesn't qualify as faith.

Belief Is Specific

Jesus was traveling to Jericho when a blind man called out, "Jesus, Son of David, have mercy on me!" (Luke 18:38). Some tried to hush him, but he would not be denied. He called out a second time. Jesus then asked him the question he asks us all, "What do you want me to do for you?" The blind man was specific, "Lord, I want to see" (v. 41).

The prayer of faith is not, "Please guide the doctors, comfort the family, and help us to believe that all things work together for good." There is no real expectation in such a prayer that God will directly intervene. This is a supporting prayer, a fallback position from what you really want, but it isn't the prayer of faith that calls on God to intervene and give you what you need. What I am getting at is that too many of us use the supporting or fall-back-position prayer as *the prayer.*

Tonight I will face people with brain cancer, bone cancer, lymphoma, and leukemia, and they don't want to hear a fall-back, risk-free prayer. They want someone to rush the throne of God and break down the gates of hell. They want a community of believers to pray specifically for supernatural healing right then and there. We all know the final choice belongs to God, but if it is already decided, then why have a prayer meeting and put everybody through a futile exercise? If we pray in faith asking

God for what we really want, there will be more healing and many miracles and the power of God will be revealed. Yes, there will be disappointments, but God tells us to keep asking. Don't give up. Don't be missing in action.

Knowing the Bible Is Not Faith

In one of his many conflicts with the Pharisees Jesus made a distinction between study and faith. He was accusing them of not believing in him because their hearts had turned against him. He told them they had never heard God's voice or seen his form, and the Word of God did not dwell in them. In other words, they didn't have a clue. They had totally missed the point by their lack of faith, and all their study had done them no good. "You diligently study the Scriptures because you think that by them you possess eternal life. These are the Scriptures that testify about me, yet you refuse to come to me to have life" (John 5:39–40).

There is no primary parallel between Christians who do believe in Jesus and the Pharisees who did not. There is, however, a parallel when Christians refuse to believe certain parts of the Scripture. Some of the most knowledgeable believers are paralyzed by stacks of information and alternative interpretations of the Bible. Knowing options can feed our fears when we must put on the line our faith in God and his Word. I am not suggesting a departure from the serious study of the Bible. But don't let the various schools of thought and refinements of Greek exegesis cause you not to pray in faith. I know the conflicts both theologically and philosophically concerning healing. I recommend believing the most and the best about what God desires to do. Don't spend your time in the world of "what God *could* do." Focus on what he *will* do in response to our faithful prayers.

What Does Faith Look Like?

There is an old story that teaches us about faith. It concerns a circus performer who would push a wheelbarrow across a high wire strung thirty feet above the ground. There was no net and the high-wire artist enjoyed goading the audience. To make things more lively, he would put some bricks in the wheelbarrow and cross over the wire and back the first time. There was of course the drum roll as he crossed and the applause on his return.

"How many of you think I can do it again?" Many applauded, and people put money in the wheelbarrow to see him do it again. On returning from his second trek, he receives thunderous applause. The suspense was building as he challenged the audience one more time, "How many of you think I can do it a third time?" The crowd went wild. "Who will be the first then to get into the wheelbarrow?" The noise drained from the crowd and nervous laughter brought the act to an end. There were no takers. Faith is like getting into the wheelbarrow.

I have been inspired by many writers, one of which is Dutch Sheets and his fine book *Intercessory Prayer*.[5] His wife had an ovarian cyst, and the doctor was not sure if it was benign or malignant. The doctor wanted to remove it to be safe, but Dutch decided he wanted to give God a chance. He asked the doctor to give him two months to pray. He prayed one hour daily for a month. He pictured the ovarian cyst shrinking. His wife's pain began to recede, which meant the cyst was shrinking. His wife finally told him that the pain was gone. A subsequent ultrasound confirmed that the cyst was gone.

That is faith, taking a different approach and making a commitment to the truth of Scriptures. This is particularly challenging when someone's life is on the line. Dutch and his wife would have submitted to surgery if the cyst had remained. How many of us would have just gone ahead with the surgery at the beginning? How many of us miss the blessing of God because we choose not to believe?

How Can We Be So Foolish?

Many had come to our prayer and healing service, a number of families for the first time. They had come expecting miracles. The family of newborn twins, one facing life-threatening surgery believed God would do a miracle. I felt powerless, more so than usual. There were various forms of cancer and nerve and muscle disorders. Some people were plagued with depression and demonic oppression. As we worshiped I called out to God for a sense of his anointing. I must be honest. I was really emotionally flat; heaven had lowered its ceiling to just above my head.

I thought, *How foolish I am to ask these people to walk the plank of faith with me! There could be great blessing but as I look into their eyes I can see the desperation: the father of three who is losing a battle with leukemia; the woman who is running from her demons; the mother of four children, three of whom have some scary symptoms; another parent waiting for a biopsy on her son's skin.* Earlier in the day my heart was palpitating more than it had in months. I had to pray, "God, I am leading a healing service and can't even get you to do anything about me." My faith seemed weak, but I spoke faith regardless of my feelings. I decided to cling to God's Word, to totally depend on him.

Two hours and many tearful prayers later, God had broken through. We had not seen any visible healings—most of the requests were such that you could not immediately tell. Some felt the same way, but we do expect God to work powerfully in healing as a result of our gathering.

But there were some amazing moments. About halfway through the evening, there were circles of people gathered around those in need, praying and ministering. Behind me was an ongoing demonic oppression issue. There were the tears, cries, moans, and groans that accompany such work. There was the woman who was fighting depression, thinking she didn't deserve to live. People were praying for her, hugging her, weeping with her. People were sensing God's presence through the spiritual gifts of others. Even those who didn't get healed right then and there know that they now have a family of people praying for them. I feel so foolish and weak at times, but I will keep on marching into the fire. I believe that is the only place where we will find his glory.

Sovereign Decision

Not everyone is healed; it could be no more than 50 percent, who, after prayer, experience physical healing. Those healed spiritually or emotionally or who are delivered from demonic oppression are more numerous than those healed of physical ailments. How do we look those who are not healed in the eye?

What hope can we give them? They continue to suffer; their families start sliding into despair.

The Redemptive Value of Suffering

We live between the worlds of power and pain. No one taught this better than an unhealed servant. "To keep me from becoming conceited because of these surpassingly great revelations, there was given me a thorn in my flesh, a messenger of Satan, to torment me" (2 Cor. 12:7).

Not everyone knows the reason he or she is sick. I think it would be safe to make that almost no one. Paul gives his theory as to why he is unhealed. He knows himself and thinks his special experiences would cause him to be conceited. Paul's theology allows for Satan to attack him and then God to use the affliction as a means to achieve humility. Can we safely say that every illness we have has a purpose? I am not sure about knowing the reason for the malady, but I am sure that God can use it to build our character. But Paul's next statement clearly shows that character building is not his heart's desire.

"Three times I pleaded with the Lord to take it away from me. But he said to me, 'My grace is sufficient for you, for my power is made perfect in weakness'" (v. 8). This must have been frustrating for Paul. He had prayed for and seen great works of power accomplished. During his ministry in Ephesus people would merely touch a cloth that had touched Paul and they were healed. Paul himself had been miraculously healed. He even raised a sleepy listener from the dead who fell out of the window during Paul's sermon (Acts 20:7–12). And now, when Paul asks three times that God remove his "thorn," God turns him down. For a man of Paul's experience, asking three times is a lot. He had been up to the third heaven and seen things he could tell no man. Yet an unhealed Paul was willing to accept his illness when he knew the reason. And then he turned toward the good that could come from it. This is not an easy process for any of us, to be the wounded healer, to pray for others and see them healed, while the old saw, "Physician heal thyself," haunts our spirit.

This is an odd compensation when compared with being healed. Based on his personal experience, he writes a theology of suffering. "Therefore I will boast all the more gladly about my weaknesses, so that Christ's power may rest on me" (v. 9).

Now wait a minute. All this so Christ's power may rest on him? Hadn't Christ's power already been present and impressive in his life? Paul makes a shift in his thinking that requires a different kind of miracle. He accepted his malady with thanksgiving. Christ's power in him to minister to others was enhanced. Humility is a prerequisite for the free flow of God's grace (see 1 Peter 5:5–6). His final statement is the paradox of living with and for God: "That is why, for Christ's sake, I delight in weaknesses, in insults, in hardships, in persecutions, in difficulties. For when I am weak, then I am strong" (v. 10).

So you can be a bald man selling hairbrushes, a liar seeking to tell the truth, an addict who preaches deliverance, as long as your heart's desire is to teach God's strength in your weakness. Jesus was wounded and died for us, but his suffering brought healing. We can be suffering from some physical malady yet be used as a powerful instrument of healing for someone else. We can boast then in God's power and plan rather than our own.

I would rather be the healed healer, not the wounded healer. I will keep asking. Paul asked three times. I top that daily. In the meantime, I and others find comfort in God's caring and purposeful strategy. I like what the late Malcolm Muggeridge said during a *Firing Line* interview with William F. Buckley: "The only thing that's taught one anything is suffering, not success, not happiness. The only thing that really teaches one what life's about is affliction."

If we are going to celebrate divine healing from suffering, we must also celebrate divine endurance in suffering. God allows his children to be tested. The models are Job and Jesus. Sometimes we are privileged to follow in their footsteps. "Have you considered my servant [put your name here]?" (Job 1:8).

During my first year as a pastor, God brought a dying woman into my life. She was a retired missionary who was dying from cancer. I visited her regularly and discovered a wonderful truth. People who die with special grace minister and teach others, especially young pastors. Her lectures to me and the advice she gave me were life changing. The *awe* factor was present in her suffering.

A Mystery

Many a skeptic has blared, "If Jesus can heal anyone, why don't you preachers empty out the hospitals?" It has been said many times by preachers, "Jesus walked by many sick people he never healed." The reality in the statement addresses the mystery and timing of God's choices. When Jesus went to the pool of Bethesda, there were many sick lying about (John 5:1–15). The people were blind, lame, and paralyzed. The man was the only one healed. Later Jesus found him and told him, "Stop sinning or something worse may happen to you" (v. 15). This was an ominous warning, also possibly a hint as to why some get sick.

A pastor went to pray for a baby born without a brain. The couple had already lost two children. The baby was not healed; it died the next day. After arriving home, the pastor learned that a woman in the church had been healed of venereal disease. This was a woman who had not been particularly repentant. The pastor felt the anger rising up inside. How could God heal a woman who did not deserve it and let an innocent little boy die? The Lord spoke to him, "Who deserves healing? I will dispense my mercy. I don't need your advice."

I have already mentioned the man in our congregation who is suffering from leukemia. His attitude has been a tremendous example of strong faith. He continues to serve in his ministry with college students, minister to his family, and teach in the church. He always smiles and has a spirit of thankfulness. So far the regular and ongoing prayers of the saints have not caused God to act in our friend's behalf, but I see God's power in this man's attitude and his heart response. That of course is miraculous, but you know what I mean, no physical touch from God is in evidence.

I watch another pastor on television who was diagnosed with prostate cancer. He started talking about God's healing power on the program and claimed his healing based on Isaiah 53:5, "by his wounds we are healed," the portion of Scripture that teaches healing as one of the benefits of being a Christian. He then asked for and was able to get another biopsy and PSA. He was found to be cancer free. I rejoice that he has been healed and it encourages me to see such works of power. But this pastor is mean and surly and treats people like lower forms of life. I want to throw up my hands and ask, "If you are willing to heal the meanest pastor I know, why not your humble and gracious servant?"

You could say that I am downright angry about the sick people in our congregation. My anger isn't safe anger. I haven't redirected it to Satan—that would be acceptable. My anger is toward God. Why is he withholding? I need to know; I want to know. I will do anything that would cause him to let the floodgates of his healing power open.

The Bible never belittles human disappointment. The Book of Job contains one chapter of restoration that follows forty-one of anguish. Job's anguish itself is a sign, an aching, a hunger for something better. And faith is, in the end, a kind of homesickness—for a home we have never visited but have never once stopped longing for. Job was able to work it out in his mind and he died a happy man.

The cross of Christ demolished the myth that life is fair. God's responsibility is to make choices; ours is to respond to him with our own. He directs: "In every thing give thanks: for this is the will of God in Christ Jesus concerning you" (1 Thess. 5:18 KJV). The only way we can give thanks in everything is to have another belief: "And we know that in all things God works for the good of those who love him, who have been called according to his purpose" (Rom. 8:28). Sorry, folks. I wish I could tell you I have discovered the Colonel's twenty-one secret herbs and spices, but it comes down to trust.

The unhealed among us look to the future. We hold on to the hope that the answer is not a no, but a not yet. We hold on to his hand, even in the pain and disappointment. We hold on to the belief that he is working some miracle with friends and family who need him. Some of us realize that it is time to enter his presence—that of course is the permanent healing.

Don't postpone your own miracle. If you need spiritual healing, the key is repentance. If you need physical healing, the key is faith and trust. If it is inner healing, open up and let him into your secret world of wounds that only he can clean and fill. If it is deliverance from demonic forces, allow God and his properly gifted children to minister to your needs. Just don't be the reason you are not healed.

11

Hearing God's Voice

Do you hear voices? This is a common question asked of troubled people. If the answer is yes, you could find yourself under a doctor's care or in a lockdown ward at your local hospital. Popular culture associates hearing voices with psychological disorders, serial killers, and religious kooks. But it is common for a follower of Christ to say, "God spoke to me; God is leading me; the Lord told me."

This is familiar language from the Bible. Many of us cut our teeth on the story of the boy prophet Samuel (1 Sam. 3:1–18). Three times in the night, God called his name. Twice he went to his spiritual mentor, Eli. Both times Eli told Samuel to go back to bed. The third time Eli realized it was God speaking to Samuel. His instructions were, go back to bed and if it happens again, say, "Speak, LORD, for your servant is listening" (v. 9).

Samuel didn't recognize God's voice because the word of God had not yet been revealed to him. Is it possible for God to speak to us and we don't recognize his voice? Samuel was young and inexperienced. What would be our reason for not hearing God's voice? Have we trained ourselves not to listen? I believe there is substantial evidence that indeed the evangelical church's unintended legacy to its people is a spiritual "tin ear." The sad result is disciples living in a spiritual news blackout. Yes, the Bible is the primary and foundational communication, but there is so much more involved in relating to a living God. Devotees to other gods may pour over the writings of Mohammed, Confucius, and Karl Marx, but those men are dead. We are in relationship with a living person, the God of the universe. He will speak to us today.

One of the most popular PBS programs on the West Coast is Huell Howeser's *California Gold*. One of my favorite episodes is about Charlie Frank, a retired elephant trainer. For many years Charlie had been the personal trainer for Neeta. Charlie and Neeta had worked in the circus for many years until they both retired—Charlie to a mobile home and Neeta to the San Diego Zoo. Charlie and Neeta had not seen each other in fifteen years when Huell Howeser took Charlie to San Diego for a reunion. There was great suspense, for no one really knew if Neeta would remember Charlie.

I was glued to the television as Charlie looked out at ten elephants and immediately was able to pick out Neeta. Huell and Charlie whispered about whether Neeta would remember. Charlie had his doubts. Charlie stood a long way off and called "Neeta, come here, girl." This huge animal turned its head and started running toward Charlie. He walked toward her and they touched. She nuzzled her trunk against the old man. Tears began to roll down my cheeks. Charlie was crying, Huell was crying, and thousands of viewers were reaching for the Kleenex. Then the most amazing thing happened. Charlie put Neeta through their entire performance routine. They hadn't seen each other in fifteen years and it was like they had never been apart.

As I wiped away the tears, what touched me was the depth of the relationship. It was about the love between old Charlie and the two-ton Neeta with an even bigger heart. Neeta knew Charlie's voice. When he spoke, it was distinct from the thousands

of voices that she heard every day. Many had called out to the
elephants, and Neeta never responded. She didn't run over to
them and nuzzle them. She never went through her routine, not
even for one person. It was Charlie's love and Charlie's voice
alone that caused Neeta to respond. Jesus said, "My sheep hear
my voice" (John 10:27 KJV). They know me. It is tragic when
mature Christians don't know God's voice.

You may respond, "I read the Bible every day"—a very fine
protest indeed. If that is true, God will speak to you every day
through his Word. God's personal touch comes in other ways as
well. He may give you specific direction through a gifted person
in the body, for example.

A young Israeli told me that he was impressed to inform me
that I would be going through the fire. That is not what I wanted
to hear, but he said it would be fire and water. That meant great
testing along with great blessing. Now that I am surrounded by
fire and water, I feel as though God has prepared me for it.
Rather than lamenting it, I am relishing it, because I know it is
part of his plan for me.

There are many people who have been taught that God is finished talking to us. He gave us everything we need in the Scriptures. The sad part of all this is that many people who believe
this do not read the Scriptures. They wait for the pastor to teach
it to them on Sunday or they listen to a Scripture lesson on the
radio. That is better than nothing, but people who are not in the
Word daily have very little chance of hearing God's voice.

The Ways God Speaks

There are a number of templates we could use to discuss how
God speaks to us.[1] F. B. Meyer, a renowned Bible teacher of his
time, spoke of God speaking through the "three lights."[2] The concept of the inner light that guides is based on Proverbs 20:27:
"The lamp of the LORD searches the spirit of a man." A more literal rendering is "the spirit of man is the Lord's lamp." God uses
our spirit as a tool of guidance. Dallas Willard puts it this way,
"God comes to us precisely in and through our thoughts, per-

ceptions and experiences and can approach our conscious life only through them, for they are the substance of our being."[3]

God speaks to us in a way that is consistent with how he has created us. And who is better qualified to use the equipment than the designer? He works through sight, sound, touch, and he sometimes has been known to use smell and taste. I like the prayer of James Dobson, "Lord, I need to know what you want me to do, and I am listening. Please speak to me through my friends, books, magazines I pick up and read, and through circumstances."

Take a few minutes every day to ask God for guidance and for him to speak to you. Believe that he is not finished talking and that he wants to guide you through various means. In this chapter I will discuss three issues. The first will be the three lights of guidance. The second is how to recognize God's voice. The third is the kind of person who hears God's voice.

The Three Lights

Circumstances

From time to time most Christians experience God speaking to them through events or situations. For some the circumstances are very special.[4] But most disciples look for God to communicate his will through the open-door, closed-door policy. I don't see open and closed doors as answers but as opportunities to pray. For example, a man gets an opportunity for a promotion in his career. He sees more money, more responsibility, and frankly, more house. Immediately he puts out a fleece. The fleece concept is taken from the experience of Gideon in the Old Testament when he responded in fear and unbelief to God's clear leading (Judg. 6:36–40). Gideon didn't even believe the first time God confirmed his direction; he wanted a second confirmation.

The person in our example uses the fleece idea because God's will is unclear. Actually he is asking for a sign, a sense of direction. He may use as the fleece the sale of his home in a certain time frame for a certain amount. Of course, if he's already taken the promotion, his true desire to know God's will is questionable. The only time we can ask God for a sign is if we wait on a decision until after God has given the direction.

An open door does not mean that a disciple should walk through it. A closed door does not mean a determined follower shouldn't persist in knocking that door down in prayer.

In the middle 1980s I was pastor of a very challenging church. There was a lot of conflict, and one day I just broke. I left my office by the side door and drove home to an empty house. I took out a legal pad and began to organize my thoughts. I was thirty-six and had a graduate degree. I made a list of other careers I could pursue. FBI agent was at the top of the list. Police officer, insurance salesman, lawyer, basketball coach were also there—a good list. I looked up the FBI in the yellow pages and called. I found out I was too tall, too old, and not a lawyer. So I crossed off FBI agent, and before long I eliminated lawyer and police officer as well. Three hours later only one thing remained on my list—Amway salesman. Amway was an open door. In fact it was the only open door I could find, but I am glad today that I didn't walk through it.

The real engine that drives the decision should be God's calling on one's life with regard to personal mission. This is determined by a sense of right fit in ministry, based on giftedness rather than an open door. God has called every Christian to ministry, implicit to that calling is submission to a spiritual authority. Every believer needs to identify his or her spiritual authority. In most cases it is the local church.

So I went to the authorities in my life and crafted a future that fit my calling. God used circumstances along with other people to help me find my way. The happy result was my involvement in church planting. Those years were as good and productive as any years I've had.

So you get fired or your business is losing its viability or you get sick. It is time to ask God, "What is it, Lord?" The people of Israel during the days of Malachi were not giving to the ministry, and God disciplined them with crop failure. It was out of that crisis that he spoke and because of their pain, they listened.

Will a man rob God? Yet you rob me.

But you ask, "How do we rob you?"

In tithes and offerings. You are under a curse—the whole nation of you—because you are robbing me. Bring the whole tithe into the storehouse, that there may be food in my house. Test me

in this," says the LORD Almighty, "and see if I will not throw open
the floodgates of heaven and pour out so much blessing that you
will not have room enough for it.

Malachi 3:8–10

God used the prophet Malachi to interpret the circumstances.
One of the three lights is circumstances, but I would not make
a decision or consider that God has spoken without the confirmation of the other two lights.

I often hear Christians say that if God's people do God's
work God's way, there will be no financial or physical needs.
I wonder how that would fly in Rwanda or other Third World
countries where Christians faithfully starve to death. This
aphorism makes it sound as though any financial problems
in the home or the church are a result of disobedience. But
no one really knows the reason for some of our dilemmas or
the answer to some moral riddles. Certainly there are cases
when financial problems are a result of disobedience, but
sometimes financial problems come as a result of obedience.
God may speak to us through a shortage of funds. It causes
individuals and institutions alike to get on their knees in
prayer.

I often hear that a church that is short of money is under a
curse and it is because the leadership isn't doing their job. Sometimes that is true, but Malachi doesn't lay the blame at the feet
of the leaders alone but attributes it to the general population.
I would say the message God is giving through Malachi is that
when individuals begin to trust God, then the windows of heaven
will open.

If the leaders teach the responsibility to tithe and do it themselves, the onus is on the people to respond. So the lack of funds
in that case would not be a lack of vision or good leadership, it
would be other factors that cause the people not to respond. The
reasons could be consumer debt, addiction to material wealth,
or a callused heart that does not respond to need. So the maxim
should go, "When God's people do God's will God's way, when
the people respond in obedience, then all needs will be met."
When financial problems strike, seek God's wisdom and ask him
to speak to you specifically. Ask him to lay before you any direct

correlation between sin and what has happened. I believe that he will.

Impressions of the Spirit

How do you determine whether you are hearing God's interior voice or just another stray thought? You are walking beside the perfume counter and you hear a voice say, "Buy that perfume." You are driving home and you hear, "Go into McDonald's. Get two Big Macs and a large order of fries." The man next to you on an airplane is being obnoxious and you hear a voice say, "Punch him out."

When we hear an inner voice, we must first ask, Does it make sense? It certainly doesn't make sense for a person taking cholesterol-lowering medication to get the two Big Macs and the large order of fries. So a lot of the inner-voice-thing is the silly thoughts that rumble around in our heads on a daily basis. When we hear from God, it is normally in response to our request for help in a personal quest of some kind. We need to hear from him to make a decision or know how to minister. This is the second light.

The second question we must ask is, Does it agree with Scripture? If you want to punch the guy out, you can be sure that Scripture says to injure a person is wrong. To be vindictive is wrong. To strike out against others is wrong.

The easy part is to dismiss the silly whimsical thoughts and the anti-Christian ideas that flow through our heads. Let's face it. There is a lot of rubble floating on the surface of our minds— the mental litter of a troubled and flawed society. It's somewhat more difficult to distinguish the voice of God from our own when we are seeking his choice among options that could all fit into his will. Let me give you three examples of people who heard God's voice and obeyed.

THE SPIRIT-FILLED USHER

I have often said that ushering itself is not a calling that can stretch your faith, but a spirit-filled usher can be a wonderful tool in the hands of God. The advantage of being committed to making disciples of every member is that ushers are included.

One of our ushers heard a voice. He was leaning against the wall during the service and saw a person he didn't know doing the same on the other side of the sanctuary. The voice said, "Go over and pray for that person." He questioned the impression. *Nah! Can't be God. The guy will think I'm crazy. If he is new, he won't come back, and if he is a regular, he will leave.* But he resisted his fear and approached the man, "I felt impressed to pray for you. Does that make sense to you?" The man teared up. He was discouraged. He had come to church to find an answer, and God delivered through the Spirit-filled usher who listened to God's voice.

THE ENTHUSIASTIC CHURCH MEMBER

Two women were having lunch at Taco Bell. One was exuding joy as she talked about her church and pastor. Her voice carried across several tables, and a man nearby couldn't help but overhear. When the man got up to leave, he stopped at their table, "Where is this church and who is this pastor you like so much?"

She spoke about the church and the pastor, and she talked about the current sermon series on special needs. The man walked out and got into his car but sat there for a moment. The woman heard that inner voice. "Go out there. He needs you." It is not normal for this middle-aged, single woman to chase down married men in the parking lot of Taco Bell, but she dashed out the door just as the man was backing out. "Wait!" she cried. "Can I pray for you?"

The man parked his car; he bared his soul, talking about his invalid wife and that he was the caregiver. He spoke of his depression and difficulties. The brave disciple then spent a few minutes praying with the man and ministered to his needs.

Too many of us miss these kinds of opportunities. We hold back and miss out on so much. We need to trust the inner voice, to experiment with it, be willing to make a few mistakes and look stupid. That is why most of us don't do it. We are afraid of failure and rejection. That is a small price to pay in contrast to the great dividends.

THE OBEDIENT PASTOR

One of our youth pastors passed a seedy looking hitchhiker on the freeway. The still small voice said, "Go back and pick that guy up." Everyone knows you don't do that, it's not safe, and there is no future in it. He passed one exit then a second, arguing with himself, trying to dispel the impression. He got off at the next exit and made his way back to the hitchhiker. He pulled over and the man got in. Three days later the man was a new Christian, had made things right with his family, and was on his way to a new life.

It is true that we will make mistakes as we listen for God's voice. I have approached people with comments I thought were from God, and they have said, "No, that is not me." Or "I don't know what you are talking about."

I look at learning to hear God's voice a lot like reading my gas gauge. It isn't entirely broken, but sometimes it will register empty right after I put twenty dollars of gas in the tank. It never registers more than is in the tank, but it does register less. I don't know for sure how much fuel I have, but I have a feel for it. Listening to God's voice through impressions is not an exact science. But the more we get tuned in, the "tin ear" of the heart is transformed into a finely tuned receiver.

Passages from the Bible

The primary source for hearing from God is the Bible, the third light. The more we read it, the greater the chances are that God will speak to us through it. But there is a significant difference between Bible study and asking God to speak to my life in a meaningful way through the Scriptures. A. W. Tozer put it this way:

> It is altogether possible to be instructed in the rudiments of the faith and still have no real understanding of the whole thing. And it is possible to go on to become expert in Bible doctrine and not have spiritual illumination, with the result that a veil remains over the mind preventing it from apprehending the truth in its spiritual essence.[5]

Our primary purpose in meditating on the Bible is to meet with Christ and hear his voice. There is a huge difference between reading and meditating. To meditate is to mull something over again and again, in the way a cow chews its cud. It includes visualizing yourself obeying God's Word and writing down various applications. It is listing changes that you need to make or people that you should speak with in response to the Word.

A few years back I was confronted with a difficult decision. I was beginning to see the fruit of my labor in my church plant. I was into my sixth year, we were growing, and I was really enjoying myself. I also had a growing interest in training leaders and many invitations to do so. My books on leadership and discipleship were opening doors and I had a wonderful opportunity presented to me of developing a plan for training leaders nationwide. I had counseled with others, I had thought through my personal mission statement, and I had spent time presenting my future to the Lord. I was torn. I wanted both the church and the training network dream.

I was walking on the beach talking to God when the story of Jesus' telling Peter and company to cast their nets out into the deep came to mind. I asked God to speak to me and I received a strong impression, *Cast out into the deep.* I couldn't shake the phrase. God burned it into my soul. I knew then and there what I should do. I returned home and made arrangements to leave the pastorate and begin the training network.

God spoke specifically to my situation. How did I know? It is an inner knowing that comes with intimacy. It is like the disciples who talked with Jesus on the Emmaus road—their hearts burned within them (Luke 24:32). It is asking the Holy Spirit to speak to you and then waiting on him. It took several weeks of prayer and meditation before God's Word burned in my soul.

The three lights have safeguards. They depend on each other and they hold each other accountable. Circumstances, strong impressions of the soul, and passages in the Bible work together so we can hear God's voice. Let's say you get a very strong urge to marry a kind, loving, attractive, rich unbeliever. The stars seem to be in alignment, the stock market is bullish, but the answer is still no! When an option opposes the plain teaching of Scripture, then no amount of impressions or other signs can make it right.

Recognizing God's Voice

Elijah was in a funk. He was on the run from Jezebel. He was filled with fear and had lost perspective. God spoke to him and told him to go stand on the mountain in the presence of the Lord. "I will pass by," he said.

> Then a great and powerful wind tore the mountains apart and shattered the rocks before the LORD, but the LORD was not in the wind. After the wind there was an earthquake, but the LORD was not in the earthquake. After the earthquake came a fire, but the LORD was not in the fire. And after the fire came a gentle whisper. When Elijah heard it, he pulled his cloak over his face and went out and stood at the mouth of the cave.
>   Then a voice said to him, "What are you doing here, Elijah?"
>
>   1 Kings 19:11–13

We live in a very noisy world. Trying to hear the gentle whisper of God is like trying to find a station on your radio in the midst of the static at 3:00 A.M. in the Nevada desert. The Lord was not in the obvious and the loud. It takes experience to sort out what he is saying. The more mature our ability to hear God's voice, the less the role played by dreams, visions, and other altered states of communication. The general character of God's voice seems to be an inner whisper, impression, or passion.

This is a subjective arena, but we *can* learn to recognize God's voice. We will know it in the way we know the voices of other intimates. They are all gone now, but I can replay in my head the voices of my mother, grandparents, and uncles. There is an imprint that is made that never leaves us. When we seek God with perseverance for a lifetime, we know his voice. Jesus said in John 10:27 that we would recognize his voice. I choose to believe him.

The Tone of His Voice

Some people talk too fast; then there are others who seem to have difficulty getting the words out. When you think of people close to you, what characteristics describe their speech patterns?

Are they fast, slow, direct, indirect, passionate, cold, demanding? In the same way, describe how God spoke to you in the past. If you describe his voice as cold, demanding, or laying guilt on you, IT IS NOT THE VOICE OF GOD. The voice of the enemy is one of shortcuts and loopholes. The prototype, of course, is his one-on-one encounter with Jesus in the wilderness (Matt. 4:1–11). Satan tried to short-circuit the redemptive rescue plan. He tempted Jesus to work miracles that contradicted the plan. Satan will come to us with a good appearance. The key to rejecting him is knowledge of God's will. When you think you hear: *All people go to heaven. You don't really need to divide people by preaching the gospel,* you know that's not from God. When you hear: *Not every believer should share his or her faith; let the gifted do it,* you know it isn't from God. You know it is not from God when you hear: *Go ahead. Marry the unbeliever.* When you get an impression to correct someone "in the Lord" but don't have the facts straight or the spiritual authority to do so, you know the directive is not from God. Jesus resisted Satan's suggestions, based on his knowledge of God's Word and God's plan.

God never attempts to convince us. He simply states the facts and makes his point. His voice is self-authenticating. It carries its own authority. It is not a debate when God speaks. It is direction. God doesn't cut deals; he doesn't lay out a series of incentives. God's tone is direct, affirming, and clear. He doesn't flower his language with frivolous compliments. He gives us what we need in a way that motivates us.

When God spoke to me with the inner whisper, *Bill, I'm going to break you. Don't run,* I took it as a loving and wondrous statement. It was clear and firm, but saturated by the Holy Spirit with love. It wasn't what I wanted to hear, but it was what I needed to know in order to hold up.

The Content of His Message

What kind of things does God say to us? As I've already observed, some people argue that the Bible tells us all we really need to know. I agree that the major strands of thought needed to live for God are provided in Scripture (2 Peter 1:3–4). But God continues to comment on his Word, and a relationship demands give-and-take; otherwise it is not a relationship. Sometimes God speaks to us because he wants to correct a false idea we have developed. The apostle Peter was convinced that mixing with Gentiles was not right. He was either against it or was unclear about if and when the Good News should be preached to the Gentiles. God provided Peter with a clear vision on the roof of Simon the tanner's home in Joppa (see Acts 10). The vision contradicted Peter's interpretation of dietary rules. The voice in the vision spoke three times before he accepted what it said. Sometimes God will show us something that seems to contradict our understanding of Scripture. At these times we need to seek him and others for clarification.

At one time I was convinced that the nine gifts of 1 Corinthians 12 were no longer meant to be a part of the church. But through a series of events that combined all three lights, God showed me I had been wrong. He taught me through other members of the body, and I experienced more power and fruitfulness when I opened my heart to the gifts. I started listening to the inner voice and when I did, God worked in ways not known to me before. God started sending people to me with messages of encouragement. People started using the gift of prophecy with each other at the end of services. God would give me phrases and thoughts at the close of services to minister to special needs. Always before I would not have been listening. I would not have even asked the questions, What do you want me to do now? Do you have a word for your church? I studied the Word diligently to determine if I was on solid ground. The interdependent, intercorrective nature of the three lights provided the parameters for my new understanding. It takes courage to say to God, "Show me where I am wrong."

The Kind of Person Who Hears God's Voice

Recently I lost my sunglasses. I searched the same places day after day, desperate to find them. I made phone calls to restaurants, checked with friends, and retraced my steps at work and home. Then it hit me. I'm more determined to find my sunglasses than I am to seek God—not in my spirit and mind but in my behavior, which was demonstrating a passion and determination that was often not directed toward God. Jeremiah put it this way:

> "For I know the plans I have for you," declares the LORD, "plans to prosper you and not to harm you, plans to give you hope and a future. Then you will call upon me and come and pray to me, and I will listen to you. *You will seek me and find me when you seek me with all your heart.*
>
> Jeremiah 29:11–13

If I want to hear from God, I must be passionate to hear from him. I am speaking now in the context of the three lights. Seeking him with passion means spending time with God by listening to his voice through Scripture. I am referring to how he speaks into our lives specific direction from his Word. This may not come during a thirty-minute quiet time every day. We must be available to God anytime, anywhere, seeking him with a hungry heart. I don't know why, but the most profound insights into Scripture and life have come to me when I am exercising, but they have come after I have spent considerable time in the Word.

Every other day I take my hand weights and speed walk toward the beach. I begin talking to God with my first step and often I do the entire three miles with no conscious thought of where I am. I pass many people and don't see them, cross several streets and don't consciously notice the traffic, go along the beach and don't hear the waves. I am deep in thought. The best insights for my sermons, the breakthroughs with people and problems I encounter, most of my major life decisions have come during my walks.

God can be speaking and we are not tuned into his voice. We would be wise to seriously deal with the thoughts that continue in our minds that have a godly ring to them, but most of us don't. As thoughts come into our minds, we need to ask God, "Do you really want me to do this?" When we let those thoughts collapse, then God looks for someone else to stand in the gap.

I want to be like the boy Samuel and say, "Lord, I am listening." I want to be like Philip when God told him "Arise and go south to the road that descends from Jerusalem to Gaza." And

Philip obeyed. I am hungry to live in a new realm of intimacy with God.

Should we expect a regular diet of impressions and specific guidance outside of reading Scripture? Once we are tuned into his voice, we can expect to hear from him daily. The kind of person who hears God's voice is a committed listener. He or she has developed the habit of recognizing God's voice and has demonstrated a willingness to obey God's voice with a brave heart.

Afterword

So what is the bottom line? What does one do with the message of this book? I am sure various suggestions will be made—some of them not very nice. This work is an invitation to join me in a quest for the fullness of God. If you, like me, have grown tired of a world of good sermons, nice music, and the right hand of fellowship, then take the plunge. Ask God to show you a pathway to seek more of who he is and what he is willing to do in your life.

If you are a leader, it all begins with the personal pursuit of God. Then you will find yourself unable to remain silent. You will want to present your desire for more to your leadership team. You can take them on a journey only if you have been there before them. Then there is the teaching of the congregation. You teach them to cultivate dormant gifts, create special forums for mutual ministry, and undergird it all with prayer, prayer, prayer, and then more prayer.

Notes

Introduction

1. Doug Bannister, *The Word and Power Church* (Grand Rapids: Zondervan, 1999), is excellent at explaining this concept. Jack Deere in *Surprised by the Power of the Spirit* (Grand Rapids: Zondervan, 1993) coined the phrase "the Silent Divorce," describing how the Word and the power parts of the church experience only periodic communication, like a divorced couple.

Chapter 1 Defining What Jesus Did

1. For example in Matthew 23, Jesus directs the seven woes specifically to the hard of heart, i.e., Pharisees and teachers of the law.

2. See 1 Cor. 6:19–20 and 2 Cor. 6:16.

3. Christian A. Schwarz, *Natural Church Development: A Guide to Eight Essential Qualities of Healthy Churches* (Carol Stream, Ill.: Church Smart Resources, 1996), 47.

4. I would recommend Bill Hull, *Seven Steps to Transform Your Church* (Grand Rapids: Revell, 1997). I have published studies that show the average evangelical church sees 1.7 adult converts a year per 100 people in attendance. The Barna Institute also published annual reports on evangelistic effectiveness. The Center for Church Effectiveness in Denver, Colorado, has studies as well (1-800-995-5362).

5. Allan Bloom, *The Closing of the American Mind* (New York: Simon and Schuster, 1987), 25.

6. My personal favorite is Lyle Schaller, *The Change Agent* (Nashville: Abingdon Press, 1972).

7. Charles Kraft, *Christianity with Power* (Ann Arbor, Mich.: Servant Books, 1989), xii.

Chapter 2 Knowing How Jesus Did It

1. The case of Peter Popoff is well-known. He was exposed as a fraud when it was learned that he wore an earpiece that was connected to his wife backstage. Mrs. Popoff would feed Peter information gleaned during premeeting interviews. This would make it appear as though Popoff was exercising the gift of prophecy. There are other documented cases that indicate the same kind of chicanery.

2. R. A. Torrey, *What the Bible Teaches* (Old Tappan, N.J.: Revell, 1898), 94.

3. Wayne A. Grudem, *Systematic Theology: An Introduction to Biblical Doctrine* (Grand Rapids: Zondervan, 1994), 549.

4. William Hendriksen, *New Testament Commentary: The Gospel of John* (Grand Rapids: Baker Books, 1954), 67, 68. There are seven "I am" passages in John's Gospel: 6:35—"I am the bread of life," 8:12—"I am the light of the world," 10:7—"I am the gate," 10:11—"I am the good shepherd," 11:25—"I am the resurrection and the life," 14:6—"I am the way and the truth and the life," 15:1—"I am the true vine." Hendriksen points out that the aorist infinitive is used to describe the birth of Abraham in 8:58. His birth was a completed act in history. The "I am" claim is present indicative, giving a timeless nature to Christ's existence. It is also very likely that John played off the LXX's (Greek translation of Old Testament) use of *ego eimi* as the name of the Deity in Exodus 3:14.

5. Grudem, *Systematic Theology*, 550.

6. Ibid.

7. Ibid., 557–58.

8. See Matthew 4:1–11 where Jesus is tempted by Satan and Hebrews 4:15, which says that he "has been tempted in every way, just as we are—yet was without sin."

9. Grudem, *Systematic Theology*, 562.

Chapter 3 Properly Relating to the Written Record

1. Karl Barth, Emil Brunner, Dietrich Bonhoeffer, and Rudolf Bultmann influenced the move away from standard orthodoxy in the later nineteenth and the first half of the twentieth centuries. Bonhoeffer is best known in popular culture for being executed by the Nazis one week before the liberation of the German death camps.

2. Rudolf Bultmann, *New Testament and Mythology: Kerygma and Myth*, ed. Hans Werner Bartsch, trans. Louise Pettibone Smith and Erminie Huntress Lantero (New York: Charles Scribner, 1958).

3. Cessationist: A person who believes that gifts such as word of knowledge and wisdom, prophecy, tongues, interpretation of tongues, working of miracles, and healing have run their course. They are no longer being given as they were in the first century. This includes the cessation of apostles and prophets to function in the way that Peter, Paul, Isaiah, and Jeremiah operated. I would agree that apostles and prophets are no longer vested with the same authority as the originals. There are also many alternative views that redefine the gifts and offices. The bottom line for cessationists, however, is that the gifts, as presented in the New Testament, are no longer available to the church.

4. Jack Deere, *Surprised by the Voice of God* (Grand Rapids: Zondervan, 1996), 251–69.

5. See 2 Timothy 3:15–17 and 1 Peter 2:2.

6. The position is that once the canon of the New Testament was closed, God would no longer speak at the same level as Scripture. This I believe to be true. The question that remains, however, is, Does God speak to us by other means apart from Scripture? I believe that he does and does so through the operation of the gifts of the Spirit. God personalizes and affirms the written record in various ways. Future chapters will address this more specifically.

7. This was done at the Council at Carthage, A.D. 397.

8. The Council of Carthage, representing the churches in the western part of the Mediterranean world, agreed with the eastern churches.

9. Thomas Jefferson was a Deist. History records that he edited a Bible and physically cut out the miracles from the pages of his Bible. This became known as the Jeffersonian Bible.

10. The Jesus Seminar is a self-appointed group that discusses Jesus' miracles, and a panel votes to determine if they really happened. It should be no surprise that most of the votes are to negate the miraculous.

11. New Horizons Ministry of Marion, Indiana, 1-800-333-4009.

12. Paul makes this same point in 1 Thessalonians 1:4–5—the Word and power together is God's intention. There have been too many cases where the preaching of the Word was not accompanied by works of power.

13. See Romans 12:1–2. Transformation begins with the renewing of the mind. In Colossians 1:9–10 Paul makes a point of *epignosis,* a reference to knowledge based on experience.

Chapter 4 Experiencing God Present with Us

1. The Great Commandment—Matthew 22:37–39; the Great Commission—Matthew 28:18–20.

2. In John 14:12–14 the only qualifier is the phrase "anyone who has faith in me."

3. The seed thought on *presence* comes from Gordon Fee, *Paul, the Spirit, and the People of God* (Peabody, Mass.: Hendrickson Publishers, 1996), 9.

4. Exodus 33 tells the story of God's anger and Moses' desire to have God present as the people were to enter and conquer the Promised Land.

5. In Jeremiah 31:31–34 Jeremiah speaks of the New Covenant: "I will be their God, and they will be my people."

6. Fee, *Paul, the Spirit, and the People of God*, 66.

7. The five transformational activities, as given in chapter 1, are 1. commitment to the apostles' teaching, 2. commitment to fellowship, 3. commitment to prayer, 4. commitment to worship, 5. commitment to outreach (Acts 2:42–47).

8. Dallas Willard, *In Search of Guidance* (San Francisco: HarperCollins, 1984), 104.

9. In 1 Corinthians 14:26, "when you come together" indicates that people are to come together spiritually prepared to share through their gifts.

10. Fee, *Paul, the Spirit, and the People of God*, 163.

11. Grudem, *Systematic Theology*, 647.

Chapter 5 Experiencing the Power of the Spirit

1. See Ephesians 5:18 and 1 John 5:14.

2. Tenney's books on the power and presence of God are very motivating. I recommend them to light or rekindle the fire in our souls for the presence of God. Tommy Tenney, *The God Chasers* (Nashville: Nelson, 1999), and *The God Catchers* (Nashville: Nelson, 2000).

3. See also Mark 1:4, 8.

4. In Matthew 28:19 those commissioned to make disciples are also told to do the baptizing. When God baptizes in, with, or by the Holy Spirit, it is a work that can be done only by a member of the triune God.

5. The Greek particle appears before each statement. My addition of no after each question is my attempt to give in English a clear understanding of the original meaning.

6. In 1 Corinthians 12:11 it is clear that the Holy Spirit determines who gets what gift.

7. Peter's confession of Christ is one of the high points of the disciple's time with Jesus (Matt. 16:13–20). There are many occasions when the disciples obeyed Jesus as master, such as in the feeding of the five thousand in John 6. They went out and preached under Christ's instructions (Matt. 10:1–42). They worked miracles (Luke 10:17).

8. See Acts 8:14–17. It is generally accepted that the phrase "and they received the Holy Spirit" indicates a visible sign that was clear and authoritative. This is followed by the observation of Simon that the Spirit had been given. Everything points to the sign being speaking in tongues.

9. Gordon Fee, *God's Empowering Presence: The Holy Spirit in the Letters of Paul* (Peabody, Mass.: Hendrickson Publishers, 1994), 720.

10. In Acts 4:8 the term *filled* is an aorist passive indicating that Peter had been filled with the Holy Spirit at an earlier point. Some would say that the point and time was Pentecost. That point also could have been five seconds before he was to speak. Regardless of what is true in this case, Peter demonstrated behavior in his life like any normal human, which required repeated fillings.

11. This clearly represents a group of already filled followers being refilled (Acts 4:31). I consider this a normal pattern for the church. We need many fresh fillings even when we are already walking in the Spirit.

12. *Homo lego,* "to say the same thing," in 1 John 1:9 is translated "confess" in most English translations.

13. John 16:8–11 says that the conviction that comes to humankind is three pronged—conviction of sin, of righteousness, and of judgment.

14. The word *metanonia,* translated "repent," most often means that after perceiving the facts, you change your mind.

15. *Flesh* refers to the immaterial nature of a person that is cursed by sin and has a bent toward sin. It is the battle that every Christian fights (see Gal. 5:16–18).

16. 1 John 1:1–3 says that fellowship is based on a relationship to a risen Christ. John states that, based on that fellowship, Christians can enjoy fellowship with one another.

17. John speaks of walking in the light, Paul of walking in the Spirit. They are describing the same process of a daily interchange with God in the light of the battle and our imperfection.

18. The church in Acts 2:41 and 47 are examples of early success. Bruce Metzger in *New Testament Introduction* (Nashville: Abingdon Press, 1965), 172, sees six phases of growth that are detailed in Acts. First, 1:1–6:7. "So the word of God spread. The number of disciples in Jerusalem increased rapidly, and a large number of priests became obedient to the faith" (6:7). Second, 6:8–9:31. "Then the church throughout Judea, Galilee and Samaria enjoyed a time of peace. It was strengthened; and encouraged by the Holy Spirit, it grew in numbers, living in the fear of the Lord" (9:31). Third, 9:32–12:24. "But the word of God continued to increase and spread" (12:24). Fourth, 12:25–16:5. "So the churches were strengthened in the faith and grew daily in numbers" (16:5). Fifth, 16:6–19:20. "In this way the word of the Lord spread widely and grew in power" (19:20). Sixth, 19:21–28:31. "For two whole years Paul stayed there in his own rented house and welcomed all who came to see him. Boldly and without hindrance he preached the kingdom of God and taught about the Lord Jesus Christ" (28:30–31).

19. From 1 Corinthians 3:10–15 and 2 Corinthians 5:9–10, we understand that the searching of the human heart is about motive and purity of action. God alone understands and is qualified to make such judgments.

Chapter 6 Understanding the Purpose of Spiritual Gifts

1. According to 1 Corinthians 12:11, the Holy Spirit makes the decisions regarding who gets what gift. First Corinthians 14:1 and 39 encourage the pursuit of gifts as a means of building up the church.

2. Some gifts seem to manifest themselves when needed but cannot be called on at will, for example, the working of miracles, gifts of healing, prophecy, interpretation of tongues. These gifts seem to need a direct move from God. It could be in answer to prayer or a divine decree.

3. See Acts 1:8; Matthew 28:19–20; Matthew 24:14.

4. Fee, *Paul, the Spirit, and the People of God,* 164.

5. Church historian Philip Schaff says, "Many opened their homes. . . . in larger cities like Rome the Christian community divided itself into several such assemblies at private houses" (*History of the Christian Church,* [Grand Rapids: Eerdmans, 1910], 474). This is mentioned as an aside in Romans 16:5 and 1 Corinthians 16:19.

6. Later we will discuss Paul's rules for such interaction.

7. This specifically refers to the unbeliever, but certainly it would be permissible for the believer to believe God is powerfully present in worship. That is what a sense of awe is about.

8. The reference is to Matthew 16:1–4, but this has nothing to do with believers needing signs to continue to be faithful. It was a challenge to Jesus from the leaders of the unbelieving opposition.

9. See footnote 19 in Experiencing the Power of the Spirit.

10. Tom Beaudoin, *Virtual Faith: The Irreverent Spiritual Quest of Generation X* (San Francisco: Jossey Bass, 1998), 95; italics added.

11. Ibid., 73.

12. Acts 8:1, 4 demonstrate that the word spread when everyone was required to leave the city except the apostles. God's genius was at work. No longer could the average believer stand back and watch the apostles perform.

13. In Deuteronomy 18:14–22 Moses says God will raise up prophets like himself. If they claim to speak for God and the prophecy does not come true, they are to be punished, in some cases stoned.

14. First Corinthians 14:27–39 calls for serious evaluation of a person who is prophesying, but there is no indication that punishment is part of that evaluation. The gift of prophecy is given no higher standard than the gift of teaching or any other gift that will be exercised imperfectly. The responsibility of church leadership is to be Berean—objective—about the matter.

15. The Grandville Sharp rule has three conditions for the two parties or functions to be one person rather than two: 1. neither is impersonal; 2. neither is plural; 3. neither is a proper name. In this case pastors and teachers are plural thus not meeting requirement 2. Daniel B. Wallace, *Greek Grammar: Beyond the Basics* (Grand Rapids: Zondervan, 1996), 270–84.

16. Fee, *God's Empowering Presence*, 707.

17. Grudem, *Systematic Theology*, 1049.

18. First Corinthians 12:31 and 14:1 both speak of being eager and striving for the greater gifts. The greater gifts are those that minister to the greatest number of people, more specifically, those that can be understood in worship. Thus they do the best job at edification.

Chapter 7 Accepting the Challenge of Unleashing the Miraculous

1. See 1 Timothy 4:7 and Titus 2:5. There are a number of passages that warn believers against gossip and spreading malicious talk.

2. Doug Bannister explains the concept of the Word and power church in *The Word and Power Church*.

3. See Romans 1:29–32, 1 Corinthians 6:9–11; Galatians 5:19–21.

4. See Ephesians 2:10. God has created good works for us to do. His desire is that we would obediently pursue them and do them. That is the basic formula for fulfillment.

5. Paul Brand and Philip Yancey, *Fearfully and Wonderfully Made* (Grand Rapids: Zondervan, 1980), 24.

6. See Philippians 2:5–8, where the humility of Christ is given as our example, and Galatians 2:20, which speaks of the flesh being crucified. Living in the power of the Spirit is the demonstration of Spirit over flesh (Gal. 5:6–18).

7. The basic idea is taken from Homileticsonline.com, Timothy Merrill, senior editor.

Chapter 8 Employing the Miraculous in Worship

1. Apollos, Peter, Christ, and Paul all had fans. Once again this demonstrates the lack of unity. Factions were based on personality and personal tastes.

2. The exhortation of Hebrews 10:24–25 to consider how to stimulate one another toward good deeds requires more than one-way communication. The "when you come together" aspect of 1 Corinthians 14:26 requires a forum for interaction. This means that venues of interaction and accountability are necessary to build up and prepare disciples for ministry.

3. Three of my books, all published by Revell, address structure, *Revival That Reforms*, 1998, *Seven Steps to Transform Your Church*, 1993, and *Building High Commitment in a Low-Commitment World*, 1996. They all speak about streamlining administrative layers and developing structure that empowers and is friendly toward mission.

4. I am assuming that "everyone" in 1 Corinthians 14:26 means everyone. No one is excluded from the responsibility.

5. See Jesus' struggle in the Garden of Gethsemane (Matt. 26:36–39) and his becoming sin (2 Cor. 5:21).

6. Grudem, *Systematic Theology*, 1049.

7. Ibid., 1050–60.

8. See 2 Timothy 3:16–17 and 4:2–4.

9. See Fee, *God's Empowering Presence*, 236–39. Fee details four ways that Paul changed the Isaiah prophecy (28:11–12) to tailor it for the Corinthians. 1. He inverts the order of "stammering lips" and "other tongues." 2. He changed "stammering lips" to "the lips of others." 3. He alters the "Lord will speak" to "I will speak." 4. He skips a considerable section in the Isaiah passage picking up at the end of verse 12 where he modifies "and they would not hear," referring to the intelligible words of the Lord, to "and even so they would not obey me."

10. *Symbiotic* means an intimate living together, an association of mutual advantage.

11. Michael Green, *Evangelism in the Early Church* (Grand Rapids: Eerdmans, 1970), 194–206.

12. See, for example, Acts 11:28; 21:4, 10–11.

13. See Acts 15:35; 18:11, 24–28; Romans 2:21; 15:4, Colossians 3:16; Hebrews 5:12. From Grudem, *Systematic Theology*, 1058.

Chapter 9 Becoming a Healing Community

1. See Acts 2:38 on spiritual healing and Luke 4:38–40 on physical healing.

2. See Mark 1:23–27 and Ephesians 6:10–16.

3. See Colossians 2:13–15 and 1 Corinthians 15:50–58.

4. See Neil T. Anderson, *The Bondage Breaker* (1990; revised, Eugene, Ore.: Harvest House, 2000); Merrill F. Unger, *What Demons Can Do to Saints* (Chicago: Moody, 1977); Mark Bubeck, *The Adversary* (Chicago: Moody, 1976); Kurt Koch, *The Devil's Alphabet* (Grand Rapids: Kregel, 1971).

5. See Mark 11:24 on faith, 1 John 3:21–22 on the importance of keeping commandments, John 15:7 on obedience in word and prayer, 1 John 5:14–15 on praying according to God's will, and Matthew 18:15–18 on the importance of agreement with others.

Chapter 10 Discovering Obstacles to Healing

1. The word *worldly* is translated from the Greek *sarkos*, meaning "flesh." This does not refer to human flesh or skin, but to the fallen part of a person's immaterial nature. It is the part of the immaterial nature that is ego-driven and is energized by sin.

2. See Ephesians 6:10–12 and 2 Corinthians 10:3–5.

3. Standard Christian cults, such as Jehovah Witnesses and Mormons, deny the deity of Christ. They represent the most common forms of departure from Christian orthodoxy. This passage is not speaking primarily of other religions and philosophies that do not have their base in orthodox Christianity.

4. In Mark 6:3 four brothers are named and then the plural *sisters* is used, which requires at least two. This adds up to at least seven children.

5. Dutch Sheets, *Intercessory Prayer* (Glendale, Calif.: Regal, 1996), 103–4.

Chapter 11 Hearing God's Voice

1. I am not including here some obvious ways God speaks, such as through creation (Rom. 1:20), conscious (2:14), and signs and wonders (Heb. 2:4). Signs and wonders are spoken about in earlier chapters—how they grab the attention of the seeker and how vital they are for today's church.

2. Found in Dallas Willard's *In Search of Guidance*, 93, Meyer taught the three lights as interdependent and intercorrective. That way they bring balance and avoid extremes. A fuller list would include phenomenon plus voice, supernatural messenger or angel, dreams and visions, audible voice, the human voice, the human spirit, or the "still small voice."

3. Ibid., 104.

4. Visions, dreams, and angelic appearances are possible. If you experience one of these, you will know it. I have chosen to focus on the more normal paranormal—God speaking through the three lights.

5. A. W. Tozer in Willard, *In Search of Guidance*, 27.

Bill Hull is a teacher and writer who is committed to helping the church return to its disciple-making roots. He is the former president of T-Net International and of Mission USA in the Evangelical Free Church of America. Bill now pastors Cypress Church in Cypress, California.